STUDIES IN IMPERIALISM

general editor John M. MacKenzie

When the 'Studies in Imperialism' series was founded more than twenty-five years ago, emphasis was laid upon the conviction that 'imperialism as a cultural phenomenon had as significant an effect on the dominant as on the subordinate societies'. With more than seventy books published, this remains the prime concern of the series. Cross-disciplinary work has indeed appeared covering the full spectrum of cultural phenomena, as well as examining aspects of gender and sex, frontiers and law, science and the environment, language and literature, migration and patriotic societies, and much else. Moreover, the series has always wished to present comparative work on European and American imperialism, and particularly welcomes the submission of books in these areas. The fascination with imperialism, in all its aspects, shows no sign of abating, and this series will continue to lead the way in encouraging the widest possible range of studies in the field. 'Studies in Imperialism' is fully organic in its development, always seeking to be at the cutting edge, responding to the latest interests of scholars and the needs of this ever-expanding area of scholarship.

Borders and conflict in South Asia

MANCHESTER
1824

Manchester University Press

Borders and conflict in South Asia

THE RADCLIFFE BOUNDARY COMMISSION AND THE PARTITION OF PUNJAB

Lucy P. Chester

MANCHESTER UNIVERSITY PRESS
Manchester and New York

distributed in the United States exclusively by
Palgrave Macmillan

Published by Manchester University Press
Oxford Road, Manchester M13 9NR, UK
and Room 400, 175 Fifth Avenue, New York, NY 10010, USA
www.manchesteruniversitypress.co.uk

Distributed in the United States exclusively by
Palgrave Macmillan, 175 Fifth Avenue,
New York, NY 10010, USA

Distributed in Canada exclusively by
UBC Press, University of British Columbia, 2029 West Mall,
Vancouver, BC, Canada V6T 1Z2

British Library Cataloguing-in-Publication Data is available

Library of Congress Cataloging-in-Publication Data is available

ISBN 978 0 7190 9136 0 paperback

First published by Manchester University Press in hardback 2009

This paperback edition first published 2013

The publisher has no responsibility for the persistence or accuracy of URLs for any external or third-party internet websites referred to in this book, and does not guarantee that any content on such websites is, or will remain, accurate or appropriate.

Printed by Lightning Source

For Margaret

CONTENTS

LIST OF MAPS

Maps appear between pages xvi and 1

1 India before partition: 1:15,840,000. In *The Transfer of Power 1942–7*. Vol. XII, ed. Nicholas Mansergh and Penderel Moon. London: HMSO, 1983, at end of volume. Reproduced under the terms of the Click-Use License.

2 Partition boundaries in Punjab: approximately 1:2,661,120. September 1948. In *The Transfer of Power 1942–7*. Vol. XII, ed. Nicholas Mansergh and Penderel Moon. London: HMSO, 1983, at end of volume. Reproduced under the terms of the Click-Use License.

3 The Radcliffe line in Kasur *tehsil* (detail). Rashid Ahmad Khan. *Map of Kasur Tehsil*: 1:126,720. Lahore: Kapur Art Printing Work, [n.d.]. British Library, India Office Records, L/P, 8J/10/117, Map 1. Reproduced by permission of the British Library.

4 Alternative boundaries: adapted from 'Partition boundaries in the Punjab'. Approximately 1:2,661,120. September 1948. In *The Transfer of Power 1942–7*. Vol. XII, ed. Nicholas Mansergh and Penderel Moon. London: HMSO, 1983, at end of volume. Reproduced under the terms of the Click-Use License.

5 Alternative boundaries: adapted from 'Partition boundaries in the Punjab'. Approximately 1:2,661,120. September 1948. In *The Transfer of Power 1942–7*. Vol. XII, ed. Nicholas Mansergh and Penderel Moon. London: HMSO, 1983, at end of volume. Reproduced under the terms of the Click-Use License.

6 Disputes over Theh Sarja Marja and Chak Ladheke. United States Army Map Service, NH 43-2, 'Lahore'. Edition 2-AMS. 1:250,000. Series U502. Washington: Army Map Service, 1963.

7 Hussainiwala headworks disputed area. United States Army Map Service, NH 43-6, 'Ferozepore'. Edition 1-AMS. 1:250,000. Series U502. Washington: Army Map Service, 1959.

8 Sulemanke headworks disputed area. United States Army Map Service, NH 43-6, 'Ferozepore'. Edition 1-AMS. 1:250,000. Series U502. Washington: Army Map Service, 1959.

GENERAL EDITOR'S INTRODUCTION

Few episodes in the decolonisation of the British Empire have aroused more controversy than the rush to independence and the partition of India in 1947. In the first half of the twentieth century, the British had appeared to do everything in their power to slow down constitutional advance, the possible grant of 'Dominion status' akin to that of the territories of white settlement, and full independence. Such developments as there had been had appeared limited and grudging, while the British had seemed to encourage the rival movement to the Indian National Congress, the Muslim League, with ultimately dangerous consequences. Such divisions had been exacerbated by the Second World War. Yet in its aftermath, and with the election of a Labour Government intent on creating a Welfare State and a reconstructed national identity in Britain, the brakes were suddenly off. A slow-moving river, constantly impeded by log jams, suddenly became a ferocious torrent as the independence date was brought forward and as the British authorities sought to get out of India as rapidly and, as they saw it, as honourably as possible.

Winston Churchill, from the point of view of the imperialist wing of his party, famously called it a 'scuttle', and much has been made of the arrogance and impatience of the last Viceroy, Mountbatten, eager on his terms to get a job done as quickly as possible and return to his naval career (and redress the alleged slighting of his father during the First World War). It was in this febrile atmosphere that India was partitioned into three geographical (and, then, two political) units involving the division of two of the most important provinces of the sub-continent, the Punjab and Bengal. It was a vast and complex task, involving huge distances, many millions of people, all sorts of assumptions about census returns, as well as geopolitical, ecological, hydrographic, political and many other considerations. Yet it was all accomplished in a period of little more than six weeks by commissions headed by a lawyer, Cyril Radcliffe, who had little previous experience of India, certainly 'on the ground', and no experience of boundary formation. It perhaps comes as no surprise that he has been excoriated by both sides and has received, in many cases, rough treatment from historians. He himself was well aware that he was on 'a hiding to nothing', but set out to do his duty by the British Establishment and the Indian authorities. Inevitably, he himself was horrified by the violence, bloodshed and 'ethnic cleansing' which his Award stimulated in the weeks following the independence celebrations. These events have been seen as one of the greatest blots on the escutcheon of the British imperial experience.

Although there has been a plethora of writings about these events, nobody has examined them in such detail and with such judicious balance as Lucy Chester. Using an extraordinary range of sources – private documents, personal interviews, many maps, official documents in Britain, India and Pakistan, as well as field work along the Punjabi boundary itself – she has produced by far the most comprehensive work on the western partition so far published. This involves a careful consideration of the background, of the work of the commissions, and of the tragic and problematic aftermath, sometimes bringing the story down to the present day. Importantly, she attempts to consider what the partition meant for real people, both those displaced and those who continued to live with the boundary line. She also analyses the nature of boundaries and the significance of maps, the latter so often illustrative of the perceptions, designs and objectives of their producers. Above all, she acutely examines the personalities involved, particularly Radcliffe, considering his background, his life history, and the influences that had gone into his make-up. Well illustrated, this book offers a more satisfying approach to the partition, particularly – but not exclusively – of the Punjab, than any previous work. It would be quite wrong to pre-empt her conclusions in this introduction, but it is intriguing that the rushed job accomplished by Radcliffe in such an astonishingly short time might have been no more effectively done if a much longer period had been spent on the Award. Many were tragically overwhelmed in the waterfall of events in 1947, but attempts at a counterfactual history fail to prove that things might have fallen out differently if any other methods had been used. The fundamental tragedy was perhaps the fact of partition rather than its execution.

John M. MacKenzie

ACKNOWLEDGEMENTS

This book would not have been possible without the generous assistance of a great many people, and I regret that I cannot name them all here. Any errors of fact or judgement remain my own.

First and foremost, my heartfelt thanks to all those in India, Pakistan and Britain who shared with me their memories of independence. In Pakistan, I am grateful to Abbas Chugtai of the Punjab Provincial Archives in Lahore for vital advice and assistance; the staff of the National Documentation Centre in Islamabad; John and Nickie Bennett, for a home away from home; Shahnaz Hasan and the Hasan family, for Urdu language training and sisterly support; Mahboob Alam, without whom I literally would never have got where I needed to go; General and Mrs Wajahat Husain and their son Kashif, for help given with great kindness; General Zarrar Azim and Colonel Adnan Janjua of the Pakistan Rangers; Dr and Mrs Habib and their daughter Arjumand, for easing my transition to Pakistan and jumpstarting my research; Ahsan Jameel and the Jameel family; Khurram Husain and the hospitable faculty and staff of the Lahore University of Management Sciences; and a number of others who asked that their names not be used but whose help was invaluable.

In India, I must thank the staff of the National Archives and the Nehru Memorial Museum and Library; the Millard family, for another home away from home; Meera and Malay Chatterjee, old friends; Prem and Abha Singh, for a miraculously comfortable stay; and Ritu Menon, for both useful advice and her own important work.

In England, many thanks go to Andrew Cook, for generously sharing his cartographic wisdom; David Blake, who offered his great knowledge of the India Office records; Christopher Beaumont, for invaluable interviews and assistance; Joya Chatterji, for helpful feedback, advice and encouragement; the staff at Cambridge University's South Asian Archive; and Sidney Sussex College, where I enjoyed a lovely term at Cambridge.

During my travels, the following fellow scholars refreshed my tired heart: Michael Bednar, Barbara Cole, Jenni Henderson, Kim Masteller and Donovan Dodrill, Matt Nelson and Cabeiri deBurgh Robinson.

At Yale, I found a cheerful and stimulating community for which I am very grateful. For practical advice and good company along the way, I am indebted to Ted Bromund, Mark Choate, Hang-Lien Nguyen, Mary Sharp, Gagan Sood, Jenni Siegel, Jeremi Suri and many others,

ACKNOWLEDGEMENTS

but most of all Jay Geller. Florence Thomas and Ann Carter-Drier supplied essential long-distance support. My deepest appreciation goes to Robin Winks, for providing early inspiration as teacher and scholar; Paul Kennedy, who always brought a sense of fun to intellectual discussion; and Charlie Hill, for his incisive comments and constant encouragement.

In addition, the following scholars generously provided valuable feedback at various stages: Matthew Edney, David Gilmartin, Ayesha Jalal, Vijay Pinch and Willem van Schendel. I am also grateful to the anonymous reviewers who provided constructive criticism that greatly strengthened this work.

For a productive, challenging and culinarily enjoyable year at Stanford, I thank my colleagues at the Center for International Security and Cooperation (CISAC): Lynn Eden, Scott Sagan, Steve Stedman and all the visiting scholars, especially Laura Donohue, Chris Lee, Alex Montgomery, Ben Valentino and Erik Voeten. Thanks also to Norman Naimark and the members of the Sawyer Seminar on Mass Violence at the Center for Advanced Study in the Behavioral Sciences. At the Stanford Libraries, I am especially grateful to Julie Sweetkind-Singer, who provided yet more evidence that there is a special place in heaven for map librarians, and to the efficient interlibrary loan department.

At the University of Colorado at Boulder, I am deeply grateful to Marjorie McIntosh, Mithi Mukherjee and Martha Hanna for pushing me to re-examine and expand my ideas and to Scott Bruce and Anne Lester, who were always ready with a sympathetic ear and a drink. Many thanks to everyone at Manchester University Press for making the publication process smooth and enjoyable.

The following organizations generously provided funding for this project: the Eugene M. Kayden Fund at the University of Colorado, the American Institute of Pakistan Studies, the Fox Fellowship Program, the Hamburg Fellowship Program at CISAC, the National Security Education Program and the Smith Richardson Foundation. Thanks for reproduction permissions go to the British Library and Her Majesty's Stationery Office.

Alana Conner and Margaret Sloane kept me afloat at key moments. My extended family has always been wonderfully supportive; many thanks to all, especially Peggy Reiber, Bryan and Tina Huey, Doug and Mary Ellen Huey, Andrew Goldhor, Robert Goldhor and Mari Shirazi. Most of all, I thank Pamela Chester and Richard Goldhor, editors extraordinaire and so much more, and Mark Huey, for his patience, encouragement and love. This book is dedicated to our daughter Margaret.

Lucy Chester

LIST OF ABBREVIATIONS

ALI	Aerial and land incursions (India Office Library)
BBC	British Broadcasting Corporation
CAB	Cabinet
EIC	East India Company
HE	His Excellency
HMSO	Her Majesty's Stationery Office
ICS	Indian Civil Service
IOR	India Office Records
LHA	Liddell Hart Centre for Military Archives
MOI	Ministry of Information (United Kingdom)
Mss Eur	European Manuscripts (India Office Library)
NAI	National Archives of India
NMML	Nehru Memorial Museum and Library
PBF	Punjab Boundary Force
P&J	Public and Judicial (India Office Records)
PPA	Punjab (Pakistan) Provincial Archives
RSS	Rashtriya Swayamsevak Sangh
TNA	The National Archives (United Kingdom)
TP	Nicholas Mansergh et al., eds, *Constitutional Relations between Britain and India: The Transfer of Power 1942–7.* 12 vols. London: HMSO, 1970–83
UN(O)	United Nations Organization

GLOSSARY

dhaya	ridge of land
dhoti	traditional folded garment for lower body
gurudwara	Sikh temple
jatha	Sikh fighting group
kirpan	edged weapon traditionally carried by Sikhs
lathi	wooden baton
mahatma	honorific title meaning 'great soul'
mohajir	immigrant to Pakistan from India
nakabandi	blockade; checkpoint
pandit	honorific title meaning 'scholar'
Quaid-i-Azam	great leader
rabi	winter or dry season crop
raj	rule; 'raj' became a popular shorthand for British rule in India
sardar	honorific title meaning 'chief'
sherwani	long coat with high collar
tehsil	mid-level administrative division
thana	lower-level administrative division centred on police station
tonga	light two-wheeled horse-drawn vehicle
vatan	native land
zail	lowest-level administrative division

NOTE ON TERMINOLOGY

Throughout this book, I refer to pre-partition India as 'British India', in order to avoid confusion with independent India. The use of this term should not be interpreted as negating South Asian agency. When referring to the leaders of the Indian National Congress and the Muslim League during the pre-partition period, I avoid the potentially confusing term 'Indian leaders', often used by contemporary British officials. I prefer the term 'nationalist leaders' or 'South Asian leaders'. For the post-independence period, it is of course proper to refer to these groups as 'Indian' or 'Pakistani'. Following convention, I also use the terms 'British Government' and 'Britain' as a useful shorthand for decision-makers within the British Government. References to 'Britain' should not be taken as a reference to the British people as a whole, who of course held a wide range of views on imperial policy and the appropriate course of British action in South Asia. For the sake of consistency I use the spelling Muhammad throughout, although this name can be transliterated in a variety of ways.

INDIA BEFORE PARTITION

The representations of boundaries are reproduced from the map in the *India Office List*, 1940, prepared by the Edinburgh Geographical Institute and printed by John Bartholomew and Son Ltd. They are not necessarily authoritative.

British India

Indian States and Territories

Scale   Miles
0 50 100 150 200 250 300 350 400

Map labels:

USSR
CHINA
AFGHANISTAN
Kabul
Peshawar
N W FRONTIER PROVINCE
Srinagar
Rawalpindi
KASHMIR & JAMMU
TIBET
Indus
Lahore
Amritsar
Simla
Patiala
Dehra Dun
PUNJAB
Quetta
IRAN
BALUCHISTAN
Kalat
Indus
Delhi
Bikaner
RAJPUTANA
SIND
Karachi
UNITED PROVINCES
NEPAL
Lucknow
Gwalior
Gorakhpur
SIKKIM
BHUTAN
Brahmaputra
ASSAM
Shillong
Allahabad
Benares
Patna
Ganges
BENGAL
Dacca
Imphal (Manipur)
Ahmedabad
Indore
Bhopal
Narbada
Jamnagar
BIHAR
Midnapore
Calcutta
Chittagong
Mandalay
CENTRAL PROVINCES & BERAR
Nagpur
Wardha
Cuttack
BURMA
ARABIAN SEA
BOMBAY
Bombay
Ahmednagar
Poona
ORISSA
Godavari
HYDERABAD
Vizagapatam
BAY OF BENGAL
Rangoon
Kistna
Masulipatam
Goa
MADRAS
MYSORE
Bangalore
Madras
Pondicherry (Fr)
Ootacamund
ANDAMAN ISLANDS
COCHIN
TRAVANCORE
Trincomalee
CEYLON
Colombo
NICOBAR ISLANDS

1 India before partition

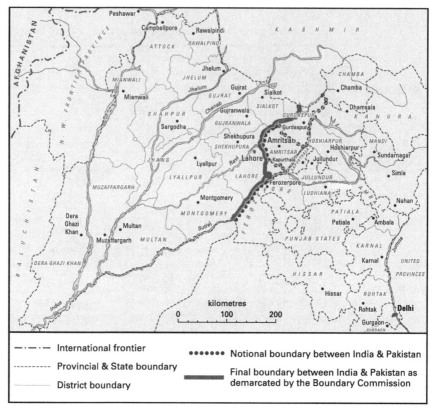

International frontier

Provincial & State boundary

District boundary

Notional boundary between India & Pakistan

Final boundary between India & Pakistan as demarcated by the Boundary Commission

2 Partition boundaries in Punjab

3 The Radcliffe line in Kasur *tehsil* (detail). Note at bottom reads:
'Attached to my Report of 12 August 1947 for reference.
Cyril Radcliffe Chairman Punjab Boundary Commission'

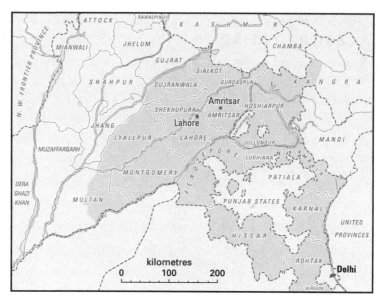

4a Sikh claim

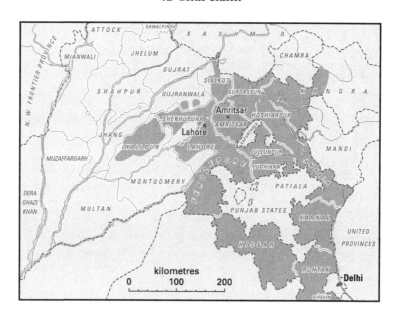

4b Congress claim

4 Alternative boundaries

Rough outlines; see Sadullah, vol. 4 for official party maps.

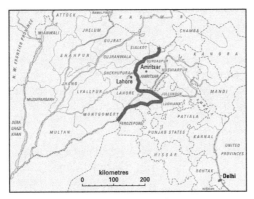

5a Sketch map line

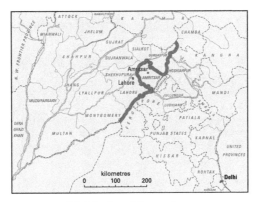

5b Notional boundary

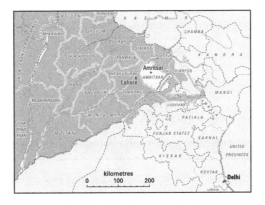

5c Muslim League claim

5 Alternative boundaries

Rough outlines; see Sadullah, vol. 4 for official party maps.

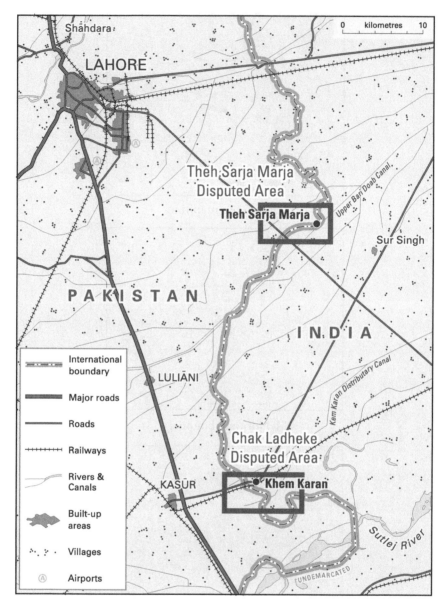

6 Disputes over Theh Sarja Marja and Chak Ladheke
Chak Ladheke, not indicated on the map, falls just south of Khem Karan

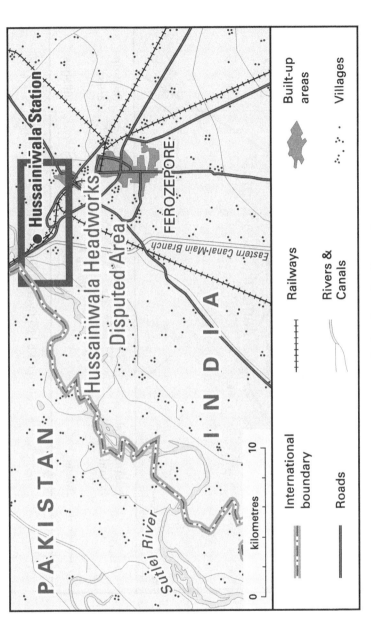

7 Hussainiwala headworks disputed area

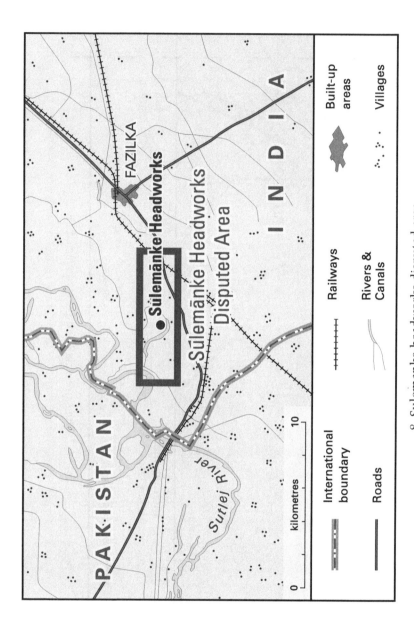

PAKISTAN

INDIA

FAZILKA

Sulemãnke Headworks

Sulemãnke Headworks
Disputed Area

Sutlej River

Railways

Rivers &
Canals

International
boundary

Roads

Built-up
areas

Villages

0   5   10

kilometres

8 Sulemanke headworks disputed area

INTRODUCTION

Shortly after independence, a Muslim traveller driving north through the newborn state of Pakistan witnessed the chaos overwhelming the border with India: 'On both sides of the road, as far as the eye could see, fires were burning and people were running helter skelter as if a flood of lava, erupting from a crater, was about to overtake them. Murree [a town near the new border with India] was all ashes and ruins and I had to stay in a burnt veranda of a burnt house where I heard the award on the 17th in a radio broadcast.'[1] Although this man's experience was a common one, he was no common traveller. He was, in fact, a member of the boundary commission responsible for drawing the boundary between India and Pakistan during the British decolonization of South Asia. The 'award' he heard via radio news was that commission's final decision. This man, Muhammad Munir, was a respected judge and a prominent member of the Muslim League, the nationalist party that had pushed hard for the creation of Pakistan, but in the end he, like so many other Indians and Pakistanis, did not learn the exact location of the new boundary until two days after independence.

This book makes two interconnected arguments. First, I argue that the boundary commission headed by Cyril Radcliffe offers a window into the complexity of nationalist dealings with colonial power structures and of colonial strategies of control, even during decolonization. I examine the nature of power relationships within the colonial state, with a focus on the often-veiled exertion of British colonial power. Specifically, I trace the reluctant cooperation of South Asian elites with British leaders in setting up the Radcliffe commission. The decisions made by these elites, operating under British pressure, in some cases ran counter to popular welfare. This work therefore seeks to add complexity to debates about the nature of colonial power and postcolonial legacies.

Second, I contend that it was not the location of the Radcliffe boundary but the flawed process of partition that caused the terrible violence of 1947. Poor preparation, especially for the flow of refugees, and the boundary commission's perceived lack of legitimacy gave both states, but particularly Pakistan, problematic origins. Rather than exacerbating these problems, surprisingly, Radcliffe's line, rushed and inexpert as it was, may in fact have minimized the violence.

In order to understand the violence and terror Munir describes, as well as when and where it occurred, we need to look more closely at the boundary commission of which he was a member. We also need to understand how it was that Munir, as well as most of his fellow commissioners, only learned of the final boundary two days after independence. Doing so will unfold the story of how the boundary was drawn, its place in the high politics of Britain's withdrawal from South Asia, and its impact on those living in the territory so abruptly and violently divided. We must begin, however, by retreating from the heat of the bloody summer of 1947 to the chill of the preceding British winter, which saw the convergence of a number of factors that dictated Britain's hasty withdrawal from South Asia.

The winter of 1946/47 brought the British empire to a point of crisis. One of the coldest British winters on record, combined with coal shortages and food limitations more stringent than wartime rationing, brought national morale to a dangerous low. British families were also clamouring for the return of soldiers scattered throughout the empire who had yet to be demobilized after World War II. In addition to these domestic woes, British leaders faced simultaneous international dilemmas. During the same period when they faced pressure to decolonize South Asia, they took the difficult decision that the Palestinian–Zionist conflict was irreconcilable and that the Palestine Mandate must be turned over to the UN. In British India, steadily worsening tensions between Muslims and Hindus and rising pressure from nationalist groups made the raj, Britain's colonial regime in South Asia, more precarious by the day. In diplomatic circles, the United States, a rising superpower no longer content to play the role of younger sibling, was pushing Britain to decolonize its imperial holdings. On top of these domestic and international troubles, the British were operating on a depleted treasury and faced the prospect of huge bills to be repaid to the United States and other wartime creditors, including India itself.

As a result, British leaders made the decision to relieve themselves of their Indian burden, and to do so quickly. Although they initially hoped to maintain a unified independent India, the level of Hindu–Muslim tension and Britain's own need for a speedy resolution drove them to accept a partition, or territorial division, of South Asia into the two new states of India and Pakistan. Over the first nine months of 1947, Britain's withdrawal from India developed with startling speed from vague future intention to accomplished fact. During the course of these nine months it became clear that, as this book will demonstrate, the British were determined to avoid projecting the image that they were handing over power under duress. On the contrary, British leaders worked hard to create the impression that the handover was proceeding in an orderly and rational manner. They did so partly out of concern for Britain's international reputation, a reputation that was more important to them than ever, given the need to impress crucial Arab allies in the Middle East and to expand the empire in new areas, such as Africa. Keenly aware of the international audience observing India's decolonization, they sought to give the partition process legitimacy by involving South Asian nationalist leaders in key decisions. At the same time, they strove to make clear that they were still firmly in control. In other words, an appearance of control, balanced with an appearance of including South Asian opinions, was central to Britain's withdrawal plans. One of the division's major problems, however, was the fact that in key areas, both geographical and logistical, no one wielded complete control, and thus chaos ensued.

These four points – haste, a veneer of order, a concern for international reputation and a conscious presentation of the process as one for which South Asians bore primary responsibility – constitute the major themes of this book, which takes the drawing of the Indo-Pakistani boundary as a window onto the end of empire in South Asia. They appear again and again in all aspects of the boundary-making process, from the belated determination that a line needed to be drawn, to the negotiations over how to draw it and to the angry but weary debates over partition's violent aftermath. The drawing of the boundary between the fledgling states of India and Pakistan provides a lens that brings into focus larger issues of colonial control, the legacy of empire and postcolonial responsibility. Although this book centres on the fascinating tale of how some 2500 miles of boundary came to be drawn, in only six weeks, by a British lawyer with no experience of boundary-making, it also analyses the complex power relationships at work in negotiations over the end of empire in South Asia. The resulting narrative combines the intrigue of high politics with the tragedies experienced by those on the ground and the influence of the rapidly transforming international scene with the role of local society, culture and tradition.

This book focuses on partition's impact on Punjab, in the north-west wing of the South Asian subcontinent. The 1947 boundary commission also drew a boundary through Bengal, in the north-east, but the Punjab division was far more violent.[2] The violence was rooted in part in demographic complexity, for unlike Bengal, which was made up primarily of Hindus and Muslims, Punjab was home to three important communities: Hindus, Muslims and Sikhs. Central Punjab was the traditional homeland of this last group. The proposal for a new boundary running directly through central Punjab angered many Sikh leaders, who feared the destruction of their community and consequently vowed to defend it. In part because of its strategic location and in part because the Sikh community is still bitterly resentful of injuries suffered during and after partition, Punjab remains a site of tension between India and Pakistan.

How did the 1947 division of India and Pakistan, which was intended to resolve conflict between religious groups, come to intensify that tension? Part of the answer lies in the drawing of the boundary that separated the two new states. I argue that the boundary commission that drew this line was not the independent judicial body it appeared to be but was influenced by the needs of a number of political parties. Surprisingly, given the commission's problematic structure and procedure, its decision was superior to any major alternative. The troubles associated with partition can be traced to the larger process of division, which was marked by chaos and hurry. Although the term 'transfer of power' is often used to describe the British withdrawal, it is a misleading phrase. As one historian notes, it implies 'not the surrender of India but her conveyance, with all that this implies in prior purpose, studied management, and mutual consent. A measured delivery to Indians of the instruments of governance, in the manner of the father handing the car keys to his son.'[3] In reality, the British departure was hasty, ill-planned and extremely bloody. And yet the British were able to present themselves as presiding over an orderly and objective process, in part because of the boundary commission's judicial, rational façade.

Although the creation of the Indo-Pakistani boundary is significant in and of itself, particularly in terms of its implications for international security, this historical episode also highlights important aspects of British methods both for maintaining colonial control and for expediting the process of decolonization. By shrewdly drawing nationalist leaders into the partition process, the British ostensibly relieved themselves of much of the burden of responsibility for the violence and chaos that accompanied independence. In reality, however, the British retained as much control as possible, even though their grip on power was rapidly weakening. British leaders also created a boundary-making process that appeared to be objective, balanced and judicial, when in fact it was fraught with conflicting political pressures. This judicial façade was important in part because it subdued potential nationalist objections to British influence over the final result of partition. It was also central to British efforts to convince international audiences – in Britain itself, in other parts of the British empire, and in the increasingly powerful and anti-colonial United States – that it was engaged in a smooth, controlled and fair decolonization. Unfortunately, this carefully cultivated image was far from the truth.

Although I have argued that nationalist leaders had less influence over the boundary-making process than the British maintained, this is not to deny the agency of South Asian actors. The nationalist leaders were fiercely independent and strong-willed men, each with his own vision of the nation's future and the best means to achieve it. They themselves decided not to take an active role in the boundary-making process, a choice that contributed to the relative lack of South Asian influence over the boundaries.[4] They were also operating under extreme pressure, which required them to prioritize their efforts, and they seem to have shared the assumption, stated as late as June, that the boundaries could be adjusted later. Furthermore, it is important to note that provincial politicians played a greater role in shaping the boundary in Bengal than in Punjab. But the fact remains that South Asians, particularly Punjabis, did not have as much input as British statements made it appear.

This project draws on a range of approaches, including international history, biography, cartographic history and borderlands studies. I conducted archival research and interviews in Britain, Pakistan and India in order to gather a balanced range of sources, including some material previously inaccessible to researchers. Interviews with colleagues and acquaintances of Cyril Radcliffe, the chairman of the 1947 boundary commission, provided insight into his reasoning and motivation. Analysis of the maps Radcliffe saw provided a previously neglected angle on the delineation of the partition boundary. Finally, the unusual combination of research in India and in Pakistan facilitated a balanced analysis of the Punjabi borderlands that straddle the Radcliffe line.

This story centres on a small number of individuals: first and foremost, Radcliffe, the man who had responsibility for the boundary line, as well as Lord Louis Mountbatten, the last viceroy of India, Jawaharlal Nehru and Sardar Vallabhbhai Patel, leaders of the Indian National Congress, and Muhammad Ali Jinnah, head of the Muslim League. (Although Mahatma Gandhi could still rally public support, his influence within the Congress Party was waning and he had little direct involvement in the partition negotiations.[5]) Evan Jenkins, the Governor of pre-partition Punjab, emerges as a Cassandra-like figure, persistently warning of the dire consequences of partition. But my argument also has a great deal to do with the sweeping drives of British imperialism, Indian and Pakistani nationalism, and decolonization. In addition to analysing the role of individual experience and choice, therefore, this book considers the influence of larger historical forces. It explores the balance between the role of individuals and that of structural influences. My conclusions about the forces that shaped the

Indo-Pakistani boundary would seem to support a structural approach, but the lessons of this particular division could be read another way. If at any point, key individuals had decided to take another path – for example, if Radcliffe had withdrawn his services once he reached India and learned of the extremely tight deadline imposed on his work – the outcome could have been dramatically different. Alternatively, if the key individuals had had different backgrounds – for example, if all the Indian leaders had not been lawyers but businessmen or engineers – the outcome could again have been very different. This argument concerns individuals attempting to do what they saw as best under the pressures of larger structural forces and as a result both struggling against and bowing to these forces.

Although the Radcliffe boundary commission is well known to every Indian and Pakistani schoolchild, only a handful of historians have examined it in any depth. Joya Chatterji's excellent 'The fashioning of a frontier: The Radcliffe line and Bengal's border landscape, 1947–52', focusing on the Bengal boundary commission, argues that the drawing of the border in Bengal was not a technical affair, but a line drawn in haste and ignorance, heavily influenced by political pressure.[6] Further-more, Chatterji demonstrates, the creation of the boundary was not a contained event, but a long-term political process, one which continues to this day.[7] She notes that the surgical analogies often used to describe partition reflect a number of misleading assumptions, including the ideas that partition was a remedy for communal violence, that it was conducted with clinical precision and that a trained expert carried it out.[8]

Few historians have attempted to situate the boundary question within the larger narrative of partition.[9] Those general histories of South Asia in the 1940s that touch on the boundary commission at all portray it as either a malicious conspiracy or an inexplicable disaster. Similarly, they paint Radcliffe either as a conspirator or as an ignorant bumbler. Many (although not all) of these conspiracy theories are based on a distortion of the established facts. The 'bumbler' school of histo-riography seems on the surface more credible. However, I argue that the peculiarities of the boundary commission must be understood in the context of British, League and Congress political imperatives. This book aims to show the boundary commission's place in the run-up to partition, particularly within the continuity of British colonial methods of control during the end of the raj.

These issues are important because the 1947 partition of South Asia remains significant on multiple levels. As an episode in imperial history, it marked the beginning of a global trend towards decoloniza-tion. For South Asian history, it meant independence for India and

Pakistan. Unfortunately, it also inaugurated Indo-Pakistani tension. Although conflict between Hindus and Muslims had existed on the subcontinent, to a greater or lesser degree, for many centuries, partition brought that conflict to the international level, and exacerbated it. The results include three wars, in 1948, 1965 and 1971, as well as the Kargil conflict of 1999. The need to resolve Indo-Pakistani tension took on greater urgency when both India and Pakistan tested their nuclear weapons in May 1998 and will continue as long as the risk of subcontinental nuclear war exists.

Although this book does not deal directly with the conflict over Kashmir, the division of Punjab relates tangentially to the Kashmir question. As a princely state, Kashmir was a semi-independent entity whose maharajah was entitled to decide for himself whether to accede to India or Pakistan. Radcliffe had no responsibility for deciding Kashmir's fate and no jurisdiction to draw any boundary in that state. However, some observers have alleged that Radcliffe gave sections of northern Punjab to India in order to provide strategic access to Kashmir.[10] These allegations are impossible to prove, but there are also indisputable geographical connections between Kashmir and Punjab, particularly the waters feeding the vital irrigation systems of both Indian and Pakistani Punjab, which originate in the Kashmiri mountains. The events of 1947 remain relevant to the prospects for peace in South Asia.

The first half of the book focuses on the high politics of the British withdrawal and of Indian and Pakistani independence, while the second half deals with the ground-level impact of the partition process. Chapter 1 provides an overview of the historical context that so profoundly affected these events, not only at the international and Indian levels, but also in local terms. Chapter 2, which covers June 1947, emphasizes the British creation of a façade of joint British–South Asian responsibility for the partition process as a key element of imperial control, even as that control slipped away. It also brings to life Cyril Radcliffe, a central character whom other historians have left as a shadowy, mysterious figure, and provides clear explanations for his motivations – and regrets. Chapter 3 takes the story into July and early August. It examines the problematic hearings and deliberations of the Punjab boundary commission, highlighting its deeply politicized nature. Chapter 4 draws on cartographic sources in order to provide a new analysis of the reasoning behind Radcliffe's final deliberations over the boundary line. It argues that because British imperial maps had been designed as tools of colonial control, they did not contain information that might have allowed the boundary commission to anticipate and prevent some of the economic and social disruptions that would wreak havoc in the months and years after partition. Chapter 5 lays out the contents and reception of Radcliffe's award, announced in mid-August, and explodes the myth of Radcliffe's independence.

After independence, the narrative moves to the local level, providing new material on life in the newly created borderlands. Chapter 6 deals with the impact of the Radcliffe line in the final months of 1947, revealing the price paid for independence by inhabitants of border areas. Chapter 7 offers an innovative counterfactual analysis of alternative lines, demonstrating that Radcliffe's line, while not ideal, resulted in less violence than any other major proposal likely would have done. Chapter 8 traces the development of the Punjabi borderlands, beginning with the first months and years of independence, particularly the Radcliffe line's initially devastating impact on the irrigation system that fed Punjab's crucial agricultural areas. Drawing on previously unseen material on government negotiations over the partition boundary in the 1950s and 1960s, as well as documents on the boundary's effect on local inhabitants of the borderlands, it continues with a detailed and hitherto unknown picture of the continuing development of these zones of interaction between Indians and Pakistanis. Chapter 9 returns to the central figure of Cyril Radcliffe, clarifying Radcliffe's motivations for accepting his impossible task, as well as the impact of that experience on his own understanding of empire. The conclusion revisits the major themes of the book and highlights policy-relevant aspects of this study of partition.

Notes

1 Muhammad Munir, *From Jinnah to Zia* (Lahore: Vanguard Books, 1980), p. 18.
2 For the Bengal boundary commission, see Joya Chatterji, *The Spoils of Partition: Bengal and India, 1947–1967* (Cambridge: Cambridge University Press, 2007), pp. 19–60.
3 Peter Ward Fay, *The Forgotten Army: India's Armed Struggle for Independence 1942–1945* (Ann Arbor: University of Michigan Press, 1993), p. 3, also pp. 520–1. Many thanks to Vijay Pinch for bringing this point to my attention.
4 Chatterji, *Spoils*, pp. 25–6.
5 Judith Brown, *Gandhi: Prisoner of Hope* (New Haven: Yale University Press, 1989), p. 369.
6 Joya Chatterji, 'The fashioning of a frontier: The Radcliffe Line and Bengal's border landscape, 1947–52', *Modern Asian Studies* 33:1 (1999), pp. 185–242 and *Spoils*, pp. 19–60.
7 Chatterji, 'Fashioning', p. 242.
8 Chatterji, 'Fashioning', pp. 185–6.
9 David Gilmartin offers an excellent critique of partition historiography in 'Partition, Pakistan, and South Asian history: In search of a narrative', *Journal of Asian Studies* 57:4 (November 1998), pp. 1068–95.
10 Alastair Lamb, *Incomplete Partition: The Genesis of the Kashmir Dispute 1947–1948* (Hertingfordbury: Roxford Books, 1997), pp. 110–11.

CHAPTER ONE

'Standing on the edge of a volcano': the historical context of partition

With conflict between Hindus, Muslims and Sikhs reaching unprecedented levels in the mid-1940s, British leaders felt compelled to move towards decolonization. Adding to the pressure driving this decision were international considerations and domestic pressures in Britain itself. When Mountbatten arrived in March 1947 as India's last viceroy, he emphasized the need for haste. The importance of the worldwide audience, however, necessitated that this speedy departure be cloaked in pretended orderliness, to quell any notion that Britain had been forced out.

Although the events of 1947 moved at high speed towards the August partition, Indian independence had not always been such an urgent goal for the British Government. The first half of the twentieth century saw a series of reforms that increased South Asians' participation in their own governance.[1] Among these were the Morley-Minto reforms of 1909, often regarded as containing the seeds of partition. By creating separate electorates for different religious communities, however, they also implanted the idea that Indian society consisted of fundamentally different groups, encouraging political leaders to identify themselves primarily in terms of communal difference.[2] Politicians found religious rhetoric useful for rallying support, sometimes with dangerous results. In the elections of 1937 and 1945-46, both the secular Indian National Congress (steered by Jawaharlal Nehru, Sardar Vallabhbhai Patel and an ageing Mahatma Gandhi) and the Muslim League, which claimed to represent South Asia's Muslims (and was led by Muhammad Ali Jinnah and Liaquat Ali Khan), played on communal themes.

With the onset of World War II, the British-controlled Government of India found itself in a difficult position. Britain declared war on India's behalf, without any pretence of consultation, and Indian political leaders and public opinion were outraged. The prospect of civil unrest loomed.[3] In 1942, with the Allies in urgent need of a reliable Indian base, Prime Minister Winston Churchill dispatched Sir Stafford Cripps to India at the head of a Cabinet delegation charged with exploring the possibility of self-government after the war. Cripps offered an implicit promise that if India fought in the war it would be granted freedom, which Congress rejected with Gandhi's memorable phrase that it was a 'postdated cheque on a failing bank'.[4] In the aftermath of Cripps's failed mission, Gandhi launched the 'Quit India' non-cooperation movement, which the British repressed violently. Notwithstanding dissatisfaction in India, Indian troops fought valiantly for the Allied cause in World War II.[5] Nehru himself, reluctant to undermine the battle against fascism, had mixed feelings about the Quit India movement.[6]

With the conflict's end, Indian leaders and people alike expected to be repaid for their wartime support with independence. In Britain, the Conservatives were voted out and the Labour Party took power, under Clement Attlee. Meanwhile, the India Office was losing patience with its viceroy, Lord Wavell. Wavell's relations with the India Office had been steadily worsening throughout 1946. Wavell, a career military man whose stolid exterior concealed a sensitive, poetry-writing bent, had led India since 1943.[7] Left with the difficult job of guiding India through treacherous postwar waters, he sent increasingly blunt warnings to London that its Indian policies were misguided and inadequate to the challenges ahead. Lord Pethick-Lawrence, Britain's Secretary of State for India, resented these warnings and paid less and less attention to them as time went on. In particular, Wavell's outline of potential partition boundaries, the first serious discussion of the issue, received little consideration. When Wavell assembled a 'Breakdown Plan', calling for a complete British withdrawal from South Asia, the British Cabinet was alarmed. In 1946, Attlee sent another Cabinet-level delegation to India in hopes of negotiating a less drastic outcome.[8] The resulting proposal, known as the 'ABC Plan', called for a loose federation to consist of three groups of provinces, each of which had the option to 'opt out' of the federation. The north-eastern and north-western groups were predominantly Muslim; the south-central group was predominantly Hindu. (For an overview of pre-partition India, see map 1.) This proposal met a curious reception. It was first accepted, then rejected, by Congress; the Muslim League initially announced that it would cooperate, but in the aftermath of the Congress decision renounced constitutional methods and declared 'Direct Action Day'.

In Calcutta, capital of the north-eastern province of Bengal, 'Direct Action Day' quickly became the 'Great Calcutta Killing'. Some 4000 Bengalis, both Hindu and Muslim, were killed and a communal war of succession began.[9] During this unrest, the north-western province of

Punjab remained relatively quiet, even though its Sikhs, Hindus and Muslims had all built up communal militias throughout the turbulent 1920s and 1930s. In March 1947, however, during the first major episode of Punjabi mass violence, Sikh militias proved largely ineffective and many Sikhs were killed. As a result, the community's leaders redoubled their efforts to organize communal armies, spurred by a desire for revenge.[10]

Punjab had played an outsized role in Indian affairs since the nineteenth century, even though it was one of the British raj's last acquisitions. The British only annexed Punjab in 1849, after overcoming staunch Sikh resistance. Initially, the new territory's strategic value lay in its geographical proximity to Afghanistan and its position astride the potential Russian invasion route. Within a decade, it took on new significance, as its inhabitants provided crucial support to the British side during the 1857 uprising. In the decades after the rebellion, the British strengthened their military position in Punjab by constructing extensive railway and road networks, in order to facilitate troop deployment.[11] They also extended the existing canal system.

The agricultural changes that grew out of these canal extensions, particularly the 1890 initiation of canal projects in the dry western Punjab, significantly affected Punjabi society. The British selected settlers from certain groups to colonize the new planned villages in the west, known as the canal colonies. Through this decades-long effort, the British state was able to reinforce the social status quo, consolidate loyalty to itself and counter unrest. Land-distribution policies also had the effect of boosting the importance of the military and moving significant numbers of Sikhs and Hindus to areas that had formerly been largely Muslim.[12] These demographic changes would have tragic consequences in 1947.

British land policies also contributed to the strength of the Punjab National Unionist Party, which represented the agricultural classes. Throughout the 1920s, 1930s and early 1940s, the Unionists, an alliance of loyalist rural landholders that included Hindus, Muslims and Sikhs, dominated the Punjab council. Even as nationalist parties, particularly the Indian National Congress, gained ground in other provinces in the 1920s and 1930s, the pro-British Unionists were able to maintain their hold on power in Punjab.

The Muslim League exerted relatively little influence in the province until the 1940s. It was roundly defeated by the Unionists in the 1937 elections. During the subsequent decade, however, the League's strength grew, and it emerged triumphant from the 1946 elections. Congress and the Unionists joined forces against it, forming a coalition to keep the League out of the provincial government. But in

[11]

March 1947, a League non-cooperation campaign against this coalition proved so effective that the Unionist-led government resigned.[13] When the provincial Muslim League proved unable to form a coalition government of its own, Jenkins imposed direct governor's rule, under Section 93 of the 1935 Government of India Act. Communal violence spiked in the following week.[14] The Unionist resignation ended an era of cooperation across religious groups (albeit confined to economic elites); the rest of 1947 would see a downward spiral into intense communal conflict.

By the beginning of 1947, Pethick-Lawrence and Attlee had lost all confidence in Wavell, regarding him as 'frankly pretty defeatist'.[15] In February 1947, Attlee asked Wavell to resign; when he refused, the Prime Minister unceremoniously sacked him. Lord Louis Mountbatten, a career naval officer and cousin to the king, was appointed in his place. Mountbatten was already acquainted with Nehru, whom he had met in 1946 while serving as the Supreme Allied Commander for South East Asia. The ambitious and forceful Mountbatten was given a June 1948 deadline by which to disentangle Britain from India. When he arrived in India in March 1947, he quickly concluded that a rapprochement between the various parties was impossible, which meant that partition offered the quickest route to Britain's withdrawal. Within a few months he decided to move the decolonization deadline up, to 15 August 1947.

The history of the demand for a separate Muslim state is too complex to address fully here, but it is important to note that Muslim League statements never specified where Pakistan's boundaries would fall.[16] By keeping the Pakistan idea geographically vague, the shrewd tactician Jinnah hoped to appeal to the largest possible constituency. He also saw that there was a tactical advantage in refusing to define Pakistan until the last possible moment.[17] In the end, this gamble backfired; when the Congress Party finally consented to partition, it did so on the condition that the provinces of Punjab (in north-west India) and Bengal (in the north-east) be divided, rather than go to Pakistan in their entirety. This decision had a dramatic effect on the outcome of partition. The Sikhs, who comprised some 13 per cent of the population of undivided Punjab, were perhaps the community most deeply impacted by partition. Rather than offer a realistic alternative that would protect their needs within India or Pakistan, however, they proposed an independent Sikh state, which both Congress and the League found unpalatable. In the absence of any defined proposals, let alone any agreed line, British authorities decided to proceed towards independence on the basis of a 'notional boundary' (see map 2). Lines were drawn through Bengal and Punjab, based solely on the distribution of Muslim-majority districts as defined in the 1941 census. As no one pretended that these lines were permanent, their administrative utility was limited at best. Anxieties rose throughout the summer of 1947, as residents of Bengal and Punjab waited fearfully for the final boundary decision.

The rush to devolve power

Of the major parties involved – the British, Congress and the League – each had powerful incentives to proceed with the handover at high speed. Britain was suffering serious financial troubles, as well as heavy international pressure to decolonize. Congress leaders were eager to take power after years of opposition, which had included long stretches in prison. As for Jinnah, his precarious health may have given him a more personal reason for desiring a rapid handover.

For the British Labour Government, a number of factors, both international and domestic, dictated the push for a rapid withdrawal. Partition was shaped not only by decades of Indian nationalist pressure on the British Government and by the rise of civil unrest in the subcontinent, but also by Britain's precarious economic position in the aftermath of World War II. After nearly two centuries as an extraordinary asset, Britain's colonial holdings in South Asia became an economic liability at a time when Britain could least afford it.[18] Domestic political concerns also swayed Britain's newly elected Labour Government, and American pressure to decolonize influenced both international and British domestic opinion against the raj. British India became a political and symbolic liability as well as an economic problem, and ridding itself of its Indian encumbrances became a priority for the British Government.

At the same time, British leaders were grappling with another problematic imperial holding: the Palestine Mandate. In December 1946, British leaders came reluctantly to the conclusion that it was impossible to resolve the conflicting World War I promises made to Zionists and to Arabs. Political considerations played a major role in this decision, for British leaders had become increasingly convinced that maintaining good relations with Arab leaders was vital to preserve Britain's position in the Middle East. Withdrawing from the mandate, renouncing efforts to support the establishment of a Jewish homeland in Palestine and handing the problem over to the UN was, to the British, the best way to avoid making decisions that would alienate Arab allies.[19] The decision to carve a sovereign Muslim state out of India was therefore taken within a larger international context in which future relations with Muslim leaders were considered a top priority.

The British were also keenly aware of the need to placate their American ally. A British military officer in India in 1947 later stressed the role of international forces in the British decision to decolonize, offering a vividly imperialist view of the pressures on the British Government:

> By 1946 the British had reached the stage at which, in pretty nearly every international discussion, they were treading on such thin ice as 'oppressors' of Indians in the eyes of the U.S.A. and Russia, that their influence at conferences was being most seriously impaired. Peripatetic Indians were prancing about England, and particularly the U.S.A., shrilling in public places the terrible oppressions carried out by the British in India.[20]

Leaving aside its dramatic pro-imperial language, this passage shows the effect of South Asian nationalist activities at a time when Britain felt the need to bolster its image as a democratic power in the eyes of its international partners. This need was particularly urgent because the United States held the key to Britain's economic future.

But the United States was not the only rising superpower on the international scene; the British were also confronted by the spectre of the Soviet Union. Russia had been British India's historic opponent in the Great Game for control of Central Asia and the approaches to South Asia. Although fears of Soviet influence on a newly independent subcontinent were a continuation of Britain's past preoccupation, the rise of communism lent added urgency to the situation. During the troubles of 1947, with many concerns competing for their attention, the British continued to devote intelligence resources to tracking communist activity in India.[21] Maintaining an image of control, even if the reality was more chaotic, may have been part of a British effort to keep the Soviet Union from sensing and seeking to fill a power vacuum in South Asia.

In addition to these rapidly developing international concerns, Britain's postwar economic woes also drove the decision to leave India. Rationing was worse than it had been during the war, and the bitter winter of 1946–47 exposed severe coal shortages.[22] In addition, India was no longer the valuable market for British manufactures it had been for so long; more significantly, India's wartime loans to Britain transformed the colony from debtor to major creditor. As a result, 'in Britain's changed and desperate economic situation in 1945, India had ceased to be an imperial asset'.[23] Given that the raj no longer benefited it, the British Government lost its desire to support the cost of the Indian administration.

Domestic political considerations also impelled the Labour Government to leave India.[24] Labour had traditionally been aligned with the Indian National Congress, and had in fact campaigned in 1945 on a platform that explicitly promised 'the advancement of India to responsible self-government'.[25] Attlee himself had a special interest in India. He had been a member of the Simon commission on constitutional reform, which visited India in 1928–29.[26] In addition, by 1947 many British administrators in India felt strong incentives to pull out. There was a growing sense that the law and order situation was beyond repair and that the British could exercise meaningful authority only a short time longer. As Mountbatten described it later, speed was required 'because the thing was breaking up under my hands. The reason was that neither side would cooperate with each other. I could feel the damn thing simmering. It's like standing on the edge of a volcano and feeling the moment of explosion.'[27] It is curious that Munir independently chose the same volcanic metaphor to describe the aftermath of Mountbatten's work.

As a result of these varied pressures, the British Government felt that it was vital to leave India as quickly as possible. The manner of leaving, however, had to be carefully considered. It was necessary that Britain should appear to hand over its colonial responsibilities in an orderly, democratic fashion, not only to reassure its American allies, but also to demonstrate to the rest of its imperial holdings that it was still very much in control. The Indian handover, as it happened, was far from orderly, but the British did their best to present it as a rational process. The Radcliffe boundary commission was central to this presentation.

Although it may seem natural to assume that the nationalist leaders wanted independence as quickly as possible, the question of why Congress and the Muslim League agreed to such a hasty transfer of power deserves careful consideration. Further study is required to explain why these leaders, after fighting for independence with such patience and determination, agreed to a number of short-sighted and misguided policies in the months leading up to partition – policies that in some cases had disastrous results. Among these decisions was the entire boundary issue, which received little consideration. Although there is evidence that the Congress and League leaders found themselves overwhelmed by the immensity of the task facing them and were happy enough to agree to what in some cases seemed like temporary solutions, this question warrants further attention. In the meantime, several suggestive themes emerge from the existing literature.

The Indian National Congress shared Britain's desire for a speedy handover, albeit for somewhat different reasons. After contesting

British rule for decades, Congress leaders were eager to attain independence. Gandhi had begun pushing for an unconditional withdrawal years earlier, with uncompromising calls to 'leave India to God. If that is too much, then leave her to anarchy.'[28] He rejected the notion that India needed British assistance to ensure the continuation of law and order after independence; the time for patience was past. Nehru later recalled feeling that Congress had to seize this prime opportunity, even if it meant partition: 'We saw no other way of getting our freedom – in the near future, I mean.'[29] Furthermore, most of the Congress leaders believed that Pakistan was not a viable state and that partition would be a temporary measure ultimately resulting in reunification.[30] Fatigue may also have been a factor. The leaders of Congress, including Nehru, who was a generation younger than Gandhi, had laboured under trying conditions for years. Many of them had endured lengthy jail terms. As Nehru, who had spent nine years in various British Indian prisons, later recalled, 'The truth is we were tired men, and we were getting on in years too.'[31] The Congress leaders were running out of time to rid themselves of the British and still have the opportunity to shape the postcolonial state.

Like the British, however, Congress feared losing its control. Authority over the Congress rank and file was slipping away, as local members grew disillusioned waiting for independence and some succumbed to communalism.[32] Patel put a different spin on the problem, arguing that because Congress was pledged to non-violence, it could not resist partition; to do so could mean the end of the party.[33] Finally, Congress leaders also feared that simmering communal tensions could explode unless drastic action was taken. Ironically, this fear of violence did not impel them to insist on more thorough preparations to deal with the possibility of post-partition killing.

The Muslim League, and particularly its leader, Muhammad Ali Jinnah, also wanted to grasp the reins of power as soon as possible. By the mid-1940s, Jinnah was obviously unwell, although it is not clear whether he knew how severe his illness was.[34] One biographer quotes Jinnah's sister, with whom he was very close, as saying, 'For several years before his death there was a constant tug-of-war between his physicians and the *Quaid-i-Azam* [Great Leader, Jinnah's preferred title]. They warned him to take long intervals of rest and short hours of hard work, but he did exactly the opposite, knowing full well the risk he was running.'[35] If Jinnah was aware that a life-threatening medical condition underlay his chronic lung problems, an even greater urgency may have impelled him during these crucial months. He died of lung disease in September 1948, having had far too little time to set Pakistan on the tolerant course he apparently envisioned.

The Sikhs, who would be profoundly affected by these plans for partition, were poorly represented in New Delhi. Baldev Singh, the Minister of Defence, was the sole Sikh member of the Partition Council. Although he took part in the negotiations over the form of independence, it was not clear to what extent he could speak for the Sikh community, who were represented by a range of political parties, none of which wielded much influence at the centre. In the end, his assurances that the Sikhs would accept the boundary award meant little in the face of Sikh fear and outrage. Other leaders, particularly the influential Master Tara Singh, wielded the real power, through their ability to conjure up mass violence in Punjab. The British claimed to be baffled by the Sikhs' acceptance of the partition plan. Mountbatten publicly said, 'I found that it was mainly at the request of the Sikh community that Congress had put forward the Resolution on the partition of the Punjab ... when I sent for the map and studied the distribution of the Sikh population under this proposal, I must say that I was astounded to find that the plan which they had produced divided their community into two almost equal parts.'[36] Some groups proposed an independent Sikh state, but their claims were ignored.[37] Evan Jenkins, the Governor of Punjab, was in regular touch with the Sikh leaders, but he deplored what he saw as their naive approach to the political questions at hand. After an interview with one leading Sikh, he described him as 'still unhappy and extremely puzzled. He and Master Tara Singh have certainly made a great mess of the whole Sikh question.'[38] The Sikhs did not share the League and Congress enthusiasm for a rapid handover, but they found themselves power-less to stop it.

Despite the motivations outlined above, there were those who felt the nationalist parties, particularly Congress, having waited so long, could afford to devote a bit more time to ensuring that independence was achieved under the right conditions. As one historian asks, 'having waited thirty years, should they not have waited a little longer, as Gandhi suggested? Perhaps they did not because they had been totally demoralized by the events of 1942 [when Congress leaders launched the Quit India movement and were jailed *en masse*] and beyond.'[39] Whatever the reasons that impelled the rush to devolve power, it is clear that all the actors involved felt the tremendous pressure of the times. By mid-1947, the Muslim League and Congress were willing to cooperate with the British in rushing through the handover.

Cartography and power in imperial India

In addition to the political context of partition, we must also examine the role of maps, for these technical documents played a central part in the partition drama. Cartographic analysis is a key element of this book. Maps were crucial tools in Britain's system of imperial control over South Asia, from the earliest days of Britain's involvement in the subcontinent.[40] Examining the relationship between cartography and imperial control illuminates the nature of that power, both at its height and at its end. The main institution responsible for British imperial map-making was the Survey of India.

In recent years, the study of cartography has moved away from a tendency to evaluate maps as scientifically accurate or inaccurate, opening up new fields of inquiry into the nature of maps as instruments of power.[41] Maps can no longer be regarded as neutral tools, but as texts that convey the biases of their makers. Properly read, maps illuminate the political character of the institutions or societies that produce or use them.

British efforts to map South Asia were limited by British perceptions of the land under their control. As a leading scholar of imperial cartography in India writes, the British cartographic archive 'described and allowed access to ... *British* India, a rational and ordered space that could be managed and governed in a rational and ordered manner'.[42] In mapping 'British India', the British actually created it. They also gave it an artificial geographical unity.[43] Ironically, dismantling that unity would be, at least in part, a British undertaking as well.

Recent cartographic research has demonstrated that maps are constructed according to political values and purposes, and the maps produced by the British raj are no exception. The British gathered knowledge about India in order to exercise power over it: 'the British mapping of India was an exercise in discipline: the British surveyed the Indian landscapes in an effort to assess and to improve them'.[44] A close look at these maps and the context in which they were produced provides useful insights into the multiple levels on which the British understood India. To British officials, the subcontinent was a theatre of war to be conquered and pacified, a territory to be controlled once conquest was complete, and a space to be administered and taxed. They also pictured it as an arena of unchanging social hierarchies and as a landscape marked by British historical achievements and sacrifices. Surveyors and mapmakers in particular understood India in scientific terms, as a domain open to being comprehensively understood in clear, categorical terms.

The Survey of India, known to its staff as 'the Department', was

[18]

responsible for producing Government of India maps of the subcontinent. Its twentieth-century work was hampered by the two world wars, both of which temporarily diverted many of its resources and most of its men.[45] In 1905, the Department was reorganized, partly in response to complaints from military authorities that its maps were not 'modern' and that military surveys were too slow. The subsequent reforms brought new policies, new printing machinery and the use of new colour techniques.[46] The Department also implemented a systematic scheme for a modern topographical survey of all of southern Asia. The territory between meridians 44° and 124°, east of Greenwich, and between parallels 4° and 40°, north latitude, was to be mapped on the scale of 1:1,000,000. These maps were subdivided into 16 'degree sheets', on the scale of one inch to four miles, which covered 1° latitude by 1° longitude. The degree sheets were in turn subdivided into maps on the scale of one inch to the mile, which covered 15' latitude by 15' longitude.[47] In 1914, however, the loss of many officers and surveyors called up to serve in World War I greatly disrupted this ambitious project. Even after the war, the Department found itself short-handed, necessitating heavy recruitment until 1925. As a result, its programmes were further delayed.[48]

The global depression of the 1930s hampered the Survey still further, as budget restrictions nearly halved it. As a former Surveyor-General noted, 'it was clear that there was no chance whatever of completing the "modern" survey of India in anything like the twenty-five years originally specified and still less, with the curtailed personnel and funds, of keeping up-to-date such maps as we had'.[49] By 1939, however, new policies had considerably accelerated map production.[50] These successes were short-lived, for the Survey not only lost many men to the mobilization for World War II but also devoted its remaining resources and staff to military needs. With Japan's entry into the war, the Department focused much of its energy on maps of eastern India and the subcontinent's eastern coast.[51] Personnel shortages were so severe that the Department brought from Britain members of the Royal Engineers who had been civilian printing tradesmen and even utilized Italian prisoners of war with experience in air surveying.[52] Land surveys were almost completely halted, except in cases of military requirement. The press of time and lack of personnel meant that air-survey techniques took the place of previous methods.

Beginning in 1943, a few civilian projects once again took priority, as the Government of India launched its 'Grow More Food' campaign in response to that year's devastating Bengal famine. This effort involved reservoir projects for which survey information was required, including the Punjab's Chenab and Sutlej valleys. This work, carried out during

1944 and 1945, relied on air surveys. During the same period, a Punjab Irrigation Party undertook an irrigation survey in the Gurgaon area, near New Delhi. Even during the war, the British authorities considered it essential to continue amassing cartographic information on Punjab, albeit on a much-reduced level.

Imperial perceptions of India as a conquered territory are unambiguously indicated by one of the most striking symbols on Survey of India maps: two crossed swords, accompanied by a date, that indicate major British battles against indigenous resistance. These icons indicate British victories, but also sacrifices; from a British perspective, they memorialize the price Britain paid to conquer, pacify and govern a distant land.[53] The region was a prize worth fighting for in part because of its revenue potential. Like the Mughal emperors before them, British officials devoted a great deal of thought and resources to the assessment and collection of land returns. From 1767 to 1905, the Survey of India was responsible for revenue surveys.[54] The creation of cadastral maps, intended to rationalize and facilitate tax collection at the ground level, was an important element of the imperial accumulation of local cartographic knowledge.[55] As cartographic historian Matthew Edney notes, 'maps were fundamental tools of rule'.[56]

Survey of India maps (like the ones Radcliffe used to indicate his final boundary decision) featured administrative divisions prominently. The basic unit of British administration, the *thana*, was an area of varying size, based on the jurisdiction of local police stations. That the range of police power marked the foundation of British administration indicates that control, through law and order, was a primary concern. Once that control eroded, as it did during the 1940s, British rule was no longer possible. Indian Army sepoys and Indian policemen were crucial to the exercise of power, for the raj depended on local collaboration to maintain relative stability. When the balance between collaboration and resistance swung towards the latter, British decision-makers were left only with the choice of when, not whether, to relinquish power.

The Survey of India's mapping efforts were also based on an attempt to understand the space of the Indian empire in scientific terms. That attempt included an emphasis on totality; the entirety of Indian space was to be included in the Survey of India's work.[57] This project implied that India itself could be completely understood, in scientific terms, and that, in addition, this complete understanding could be transferred to the map-reader through the cartographic medium. The Survey of India's vision of the subcontinent also placed it within an international scientific context, as demonstrated by efforts in the early twentieth century to link its surveys and maps with those of neighbouring countries, including Persia and the Russian empire.[58]

However, British understanding of the subcontinent coexisted with serious misunderstanding. Official dealings with Indians on social and religious matters demonstrated a lack of comprehension of the range and nuance of Indian identities. Many British administrators regarded India as a land of strict social hierarchy and religious division.[59] This view did not allow for an understanding of India as a space of complex social relations between individuals and groups with multiple layered identities. This misapprehension, often construed as part of a strategy of 'divide and rule', contributed to the political fissures that resulted in partition. As we will see, it also influenced the boundary-making process itself, for the information provided to Radcliffe reflected the raj's lack of comprehension of Indian society. The census data and gazetteers that Radcliffe perused portrayed a land in which people identified themselves in categorical terms, as Hindu, Muslim, Sikh etc. They did not reflect local understandings of an individual or community's various identities or the interplay of religious affiliation, kinship ties, political associations and economic links. By demonstrating that Hindus, Sikhs and Muslims lived in intermingled communities, the information Radcliffe saw did make clear that these three groups could not be divided easily; unfortunately, the reality on the ground was even more complex than Radcliffe's documents showed.

Finally, Survey of India maps depicted the subcontinent as a unified space – unified, of course, under British rule. This apparent unity was deceptive, however, because the Indian empire was actually cobbled together from a combination of states headed by princes under Britain's indirect rule, and provinces directly ruled by the British. Administrative boundaries were vital to this image of unity. They marked British-created units of governance, units that reported to the colonial centre, New Delhi. As such, these administrative lines were a marker (on maps, if not on the actual terrain) of the legacy of rational governance and law and order that British colonialists imagined themselves leaving to independent India.

In short, British maps displayed select elements of Indian terrain as the British understood them and as they pertained to British interests. It is ironic that these fundamentally imperial maps were used to draw up the end of empire. A new survey producing new maps for the postcolonial states would have been more appropriate than a continued reliance on maps produced for specifically colonial purposes, but the timeframe imposed in Delhi did not allow it. It is true that Survey of India maps contained a great deal of information, but they also left out a great deal, such as trade patterns and kinship bonds. The Survey's maps did not capture the diversity of relationships, within and across these boundaries, that would be disrupted by partition. As a result, Survey maps were useful only up to a point. They were invaluable as tools to help the British control British India as they understood it, but they did not display the kinds of information that would allow the division of India with the minimum disruption – or, perhaps, demonstrate that a minimally invasive procedure was not possible. Even on local revenue survey maps, the villages that were home to the vast majority of South Asians appeared only as blank space, outlined by administrative boundaries (see for example map 3). The voices of those living in those villages, voices that might have argued for a different boundary line, were stilled by this cartographic silence. This silence stands in stark contrast to the British portrayal of partition as a process that drew heavily on South Asian input.

Notes

1   Thomas Metcalf, *Ideologies of the Raj* (Cambridge: Cambridge University Press, 1995), p. 223.
2   Metcalf, *Ideologies*, pp. 224–5.
3   Barbara D. Metcalf and Thomas R. Metcalf, *A Concise History of India* (Cambridge: Cambridge University Press, 2002), p. 200.
4   Metcalf and Metcalf, p. 202.
5   Others fought beside the Japanese in the Indian National Army, an episode addressed by Fay.
6   Michael Brecher, *Nehru: A Political Biography* (London: Oxford University Press, 1959), p. 259.
7   For a full biography of Wavell, see Victoria Schofield, *Wavell: Soldier and Statesman* (London: John Murray, 2006).
8   Lamb, *Incomplete Partition*, p. 23.
9   Metcalf and Metcalf, p. 213.
10 Khushwant Singh, *A History of the Sikhs*, vol. 2 (Princeton: Princeton University Press, 1966), pp. 265–73.
11 For the importance of the military in Punjabi society, see Tan Tai Yong, *The Garrison State: Military, Government and Society in Colonial Punjab, 1849–1947* (New Delhi: Sage Publications, 2005).
12 Imran Ali, *The Punjab under Imperialism, 1885–1947* (Princeton: Princeton University Press, 1988).
13 David Gilmartin, *Empire and Islam: Punjab and the Making of Pakistan* (Berkeley: University of California Press, 1988), pp. 222–3.
14 Ian Talbot, *Khizr Tiwana, the Punjab Unionist Party and the Partition of India* (Richmond: Curzon Press, 1996), pp. 160–1.
15 Francis Williams, *A Prime Minister Remembers: The War and Postwar Memoirs of The Rt. Hon. Earl Attlee* (London: Heinemann, 1961), p. 209.
16 For the development of the Pakistan demand, see Khursheed Kamal Aziz, *A History of the Idea of Pakistan*, 4 vols (Lahore: Vanguard Books, 1987).
17 Ayesha Jalal, *The Sole Spokesman* (Cambridge: Cambridge University Press, 1985), p. 119.
18 P. J. Cain and Anthony Hopkins, *British Imperialism: Crisis and Deconstruction, 1914–1990* (London: Longman, 1993), p. 196.
19 See Wm. Roger Louis, *The British Empire in the Middle East, 1945–1951* (Oxford: Clarendon Press, 1984).

20 Francis Tuker, *While Memory Serves* (London: Cassell, 1950), p. 505.
21 See for example the Government of India's fortnightly reports for Punjab, September–December 1947, in which 'Communists' is a primary category, along with 'Communal' and 'Refugees'; NAI 10(16)-PR/47.
22 T. E. B. Howarth vividly describes these privations in *Prospect and Reality: Great Britain 1945–1955* (London: Collins, 1985), pp. 45–61.
23 Cain and Hopkins, *Crisis and Deconstruction*, p. 196.
24 It is also possible that the speed with which Labour rushed through the withdrawal was related to fears that the Conservative Party, led by Winston Churchill, who remained a staunch opponent of decolonization, might return to power. However, polls in 1946 showed that the Conservatives, who had yet to recover from their unexpected defeat in 1945, lacked the popular support to unseat Labour. Henry Pelling, *The Labour Governments, 1945–51* (London: Macmillan Press, 1984), p. 72.
25 'Let us face the future' (New York: League for Industrial Democracy, 1945), p. 29.
26 Robin J. Moore, *Escape from Empire: The Attlee Government and the Indian Problem* (Oxford: Clarendon Press, 1983), pp. 1–2.
27 Larry Collins and Dominique Lapierre, *Mountbatten and the Partition of India* (New Delhi: Vikas Publishing House, 1999), p. 73.
28 *Harijan*, 24 May 1942, cited in *The Collected Works of Mahatma Gandhi*, vol. LXXVI (New Delhi: The Publications Division, Ministry of Information and Broadcasting, Government of India, 1979), p. 119.
29 Brecher, *Nehru*, p. 377.
30 Brecher, *Nehru*, p. 377.
31 Leonard Mosley, *The Last Days of the British Raj* (New York: Harcourt, Brace & World, 1962), p. 248.
32 Michael Edwardes, *Nehru: A Political Biography* (New York: Praeger Publishers, 1971), p. 196.
33 B. Krishna, *Sardar Vallabhbhai Patel: India's Iron Man* (New Delhi: HarperCollins, 1996), p. 278.
34 Patrick French, *Liberty or Death* (London: HarperCollins, 1997), pp. 364–5.
35 Hector Bolitho, *Jinnah: Creator of Pakistan* (London: John Murray, 1954), p. 219.
36 Nicholas Mansergh et al., eds, *Constitutional Relations between Britain and India: The Transfer of Power 1942–7*, vol. XI (London: HMSO, 1982), p. 112. Hereafter, I have abbreviated volumes from this series as *TP*, followed by volume and page number.
37 Singh, *History*, p. 272.
38 *TP* XII p. 431.
39 Brecher, *Nehru*, p. 380.
40 Lucy P. Chester, 'The mapping of empire: French and British cartographies of India in the late eighteenth century', *Portuguese Studies* 16 (October 2000).
41 J. B. Harley was perhaps the driving force behind this shift; *The New Nature of Maps* (Baltimore: Johns Hopkins University Press, 2001) collects seven of Harley's most important articles.
42 Matthew Edney, *Mapping an Empire: The Geographical Construction of British India, 1765–1843* (Chicago: University of Chicago Press, 1997), p. 34. Emphasis in original.
43 Edney, p. 16. In tracing the evolution of 'frontiers into boundaries', Ainslie Embree notes that British imperial insistence on defining India's borders played, albeit unintentionally, a vital role in the independence movement. Ainslie T. Embree, 'Frontiers into boundaries: The evolution of the modern state', in *Imagining India: Essays on Indian History*, ed. Mark Juergensmeyer (Delhi: Oxford University Press, 1989), p. 82.
44 Edney, p. 334.
45 For the Survey's earlier history, see Edney.
46 Oliver Wheeler, *The Survey of India during War and Early Reconstruction, 1939–1946* (Dehra Dun: Survey of India, 1955), p. 2. Wheeler is the primary source

for information on the Survey of India during the first half of the twentieth century. The paucity of information for this period may be explained by the disruptions of World War II and South Asia's subsequent partition, which likely deterred other would-be chroniclers.

47 W. M. Coldstream, *Records of the Survey of India, Vol. XII: Notes on Survey of India Maps and the Modern Development of Indian Cartography* (Calcutta: Survey of India, 1919), p. 2.
48 Wheeler, p. 3.
49 Wheeler, p. 5.
50 Wheeler, p. 16.
51 Wheeler, p. 48.
52 These prisoners, who were assigned to civil projects, did good work and the Department was sorry to lose them when they were repatriated in 1945 (Wheeler, p. 73).
53 Indian views of these battles are rather different, and not only from the losing side; many 'British' casualties of these confrontations were of course Indian sepoys.
54 In 1904, the Government of India transferred responsibility for the cadastral surveys on which revenue collection depended to the provinces. Prabhakar Mishra, 'Cadastral surveys in India – A critique', www.gisdevelopment.net/application/lis/policy/lisp0001.htm, accessed 3 March 2008.
55 A cadastral survey measures plots of land for taxation purposes.
56 Edney, p. 295.
57 Edney, p. 17.
58 Sidney Gerald Burrard, *Completion of the Link Connecting the Triangulations of India and Russia 1913* (Dehra Dun: Trigonometrical Survey, 1914).
59 Bernard Cohn, 'The census, social structure and objectification in South Asia', in *An Anthropologist among the Historians and Other Essays* (Delhi: Oxford University Press, 1987), pp. 224–54.

CHAPTER TWO

'This is your country and it is up to you to decide': the façade of South Asian responsibility

British leaders were astonishingly slow in grappling with the problem of determining a new international boundary line.[1] Even after accepting that they could not leave India without clearly identifying the entity or entities that would take control, a project that would require defining the boundaries of those entities, the British do not seem to have appreciated how important, let alone how difficult, this task would be.[2] It was not until the summer of 1947 that British and South Asian decision-makers began serious discussions about the format and procedure of a boundary commission. Once the negotiations over the commission's structure began, however, the leaders involved reached agreement surprisingly quickly.

It is important to recognize, however, that this agreement came about under heavy British pressure. Despite the fact that the nationalist leaders appeared to have primary responsibility for the partition process, the British attempted to maintain the upper hand throughout. As the law and order situation disintegrated and control became increasingly difficult, British leaders had to engage in a precarious balancing act. On the one hand, they sought to portray the nationalist leaders as responsible for key decisions, while on the other they felt compelled to convince their own domestic and international audiences that they were still in control. In early May, Mountbatten urged that Britain should 'put the responsibility for any of these mad decisions fairly and squarely on the Indian shoulders *in the eyes of the world*' and advocated a plan that would 'place the responsibility for dividing India *conspicuously* on the Indians themselves'.[3] Worldwide perception was a key factor in the viceroy's calculations, and the boundary commission would play an important role in Mountbatten's effort to stage-manage partition.

Although well-established procedures were in place by the 1940s to guide the delimitation of international boundaries, the Punjab

[25]

commission diverged widely from the established format and methods. Briefly summarized, the commission's general outline was as follows. There would be two boundary commissions, one for Punjab and one for Bengal. Both commissions would be chaired by the same man, Sir Cyril Radcliffe, a British barrister who had earned respect for his intellectual abilities, but who had never been to India. The theory was that ignorance of India would equal impartiality. Each commission would consist of four South Asian judges; these judges were to be selected by the bitterly opposed Congress and League, which nominated two men each for both commissions. It was agreed that for the Punjab commission, one of the Congress nominees would be a Sikh. These men were all judges versed in criminal law. There was no requirement that they have any particular geographical expertise or any knowledge of the problematic precedents for partition. The commission gathered information by means of public hearings at which Congress, the Muslim League and a few other interested parties presented their views on where the boundary line should fall. In the end, the commission's format and the judges' strong political loyalties left Radcliffe responsible for all the most difficult decisions in Punjab.[4]

The commission's terms of reference directed it to 'demarcate the boundaries of the two parts of the Punjab on the basis of ascertaining the contiguous majority areas of Muslims and non-Muslims. In doing so, it will also take into account other factors.'[5] These terms, with their vague reference to 'other factors', allowed the chairman enormous leeway. However, after the final boundary, known as the 'Radcliffe award', was announced, all sides complained that Radcliffe had not taken the *right* 'other factors' into account.

The Punjab boundary commission was ostensibly a judicial body organized to hear proposals; it lacked the mandate or the means to gather geographic or demographic information for itself. The commission was formed without the benefit of technical advice; it was, instead, deeply influenced by the judicial background and values of many of the South Asian leaders. Almost to a man, the various nationalist leaders were British-trained lawyers. Nehru, Patel, Jinnah and Liaquat Ali Khan, not to mention Gandhi, had all been called to the bar in London. Jinnah had even practised law there for several years, during his hiatus from South Asian politics. The commission's judicial format contrasted oddly with the prevailing wisdom on drawing boundaries, which called for the use of trained experts with local knowledge.[6] But to men whose professional experience outside politics was dominated by legal training and practice, a legal structure may well have seemed like the ideal means of dealing with a controversial problem.

Negotiations over the formation of the boundary commission

Despite the importance of establishing the territorial limits of the two new states, serious negotiations over the format and procedure of the boundary commission did not begin until early June 1947. On 2 June, Baldev Singh wrote to Mountbatten to lay out the Sikh leaders' views on the boundary commission. He was responding to an advance draft of the British Government's momentous 3 June statement, which contained the definitive announcement that India would be divided and that a commission would be established to define the necessary boundaries. In this letter, Singh expressed the anxiety felt by his fellow Sikhs and asked that the commission be required to include 'as large a percentage of Sikh population as possible' on the Indian side of the border.[7] Meeting with the South Asian leaders the following day, Mountbatten noted the Sikh complaints but did not respond directly; instead, he emphasized that the commission's terms of reference 'would be drawn up in co-operation with all parties'.[8] From an early stage, British officials in Delhi made little effort to ensure that their solution would satisfy the Sikhs, the community it would impact most heavily.

In his statements to the press following the 3 June announcement, Mountbatten took pains to portray the partition decision and particularly the boundary settlement as the responsibility of the various nationalist parties. He expressed astonishment that 'it was mainly at the request of the Sikh community' that Congress demanded Punjab be divided between Muslim and non-Muslim areas, noting that this plan would divide the Sikh homeland in two.[9] Mountbatten declared that he had been unable to find a solution to this dilemma and could only say that

> the leaders of the respective communities shall appoint a commission which will draw up the terms of reference of the Boundary Commission which has been suggested in the Plan. The Boundary Commission shall have representatives of all the parties. So far as it is humanly possible there will be no interference or dictation by the British Government. If we can be of service in advancing impartial views and helping in this work, we shall not be afraid to do so, but this is your country and it is up to you to decide what to do with it.[10]

This passage lays out key elements of the British Government's plan. The partition was to be perceived as a South Asian undertaking, with British officials acting only as steady and impartial guides. Although Mountbatten acknowledged key flaws, such as a failure to cushion partition's blow for the Sikhs, he portrayed these failings as the fault of the various nationalist leaders themselves, including Sikh representatives. In reality, the British Government had a much greater hand in shaping the boundary-making process than Mountbatten's public statements indicated. In the same speech, Mountbatten also emphasized that the rapid pace of the division was the result of a joint decision. He asserted, 'after a while it became apparent to me that next to an acceptable solution or settlement all leaders wanted speed in the actual transfer of power. All leaders were anxious to assume their full responsibilities at the earliest possible moment, and I was anxious to let them do so.'[11] All in all, Mountbatten portrayed the process as a joint venture, in which the nationalist leaders were responsible for the key decisions.

Sikh leaders reacted to the 3 June partition plan with dismay and militant leaders warned that only a boundary favourable to the Sikhs would meet with Sikh cooperation. On the same day that Mountbatten portrayed the boundary problem as one to be solved collaboratively, the prominent militant Sikh leader Master Tara Singh announced that the Sikhs' acceptance or rejection of the 3 June plan would depend on the terms of reference given to the boundary commission.[12] Furthermore, he demanded that the dividing line follow the Chenab River in central Punjab, in order to allot the city of Lahore and a number of Muslim-majority districts to India.[13]

Although the 3 June plan declared that the division would take place on 15 August, the partition process was changing almost daily. Far from having a clear plan in mind, Mountbatten and his aides were engaged in a constant process of clarifying details and resolving the most immediate problems. For example, as June wore on, negotiations over the format of the boundary commission became entangled with the discussions over the Arbitral Tribunal that would settle partition-related disputes. On 5 June, at a meeting that included Nehru, Patel, Jinnah, Liaquat and Baldev Singh, Mountbatten suggested a member of the legal profession be brought in to chair, or 'umpire', the Arbitral Tribunal. The meeting minutes record Mountbatten (referred to as 'His Excellency') stating that 'the Umpire should be somebody agreed to by both sides – somebody who was willing to give true and fair service. HIS EXCELLENCY suggested that a man experienced in judiciary affairs would be most suitable. With this suggestion there was general agreement.'[14] This statement reveals two important aspects of the partition decision-making process. Mountbatten's reference to 'both sides' dramatically oversimplified India's complex political scene, demonstrating that the viceroy was thinking primarily in terms of satisfying Congress and League demands. In his mind, it seems, the

Sikhs were not important enough to warrant independent consultation. India-wide, it is true that the Sikhs were a tiny minority; in Punjab, however, they were a force to be reckoned with. In addition, this discussion marks an early example of the general feeling among the party leaders that individuals with a judicial background were likely to provide 'fair' and 'true' decisions.

Shortly after this meeting, Mountbatten informed Listowel at the India Office that he might request a member of the Judicial Committee of Britain's Privy Council to chair the Arbitral Tribunal. Mountbatten specifically noted that 'men with previous experience of India, such as Jayakar and Beaumont, would not be acceptable'.[15] The implication was that the various political parties would perceive any British official in India, including members of the Indian Civil Service, as biased towards either Muslims or Hindus and Sikhs. This restriction automatically removed from consideration those Britons who had the most relevant expertise. The appearance of objectivity was a major concern for Mountbatten, ranking as a higher priority than the recruitment of officials with local expertise in the areas to be divided.

Another important theme hinted at in these early discussions was the role of Punjabi infrastructure, particularly the irrigation system. This consideration would emerge as central in Radcliffe's later deliberations. In the same 5 June meeting that addressed the chairmanship of the Arbitral Tribunal, Mountbatten made a noteworthy side-comment. During the 5 June meeting that marked the initial exploration of the boundary commission structure, Mountbatten 'added that the State of Bahawalpur would have to give evidence before the Western Boundary commission, in connection with arrangements for water supplies for that State'.[16] This statement indicates that Mountbatten (or his staff) was already thinking in terms of the importance of water-supply infrastructure, even at this relatively early point in the official discussions.

On 7 June, Mountbatten held another meeting, with the Dewan of Bahawalpur, that was even more directly related to the issue of irrigation. The Dewan emphasized the water-supply and irrigation problems that partition posed for his state, which bordered Punjab. Mountbatten's notes record that he asked his staff to stay in touch with the Dewan, indicating that the viceroy thought this question would remain important. At this same meeting, Mountbatten discussed the membership of the Arbitral Tribunal and the boundary commission with Jinnah and Liaquat. According to Mountbatten's notes, Liaquat suggested that the Arbitral Tribunal chair 'be a member of the Judicial Committee of the Privy Council, preferably without previous experience of India'. Jinnah, however, took a different approach in his suggestions about the boundary commission chairs (at this point in the negotiation, the assumption was that the Bengal and Punjab commissions would each have their own chairman). Rather than suggesting a legal expert, he noted that these men 'should be people with experience of the broad principles whereby boundaries were demarcated'. Mountbatten agreed to this proposal and said that he would 'suggest to the Congress leaders that all three members of each Boundary Commission should be provided by U.N.O.', a reference to the fledgling United Nations Organization, founded in October 1945. In this format, 'Representatives of Congress, the Muslim League and other interested parties would be in attendance on the Commissions as expert assessors – probably 3 from each side of each partitioned Province.'[17] These proposals indicate that the boundary commission might have taken a completely different direction, with a far greater emphasis on boundary-making expertise and impartial outside participants, than it eventually did. With the partition deadline looming, however, the push for a quick transfer of power soon superseded any desire for a boundary commission staffed or even advised by experts.

By 9 June, Mountbatten was already concerned that involving experts and/or the UN, as the League had suggested, might interfere with the need for a quick boundary decision. He cabled Listowel,

> the Muslim leaders thought the best arrangement would be to have three entirely impartial Non-Indians with experience of this kind of work, e.g. perhaps an American, a Frenchman and an Englishman, to form the Commissions themselves, and for the various interested parties to have expert assessors attached to the Commissions. They suggested that perhaps UNO might be able to help, and personally I cannot think of any better arrangement. The trouble is the time factor, since it is extremely important that the commissions should report before 15th August.

Mountbatten concluded with further emphasis on the time problem, noting that 'it would be immensely helpful if you would start thinking about how the necessary experts are going to be provided in time'.[18] Mountbatten's correspondence demonstrates that the desire for a quick settlement was, for him, a higher priority than recruiting expert or impartial personnel. It also reveals his assumption that officials in London shared this view.

The following morning, 10 June, Mountbatten discussed the Muslim League suggestion that the UN provide the boundary commission staff, as well as expert assessors, with the Congress leadership. The viceroy reported that 'Pandit Nehru at first seemed doubtful. He felt that too much delay would be involved, but when I pointed out that we could telegraph off to U.N.O. straight away and get the chosen representatives flown to India, he said that he would further consider the matter and let me know his views.' On the question of expert assessors to be attached to the commissions, the group considered selecting five assessors: a western Punjab Muslim, an eastern Punjab Hindu, a Sikh, and one representative each for the future Pakistan and 'Hindustan'. In Bengal, where there was no significant Sikh population and the demographic division would be simpler, relatively speaking, there would be only four assessors.[19]

British officials were beginning to realize just how important the boundary question would be. At a staff meeting later that day, Mountbatten's chief of staff, Hastings Lionel 'Pug' Ismay, made the crucial point that 'it would be essential to obtain the agreement of the Indian Leaders that they would abide by the decisions of the two Boundary Commissions'. Mountbatten assented and made plans to take up this point with the party leaders at the next opportunity.[20] The leaders agreed. After independence, this agreement to accept the boundary commission decision, regardless of its content, proved critical in preventing legal challenges to the Radcliffe award.

In the meantime, Nehru had consulted further with his Congress colleagues and emerged with renewed opposition to the idea of involving the United Nations. In a personal letter to the viceroy, he wrote,

> We have thought over this matter and we think that this suggestion is not feasible or practicable. This would involve considerable delay. The UNO headquarters would probably have to communicate with each member Government and a long time would elapse before a choice could be made. It is possible that the ultimate choice might not be a very suitable one. There are other considerations also which militate against this proposal. We, therefore, would not welcome it.[21]

Having discarded the idea of involving the UN, Nehru put forward another proposal, apparently raised at the same morning meeting (although not mentioned in Mountbatten's record of the discussion). This proposal, that the commission have an independent chair and four members, two nominated by Congress and two by the League, proved to be the commission's final form, illustrating that nationalist leaders did have at least some influence over elements of the boundary commission's formation. Nehru also stipulated that 'the four persons nominated by the Congress and the Muslim League should be persons of high judicial standing',[22] again highlighting his belief that judicial training provided the best background for such a task.

Nehru's proposal was significant in another way; it originated from the principles that the commission members should be political nominees and that Congress and the League should have equal representation. The final shape of the commission was still in flux, however, as demonstrated by Nehru's proposal that the four commissioners elect their own chairman. If agreement between the commissioners proved difficult, he suggested, Congress and League party leaders would agree on a nominee. Only ten weeks before partition, the identity of the boundary commission chairman was far from settled.

Meanwhile, Listowel was making inquiries as to a suitable jurist to chair the Arbitral Tribunal. He requested suggestions from the Lord Chancellor (head of the judiciary), noting that the term of service required might be two years or even longer.[23] He referred to the need to find an individual of 'the highest standing', presumably so that he would possess enough authority to withstand attempts at interference.[24] Appointing a well-known individual as chairman would also lend prestige to the boundary-making effort, allowing the British to present themselves as devoting their best men to this important task.

On 12 June, Nehru reported yet another snag. In reply to Mountbatten's request that Congress draft terms of reference for the boundary commission, he conceded that Congress leaders had been unable to arrive at satisfactory language. He noted, 'there are all manner of factors which have to be considered. If we try to make a list of them, it is either too short or too long. It is better, therefore, to leave the matter to the Boundary commission itself. They will, no doubt, take into consideration all factors they consider relevant.'[25] In the end, Congress's final draft merely reproduced the language of Britain's 3 June announcement. For the Punjab, the proposed terms were: 'The Boundary Commission is instructed to demarcate the boundaries of the two parts of the Punjab on the basis of ascertaining the contiguous majority areas of Muslims and non-Muslims. In doing so it will also take into account other factors.'[26] This formulation would serve as the commission's final terms of reference.

Nehru's letter referred yet again to the necessity for speed, making it clear that Congress had intentionally proposed vague terms of reference in hopes that this leeway would allow the commission to work more quickly, with relatively few limitations to consider and a relatively simple mandate to follow. In this instance, however, Nehru made clear that his desire for speed did not indicate a desire for a speedy *final* outcome. On the contrary, he assumed that any boundaries the commission determined could be modified after independence, if India and Pakistan agreed to do so. Making such changes, he wrote, 'is likely to be a fairly lengthy process involving the ascertainment of the wishes of the people concerned in any particular area affected'.[27] The assumption that the boundary commission's decision would prove only a temporary solution may have allowed the party leaders, burdened with many pressing problems, to pass quickly over the border question.

Nehru reiterated his opposition to the idea of using UN commissioners when the Congress and League leaders met with Mountbatten again on 13 June. Despite his famous tenacity, Jinnah agreed readily enough. He expressed once again his preference for a plan that involved the UN, but said that he was willing to accept the second option of Congress–League nominees. He even introduced some wit into the tense proceedings by noting that his initial distaste for this plan stemmed from the fact that 'he had wanted, if possible, to avoid lawyers. There was always trouble when two or more lawyers got together.'[28] In response, Mountbatten noted that it might be possible to incorporate some expertise on boundary-making by attaching advisors to the commission, possibly advisors provided by the UN. Jinnah was apparently satisfied with this vague suggestion (which was in the end discarded), or perhaps he simply did not feel strongly about the issue. In any case, Jinnah's remark, coming as it did from perhaps the most eminent lawyer in a room full of lawyers, suggests that the League leader had a better sense of humour than is often credited. However, it also highlights the fact that Jinnah was just that: a lawyer in a room full of lawyers, hashing out a plan that would draw in yet more lawyers. The process of boundary delineation was deeply influenced by the legal milieu in which it was formed.

This 13 June discussion proved to be decisive, for it concluded with a number of agreements on the commission's final form. The leaders agreed that each commission would consist of two Congress nominees and two League nominees, with an independent chairman, that all these men would be 'of high judicial standing' and that Congress would include a Sikh among its nominees for the Punjab commission. Nehru and Jinnah further agreed to send Mountbatten the names of their nominees and to consider the draft terms of reference, in the form Nehru had proposed the previous day.

On the same day, in London, Listowel wrote to Mountbatten about the progress of his search for a judge to chair the Arbitral Tribunal. Noting that the members of the Judicial Committee of the Privy Council were all over sixty (too old, in his view, to undertake the work required) and that High Court Judges were in high demand and could not be spared, he suggested Sir Cyril Radcliffe. Enthusiastically describing Radcliffe's qualifications, he wrote that 'apart from his great legal abilities, he has just the right personality and acquired during the war administrative experience which would be likely to be of great assistance to him. Of course, he may well feel unable to leave the Bar, even temporarily, so soon after returning to it, however worthwhile your job can be made to appear, but there is just a possibility that he might be attracted to it.'[29] This passage suggests that Radcliffe's 'personality' and prior experience played a role in his selection to go to India. Listowel also emphasized the need to portray the work in India as 'worthwhile' in order to attract Radcliffe to it and demonstrated a faith that he would carry it out reliably.

Listowel also noted that he was looking into the question of involving the UN in the boundary settlement. The problem of international perceptions of Britain's handling of its withdrawal from India loomed large. 'Clearly,' he wrote, 'the handling of this Boundary Commission business is going to be of crucial importance.'[30] This reference to the issue's 'crucial importance' contrasts sharply with the British Government's previous lack of attention to the boundary question – as well as the Congress and League failure to address it with any specificity. It may be significant that Listowel here emphasized the 'handling' of the boundary commission, rather than the result produced. For the British, it could be argued, the exact location of the boundary line mattered less than the international perception that they had ended their rule in India effectively and with due regard for democratic principles. Listowel also foreshadowed some of the problems that would confront the boundary commission, observing that the Sikhs in particular seemed likely to commit themselves to demands for a particular boundary line. Such a tendency, he warned, could be dangerous, 'since, once claims of this kind have been staked out, withdrawal is apt to prove difficult without loss of face'.[31] Listowel's words proved prescient.

Less than half a mile across London, at the House of Lords, the Lord Chancellor was also thinking about the Indian problem. He wrote to Listowel that day to report on his meetings with Radcliffe. With a lengthy arbitration process in mind, Jowitt had warned Radcliffe on 12 June 'that he might have to stay very much longer than the six months indicated in the telegram'. Radcliffe returned on the 13th to say that 'he was so impressed with the importance of the task that he was prepared to undertake it'.[32] Back at the India Office, Listowel cabled Mountbatten late that same evening with further information on the Foreign Office's views on the composition of the boundary commission. His telegram conveys the impression of distinct Foreign Office alarm at the idea of the UN taking a hand in the Indian boundary question, listing objection after objection to the proposal. In terse telegraphic style, Listowel wrote, 'Reference to U.N.O. General Assembly in matter of this kind is not recommended by Foreign Office,' adding that practical problems would prevent the UN speedily providing a commission. The Secretary General, Listowel continued, 'might be asked to suggest names from international field, but in this event his choice might well be governed by considerations other than that of obtaining best men'. This rather vague warning may refer to fears that the largely anti-colonial UN was unlikely to have British imperial interests at heart when forming such a commission. Listowel added, 'latter difficulty would indeed apply in event of matter being referred to any organ of U.N.O.; and possibility cannot be ruled out that Russians and other Slav States would create other political difficulties. Moreover, appeal to U.N.O. would suggest that we ourselves had proved incapable of transferring power without recourse to that body.'[33] This last sentence goes to the heart of the problem, from the British perspective. With their global empire in the balance, the British were determined to demonstrate that they could handle the decolonization of India without any foreign assistance. Reliance on the UN, or even the appearance of such reliance, could damage Britain's image in the rest of its colonial holdings, domestically and in the eyes of its Allies, particularly in the Middle East.

Mountbatten by this time was equally eager to avoid involving the UN. He cabled Listowel with the results of his 13 June meeting with the nationalist leaders, at which, he said, 'it was decided, in view of the time factor, to drop the suggestion that the boundary commission should be composed of persons obtained through U.N.O.'. He concluded, 'please therefore take no further action on the suggestion that U.N.O. should be approached'. On 19 June, Mountbatten passed along a somewhat censored version of the Foreign Office's objections to Jinnah, emphasizing the difficulty of obtaining a speedy result through the UN.[34] On the 20th, Listowel responded to Mountbatten with the observation that 'I am glad that the idea of consulting U.N.O. about the composition of the Boundary Commissions has been abandoned and it will probably be best if a reference even to the President of the International Court of Justice is also avoided as it would inevitably involve delay.'[35] The British Government had realized that international participation in this delicate decision was not desirable. It was vital for Britain's reputation as a world power that it manage the South Asian partition on its own.

The final piece of the puzzle, the chairmanship of the boundary commission, began to fall into place a few days later. While meeting with Mountbatten, Jinnah informed the viceroy that the Congress Party's proposed terms of reference would be acceptable, but that he thought it unlikely that the parties could agree on two chairmen, one for each of the Punjab and Bengal commissions. According to Mountbatten's version of the conversation, Jinnah suggested that a 'distinguished member of the Bar from England might come out as an independent

Chairman for both Commissions and that his decision should be final'. At this point, Jinnah apparently proposed that the chairman of the Arbitral Tribunal might arrive in India early and chair the boundary commission before beginning his work as arbitrator. Mountbatten informed Jinnah, in confidence, that Cyril Radcliffe had been proposed to head the Arbitral Tribunal. Jinnah replied that he would need time to consider Radcliffe's suitability as boundary commission chair, but that he 'knew of him and of the high reputation which he held at the Bar'. The next day, Jinnah wrote to Mountbatten and indicated that Radcliffe would make an acceptable boundary commission chair. 'I hope,' he wrote, 'that you will be able to persuade the Congress to accept my suggestions which are fair and which will lead to finality in the shortest possible period.'[36] Once again, Jinnah made it clear that a quick decision was his top priority.

Mountbatten presented Jinnah's suggestion of a joint chairman during his 26 June meeting with some of the nationalist leaders. Noting that 'all parties had unanimously expressed the opinion that it was most desirable that the Boundary Commissions should finish their work by the 15th of August', Mountbatten argued that there was not enough time to ask the commissioners to elect their own chairmen. Instead, he put forward Radcliffe's name, observing that if another suitable candidate could not be found, Radcliffe might chair both boundary commissions.[37] Outside of Mountbatten's confidential discussion with Jinnah, the viceroy and the party leaders had previously discussed Radcliffe only as a candidate for the Arbitral Tribunal position. The date of 26 June marked the first time that British officials openly suggested Radcliffe as a boundary commission chairman.

Mountbatten went on to laud Radcliffe's abilities, affirming that he was 'a man of high integrity, legal reputation, and wide experience'. This last comment was a bit disingenuous; Radcliffe's experience was certainly wide, but it did not include any work relevant to boundary delineation. The party leaders present apparently responded favourably to this suggestion and agreed to discuss it with their colleagues. However, Mountbatten's 27 June letter to Listowel, an enthusiastic appraisal of the possibility of Radcliffe's appointment as arbitrator, indicates that British officials still thought of Radcliffe as a candidate to head the Arbitral Tribunal. Mountbatten noted that he had a prior acquaintance with Radcliffe, writing, 'I saw a certain amount of him when he was Director-General at the Ministry of Information during the war and formed a high opinion of him.'[38] It is unclear exactly what Mountbatten knew of Radcliffe, but clearly at the time he thought him well suited to the difficult task of arbitrating partition-related disputes.

Mountbatten also discussed the possibility of Radcliffe's chairing the boundary commission as well, describing this proposal as 'purely tentative'. At this stage, Radcliffe's position as boundary commission chair was far from settled. The point of greater significance here is the fact that Mountbatten's letter to Listowel presented a slightly skewed version of Jinnah's reaction to this suggestion. He wrote, 'Jinnah has suggested that Radcliffe, if he proves acceptable, might perhaps serve in the first instance as Chairman of both Boundary Commissions to sit only to settle disputes within the Commissions.'[39] In fact, it was Mountbatten who brought Radcliffe's name into the discussion, although Jinnah had (according to Mountbatten's notes of their meeting) suggested that the Arbitral Tribunal chair might come out early to serve as boundary commission chair. The discussion of Radcliffe as boundary commission or Arbitral Tribunal chair, although accepted by the nationalist leaders, was initiated by the British. Even at the time, however, Mountbatten was careful to portray this decision as resting largely with the nationalist leaders. This step was part of a larger pattern of presenting the entire boundary commission format as one proposed and approved by the nationalist leaders, rather than the British.

Additional discrepancies in contemporary documents confuse the question of who proposed Radcliffe's name as boundary commission chair. The contrast comes out clearly in a comparison of Mountbatten's personal report of 27 June, which describes his morning meeting with the Partition Council, with the minutes of that meeting. Mountbatten's version states, 'The question of the Chairman has been causing a lot of trouble. At the first meeting of the Partition Council held to-day *Jinnah's* proposal [emphasis added] was accepted by Congress, namely that Sir Cyril Radcliffe should be appointed as the chairman of both Boundary Commissions with a final casting vote, as this was considered to be the only way in which the boundaries could be definitely settled before the 15th August.' The minutes for this meeting, however, record that the nationalist leaders accepted *Mountbatten's* proposal that Radcliffe be accepted as boundary commission chair.[40] These different versions, one asserting that Jinnah suggested Radcliffe's name and one making clear that it came from the viceroy, may reflect Mountbatten's desire that history record this aspect of the partition process as South Asian-initiated.

Having accepted Radcliffe as boundary commission chair, however, the party leaders now found his participation in the Arbitral Tribunal objectionable. Mountbatten's report states, with evident exasperation, 'we have reached a complete stalemate about the Arbitral Tribunal. Jinnah would like Radcliffe to be the Chairman; but Congress opposed this (apparently under the impression that he is a Conservative and therefore likely to favour the League!).'[41] The Labour Party was Congress's traditional ally in London, while the Conservative leader, Winston Churchill, had throughout the 1940s condemned any discussion of decolonization as a cowardly abandonment of imperial duties. Mountbatten, focused as always on reaching consensus (real or apparent) as quickly as possible, was frustrated by this temporary setback.

In a cable sent the same day that summarized the more urgent points made at this morning meeting, Mountbatten again wrote, 'both parties agreed that it was of the utmost importance that the Boundary Commissions should finish their work by August 15th and they felt that there would be no great difficulty in achieving this object, provided a really first-class Chairman could be made available'.[42] This passage not only highlights Mountbatten's characteristically optimistic assessment of the potential difficulties involved in resolving the boundary question, but also demonstrates once again his eagerness to emphasize that Congress and the League shared the British Government's desire for a rapid transfer of power. In an interesting contrast, however, this cable also hints at difficulties ahead. Mountbatten noted that he had proposed that Radcliffe serve as boundary commission chair and then stay on to serve as head of the Arbitral Tribunal. The nationalist leaders were uncomfortable with this suggestion, he reported, since they agreed that 'the report of the Boundary Commissions would almost inevitably upset one party or the other or both, whose confidence he [Radcliffe] would thus lose'.[43] These fears of trouble in connection with the boundary award would soon be realized.

On 28 June, another potential problem arose when Liaquat Ali Khan wrote to Mountbatten with the League's suggested terms of reference. These terms were largely the same as Congress's suggestion, except for one significant difference. Like Congress's version, the League's draft of the Punjab terms of reference read, 'The Boundary Commission is instructed to demarcate the boundaries of the two parts of the Punjab on the basis of ascertaining the contiguous majority areas of Muslims and non-Muslims.' However, the League's second line eliminated the clause 'In so doing', stating simply that 'The Commission will also take into account other factors.'[44] As George Abell, Mountbatten's private secretary, pointed out, the League's proposed change would give the commission far more leeway in making its decision, removing the emphasis on population figures as the primary factor to be considered.[45] Under the League's wording, 'contiguous majority areas' would carry no more weight than 'other factors'. Ismay met with Jinnah and Liaquat Ali Khan that evening, firmly pointing out that Jinnah had agreed to the Congress-proposed terms at his meeting with Mountbatten on 23 June. Ismay made it clear that the chances of amending the terms at this late date were slim.[46] The next day, Mountbatten wrote a stiff note to Jinnah about the 'complete misunderstanding on this matter'. He observed that Jinnah had explicitly agreed to the Congress-proposed terms on 23 June and had raised no objections to them when they were discussed at the 27 June meeting of the nationalist leaders. Noting yet again that 'you yourself have always emphasised the necessity for speed', Mountbatten asserted that he had 'therefore gone ahead as fast as possible'. The terms of reference, as proposed by Congress, were scheduled to be announced the next day in both India and Britain. Mountbatten concluded, 'I am sure that you will agree with me that we ought not to incur the delay which would result from re-opening this question, particularly as I understand that you told Lord Ismay that your amendments were really more a matter of form than of substance.'[47] Jinnah and Liaquat let the matter drop.

On 30 June, the Government of India announced the formation of the Punjab and Bengal boundary commissions, giving the terms of reference as Congress had proposed them. These deceptively simple instructions ran, as noted above: 'The Boundary Commission is instructed to demarcate the boundaries of the two parts of the Punjab/Bengal on the basis of ascertaining the contiguous majority areas of Muslims and non-Muslims. In doing so it will also take into account other factors.'[48] On the surface, the principal concern of both Britons and South Asians in the government was the category of religious identity. Less clear is the question of what 'other factors' indicates. This ambiguity was intended to allow the commissioners flexibility to accommodate concerns that might emerge during their deliberations and to ensure that excessively restrictive terms did not slow down the boundary-creation process. The obvious factors included administrative needs, geographical features, and communication and irrigation infrastructure, but as one historian notes, 'it was also open to the Commissions to take into account less tangible influences'.[49] After satisfying the primary requirement to divide religious majority areas, any consideration was fair game.

The terms of reference also reveal the lack of geographical knowledge available to the nationalist leaders and to the British officials responsible for the original wording of the 3 June statement, from which these terms were drawn.[50] The instruction to '*demarcate* the boundaries'[51] demonstrates the dearth of expert geographical input at any stage. Although the conventional definitions and everyday usage of the terms 'demarcate' and 'delimit' are very close, they mean entirely different things in the context of boundary-making. Demarcation refers to the process of marking a boundary on the ground. Delimitation, by contrast, means, as a contemporary authority on boundary-making had written only two years earlier, 'the choice of a boundary site and its definition in a treaty or other formal document. It is a more precise step than the general allocation of territory which preceded it, but less precise than the demarcation which usually follows.'[52] As one participant acidly observed, 'I do not think that anyone really expected these eminent but sessile judges to go around in *dhotis* and *sherwanis* [traditional Indian garb] digging holes and putting up concrete markers, which is what "demarcating" means.'[53] The Radcliffe commission was clearly concerned with delimitation, not demarcation; demarcation was left to India and Pakistan, after independence.

The eminent judges in question were named in the 29 June announcement. Listing the chairman as 'to be appointed later', the text noted that 'it is intended to appoint the same person as Chairman of both the Boundary Commissions'.[54] Although his name was not included in the public statement, Cyril Radcliffe's position as head of the boundary commissions drawing the new Indo-Pakistani line was finally settled.

Cyril Radcliffe's service to the state

Despite Radcliffe's central role in the boundary-making process, few historians have offered more than a cursory appraisal of Radcliffe the individual. The fact that the format and procedure of the boundary commission were based on the assumption that its chairman would be an unbiased and objective judge, however, makes a study of Cyril Radcliffe's character and experience vital to understanding the results his commission produced. In agreeing to Radcliffe's selection as commission chair, the Muslim League and Congress apparently failed to appreciate where his expertise, talents and true loyalties lay. Radcliffe was obviously not an independent expert with boundary-making experience, but neither was he a completely objective and ignorant newcomer. On the contrary, he was a loyal servant of the British Government who had previously demonstrated his dedication to the interests of the British state. One historian describes him as 'the eternal fireman' and 'the man to whom Governments turned to put out the flames'.[55] I argue that Radcliffe's work as boundary commission chair fitted a lifelong pattern of loyal service to the British Government in times of need.

Although Radcliffe's disinterested stance may have been open to question where British interests were concerned, his intelligence was not. Highly respected in British legal and governmental circles, Cyril

Radcliffe was widely regarded as one of the finest minds of his generation. When Christopher Beaumont, his secretary on the boundary commission, went to Victoria Station to meet him for the first time, he had no idea what Radcliffe looked like. He felt confident, however, that he would recognize him as the 'most intelligent looking man in the room' – and he did.[56] By 1947, Radcliffe was a very successful barrister, earning some £40,000 to £50,000 annually, the equivalent of over a million pounds in 2008. Lord Chancellor Jowitt, noting that Radcliffe would lose money if he accepted the boundary commission job, wrote to the Secretary of State for India, 'you will therefore see, if he does go out [to India], that so far as the money side of the matter is concerned he places us under an immense obligation to him'.[57] Jowitt had reason to believe that Radcliffe would accept the job despite the prospect of financial loss; he had previously proven himself a civic-minded man, serving at the Admiralty and later the Ministry of Information throughout World War II. Although Radcliffe bemoaned the use of the term 'Establishment' as an 'inane cliché',[58] his friends and other observers described him as the consummate Establishment man.

Any biographical study of Radcliffe is limited by the paucity of primary sources bearing on his life. His lifelong habit of destroying papers complicates the historian's task. Radcliffe's stepson describes him as the most thorough destroyer of papers he has known.[59] With the aid of Radcliffe's surviving speeches and writings, however, it is possible to analyse his motivations for public service and his perceptions of Britain's role in India.[60] In one of these lectures, Radcliffe noted that 'much of the interest of history lies in wondering why things could not have happened differently'.[61] This section addresses precisely this point. Why didn't Radcliffe, arguably the one individual with the greatest control over the outcome of the Indo-Pakistani boundary-making process, operate differently? Why not refuse to take on the task, since it lay so far outside his previous experience and expertise? Why not resign from the post once it became clear how difficult the job would be? And finally, why did he remain silent about his work in India, refusing to shed light on this perplexing episode of history? I argue that the answer lies in Radcliffe's devotion to duty, specifically duty to the British state.

Radcliffe was born on 30 March 1899, at Llanychan, Wales. His father was a soldier, his mother a solicitor's daughter. Radcliffe inherited a strong legal tradition from his mother's side of the family: his cousin, grandfather, two uncles and great-grandfather all worked in the legal profession. In his immediate family, there was an equally strong emphasis on military service: in addition to his father, two of Radcliffe's three brothers were professional soldiers.[62]

Radcliffe's family followed the traditional path of sending him to boarding school for his secondary education. He enrolled at Haileybury College in 1912, thus observing the first years of World War I from the perspective of a public schoolboy. Haileybury was very much part of the British established order, having been in earlier years the training ground for aspirants to the ranks of the East India Company, which annexed much of the Indian subcontinent during the seventeenth and eighteenth centuries before the British Crown assumed control in 1858.[63] Radcliffe's contemporaries included boys from India and other parts of the empire.[64] At Haileybury, he might even have known of the older Clement Attlee, a fellow Old Haileyburian who, many years later, presided as Prime Minister over Britain's withdrawal from India.[65] It seems likely that Radcliffe emerged from his Haileybury years with an appreciation of the importance of the British empire already shaping his worldview.

The other major influence on Radcliffe's adolescent years was World War I. Radcliffe was fifteen and had been at school for two years when the war began in August 1914; he was too young to fight, but some of his older schoolmates left for the front. Years later, writing in the school magazine, he recalled that 'only nine months or so separated the Prefect crossing the Quad from the young officer in the trenches and many of them would hurry back, on their scanty leaves, to re-visit the buildings, the fields, and their friends. Often it was to be a last visit.'[66] For Radcliffe, the loss of friends and acquaintances in World War I had a lasting effect. In his final year at school, Radcliffe was appointed Head Boy.[67] This honour cannot have been much consolation for the fact that Radcliffe's own house at Haileybury was particularly hard-hit; of the forty-six boys resident when he came to school in 1912, twenty died in the war.[68] But the fact that Radcliffe served as president of the Haileybury Society in 1952 is testimony to the lasting connection he felt to his school.[69]

Radcliffe's own thoughts on the influences that form an individual's worldview shed light on the forces that shaped him. In his late sixties, he wrote, 'One's thought ... is much more a disposition or approach towards the observed world which is conditioned by one's natural make-up and continuing experiences, of which the earlier are probably the more formative; and I doubt very much whether, although one's thought, in this sense, may be deepened and enlarged by later experiences, it is likely to be changed by them in any significant or revolutionary way.'[70] Radcliffe asserts here that an individual's reason is affected by life experience, particularly early experience. Since Radcliffe's work throughout his life, both as a barrister and as a public servant, was guided by reason, we can conclude that Radcliffe's early experiences had an important effect on his later work.

Radcliffe's primary influences, I argue, were fourfold: his family, which emphasized military service and duty; his adolescent development in a public school environment that stressed loyalty to the state and the Establishment; the Great War, which reinforced his appreciation of state service and of the need for sacrifice; and his postwar years at Oxford, which launched him into the professional world of the Establishment.

In appraising the influences at work in Radcliffe's mind, it is worth noting that the passage below follows immediately on Radcliffe's argument that early influences are most lasting:

> As I get older I become increasingly aware of the fact that my own reaction to life was formed by the War of 1914–18, the impact of which I met first as a schoolboy rather older than my years and later in the Army ... What stands out so clearly, so clearly that it remains as the dominant impression, is a certain uncomplainingness, an acceptance, without dramatics and without self-pity, of their sad and untimely fortune ... I have carried with me into the long years of growing up a settled admiration for that special kind of courage that, without illusion, sustains an unequal burden to whatever the end may be.[71]

This passage reveals a great deal about Radcliffe's character. First and foremost it demonstrates his belief in the importance of duty. Second, and most striking, is his belief that one should attempt to carry out one's duty even when confronted by great, perhaps insurmountable, difficulties. It is also worth noting that the particular duty that he singles out for praise, the example that he says he has carried with him throughout his life, involves service to the British state.

Radcliffe himself never saw combat. His poor eyesight – he wore thick spectacles throughout his life – kept him from the front lines. Having finished school, Radcliffe was called up in 1917 and served in the Labour Corps in France from 1918 to 1919. His duties there would have included repairing roads and communications.[72] Labour Corps members undertook difficult tasks in sometimes dangerous conditions, even working under fire.[73] In keeping with his insistence that early experiences shape later reasoning, it is tempting to speculate that Radcliffe's years in the Labour Corps drove home the importance of bridges, roads, railroads and other infrastructure. That early influence may have shaped his decisions in 1947, which profoundly affected local and provincial infrastructure networks.[74]

After returning to England, Radcliffe took up a scholarship at New College, Oxford, where he read classics. At Oxford, Radcliffe began to recover from his wartime experiences. One New College friend observed, 'Even Cyril Radcliffe, who knew exactly what he wished to do and set about it with quiet determination, had lost dear friends and needed something or someone to take their place. Under a gentle irony he hid a desire for some peaceful, secure affection and hoped to regain the happiness which he had enjoyed in his childhood with his remarkable mother and three brothers.'[75] This friend also recalled Radcliffe's puckish sense of humour, used to tease a somewhat inadequate history tutor: 'Cyril Radcliffe and I used to invent quotations from an imaginary Greek historian called Aristomenes of Tauromenium, and Casson would either nod his head knowingly or say, "I had forgotten that."'[76]

While still an undergraduate, Radcliffe progressed towards a legal career by gaining admittance to the Inner Temple, with the support of his uncle, already a member. After taking a first-class degree at Oxford in 1921, Radcliffe accepted a fellowship at Oxford's prestigious All Souls College. It was yet another step in Radcliffe's life-long journey from one Establishment bastion to the next, as he moved from undergraduate life at Oxford to London's Inner Temple.[77] Radcliffe later recalled that All Souls 'did seem to me to represent something that might now be called a senior branch of the Establishment'. Even at this young age, Radcliffe was mixing with Britain's most powerful men, for the non-resident fellows of All Souls generally included, as Radcliffe noted,

> a minister or Secretary of State (nothing so eye-catching as a Prime Minister), an archbishop and here and there a bishop, the permanent head of this department of State or that (preferably Treasury or Foreign Office), one or two headmasters from really important schools, the editor of *The Times* and someone from the inner circle of the City: and, of course, several of the leading lawyers of the day. One awaited with some trepidation the Saturday afternoon arrival of so much eminence.[78]

Radcliffe spent only occasional weekends at All Souls, however, preferring to concentrate on his legal practice. Called to the bar in the Inner Temple in 1924, Radcliffe 'took silk', becoming a King's Counsellor in 1935, and rapidly established himself at the top of his profession.[79]

Those historians who discuss Radcliffe's personal history at all often state that Radcliffe knew nothing about India before he took on the boundary commission work in the summer of 1947. In fact, Radcliffe did have a personal connection to the subcontinent. Geoffrey, the closest of his three brothers, died in India on 30 December 1938, at the age of forty-two.[80] It seems likely that he was buried in Calcutta, for Radcliffe visited that city's South Park Street Cemetery in 1947. Shortly after his return to Britain, Radcliffe gave a rather mournful BBC talk, musing on Britons buried in India, their sacrifices for the empire and how quickly the British people tended to forget that sacrifice.[81] Family tradition also holds that Radcliffe may have been involved professionally in India-related cases before 1947, but concrete evidence of such a connection remains to be uncovered.[82]

The year 1939 brought the uncertainty of World War II but also, for Radcliffe, more settled personal circumstances. Radcliffe remained single until relatively late in life, but in December 1939 he married Antonia Tennant. Tennant was freshly divorced from John Tennant, a partner in a stockbroker firm that included the Conservative politician Bob Boothby, a friend of Radcliffe from their Oxford days. Antonia Tennant and Radcliffe first met at a country house party hosted by Boothby. Tennant herself came from an upper-class family; her father was the first Baron Charnwood and a Member of Parliament. She had two young sons, Anthony and Mark, by John Tennant, and Radcliffe seems to have had a good relationship with the boys.

During the war years, however, Radcliffe had little time to savour the joys of family life. A government friend saw him making sandbags on the Mall in central London during the early days of World War II, and Radcliffe's contacts arranged for him to join the Admiralty, in a position more in keeping with his intellectual powers. He served out the war in government service.[83] In early 1940, Radcliffe shifted to the Ministry of Information (MOI), where he supervised the Government's censorship effort, rising quickly to Director General, a post he held for the remainder of the war.

Contemporary observers and historians appraising Radcliffe's tenure at the MOI consistently describe his work in glowing terms. Not only was his intelligence of the highest calibre, he was 'supremely efficient' in handling the many administrative problems facing MOI when he arrived.[84] After joining the Ministry in April 1940, as the Controller of News and Censorship, Radcliffe quickly settled in at its labyrinthine home at London University. In December of the same year, he was promoted to Deputy Director General, assisting his friend Walter Monckton, who was Director General.

MOI was an improvised ministry intended to meet wartime needs.[85] Its responsibilities included censorship, which was imposed on communications leaving the country and was undertaken voluntarily by domestic newspapers, and propaganda, both in Britain and overseas.[86] In the early years of the war, however, it handled these responsibilities poorly. Its clumsy and inconsistent censorship generated resentment among reporters and its home front propaganda was ineffective in boosting morale. In early 1941, Radcliffe and Monckton bluntly laid out the MOI's deficiencies. They asserted that the Ministry could not function without control over all forms of propaganda, access to all information given to the Foreign Office and the military services, and authority over the publication of official news. 'Not one of these conditions', they concluded, 'is fulfilled at present.'[87] The MOI supervised its own 'white' propaganda (openly identified as originating in Britain and usually carried out by the British Broadcasting Corporation (BBC)), but 'black' propaganda (which concealed its British origins) was controlled by a number of different divisions and issued from a range of stations.[88] In addition, Radcliffe and Monckton argued that MOI required full access to confidential information in order to offer proper guidance to the press on the types of stories that should not be published.

The situation remained unsatisfactory through 1941. When Brendan Bracken replaced Duff Cooper as the Minister of Information, Monckton requested a transfer to a new posting. He wrote, 'Since the Ministry has had all too little power and authority, I have had to do my work depending solely on the maintenance of good relations with other departments of state and with the press. I have no stomach for a battle on both fronts without the necessary weapons under a government which has no real faith in the Ministry or its work.'[89] Despite Monckton's glum outlook, MOI's position improved markedly under Bracken. The new Minister of Information brought to his post a great many qualities, including his close relationship with Winston Churchill, that enabled him to make a surprising success of this hitherto thankless position. However, Radcliffe's contributions were also crucial to MOI's rising fortunes.

When later that year Radcliffe himself was appointed Director General, he worked closely with Bracken. Radcliffe made his mark behind the scenes, beginning with the influence he exerted on Bracken's wholesale reorganization.[90] Such was the reliance his colleagues placed upon him that his actual responsibilities at various stages were greater than his official assignments. Bracken often handed day-to-day responsibility for the entire ministry over to Radcliffe, preferring to remain at his country house to nurse the exhaustion that afflicted so many overworked government servants, Radcliffe included.[91]

Some of MOI's problems were intrinsic to its mission, particularly as it was undertaken in a democratic society. Its censors were men with no previous experience of this kind of work. Their results were often inconsistent. In the war's early years, reporters were intensely frustrated at the censors' inability to appreciate their need for speed in order to publish news while it was still news. These problems resolved over time, due partly to experience and partly to Radcliffe's influence: 'Radcliffe had formulated an exact and workable set of principles prescribing *inter alia* that it was no part of the censors' task to ban statements of opinion or to have regard to the use that the enemy propaganda might make of information.'[92] Radcliffe came to be widely respected as an administrator.

MOI's effectiveness grew significantly from 1940 onwards, due in large part to Radcliffe's quiet but effective work. Applying his legal skills to MOI's many problems, he improved the Ministry's organization and clarified its function. As one historian writes, 'he brought to his new work the Chancery barrister's faculty for lucid dispassionate judgement and resolute decision, as well as organizational skill of a sort rarely found among lawyers'.[93] He resolutely fought any attempt to infringe on the Ministry's role. Yet even in his dealings with politicians and with the interdepartmental squabbles that are an inevitable part of official work, he was straightforward; 'he eschewed intrigue and stamped a certain high-minded quality on all he touched'.[94] Radcliffe greatly preferred an open approach.

Radcliffe's dislike of official scheming was characteristic. Bracken, whom Radcliffe dubbed 'the great arranger',[95] was occasionally a source of annoyance in this regard. Radcliffe recalled, 'I sometimes found him exasperating, owing to a certain indirectness in the way in which he approached his objectives.'[96] Some of this reluctance to take a firm stance was inherent in Bracken's job, for he was constantly under pressure from Churchill to suppress newspaper reports hostile to the Americans.[97] This interference ran against Radcliffe's principles: 'Radcliffe, forever the purist, resented this. He consistently opposed the suppression of information, however embarrassing to the government, on any ground other than military security. There were basic principles such as the veracity of propaganda or impartiality as between journalists that he was not prepared to barter to meet any passing political convenience.'[98] Given Radcliffe's reputation for directness and dislike of subterfuge, it is all the more ironic that his work in India stands for many as a prime example of 'perfidious Albion' at work.

Radcliffe took an active part in managing the British Information Services in the United States, at one point sacking the head of the New York office and choosing a replacement who greatly improved Britain's American publicity campaigns.[99] Given American dislike of foreign propaganda, MOI work in the US was a tricky business. The MOI also had to contend with hostile American attitudes about the British role in India, sentiments of which Radcliffe was well informed.[100] When Field Marshal Wavell was made Viceroy of India in 1943, a *New York Times* reporter inquired at an MOI press conference 'whether the appointment of a military man indicated that India was about to be turned into a police state'.[101] Radcliffe was therefore well aware of critical American attitudes towards British colonial rule in South Asia.

Despite these difficulties, by 1944 matters at the MOI had improved so much that a report by the Treasury concluded: 'The Ministry of Information made an unfortunate start, but in the light of experience they have now built up an organization and developed a technique, which are impressive in the extreme. There is a thoroughness and solidity, combined with flexibility and enterprise, which are the hall-marks of administrative efficiency.'[102] Bracken enjoyed such praise but unhesitatingly gave credit to Radcliffe.[103] However, the press of work left Radcliffe exhausted by the war's end. A friend who saw him in the summer of 1945 noted that Radcliffe was 'delighted to be free again. Already he looks much better. Wise man that he is, he is taking three months' full leave before he returns to the Bar in October.'[104] After years of hard work, Radcliffe had earned a rest.

Once recovered, Radcliffe resumed his lucrative legal practice. In mid-1947, however, as we have seen, the British Government prevailed upon him to make a temporary return to public service, as chairman of the Indian boundary commissions. Radcliffe was reluctant to leave his wife for the long period of travel that he anticipated, and he negotiated Government of India-paid passage for Lady Radcliffe and the boys as a condition of his service, expecting that they would join him during school holidays.[105] As it was, Radcliffe was in India for such a brief period that there was no opportunity for Lady Radcliffe to join him. Radcliffe did not enjoy his time in India, but it did give him an opportunity to apply the loyalty and skills developed in his previous work.

Radcliffe's experience at the MOI had given him a keen appreciation of the importance of public opinion – and of the ways in which public opinion might be swayed. He was convinced that greater openness, rather than tighter restrictions on press reporting, was vital to sustaining the morale of the British people. In late 1942 he had lent his support to demands that the BBC be allowed greater latitude in providing more vivid and immediate reporting in order to involve the public in the progress of the war.[106] Radcliffe's experience with public relations gave him an understanding of the need to give the public the right sort of information to generate support.

Perhaps more significantly, Radcliffe's position in the MOI had also given him access to intelligence reports. Concurrent with Radcliffe's appointment to the MOI in April 1940, Postal and Telegraph Censorship, a division that gathered intelligence information globally, joined the Ministry.[107] In his role as Controller of News and Censorship, Radcliffe had seen these reports, which included information on Indian politics and the activities of Indian leaders abroad. There is no evidence that Radcliffe gave Indian intelligence particular attention, but he would certainly have had more knowledge of the Indian scene than is generally believed. As a member of the post-World War II Establishment, Radcliffe shared many of the values that underlay British imperialism.[108] I argue that his keen sense of loyalty to British interests shaped his work as boundary commission chair.

The Indian Independence Bill

As Radcliffe prepared for his voyage to India, the British Government began to speed up its withdrawal. On 4 July, the government introduced an Indian Independence Bill in the British House of Commons. This bill included a clause that ultimately rendered Radcliffe's decision binding on both India and Pakistan. This clause's final form was influenced by Muslim League complaints that the draft bill was unclear on this subject. Noting that Congress and the League had both agreed to accept the boundary commission decision as final, the League demanded clarification that Mountbatten was similarly bound to accept the award. The League called for a provision in the bill 'making the awards of the Boundary Commission final and binding on the two dominions [India and Pakistan] so that the boundaries are determined strictly in accordance with the terms of the awards of the Commissions concerned'.[109] Congress had earlier raised similar objections to the draft bill,[110] and the final version reflected the concerns of both Congress and the League. It stated: 'The boundaries of the said new Provinces shall be such as may be determined, whether before or after the appointed day, by awards of boundary commissions appointed by the Governor-General in that behalf.'[111] This wording ensured that Radcliffe's award would be final.

Listowel described for Mountbatten the somewhat chaotic scene in London, where the final version of the Indian Independence Bill was prepared and printed in the early morning hours of 4 July. He also noted his pleasure at Radcliffe's acceptance of the position of boundary commission chair, observing that Radcliffe 'is approaching the whole matter in a most public-spirited manner and will, I have little doubt, fill the rôle admirably'.[112] Listowel did not say so explicitly, but Radcliffe's 'public spirit' was, as I have argued, a vital element of his qualification for that role. Listowel also reported that Radcliffe planned to leave for India on 6 July and that Lady Radcliffe planned to follow him out about ten days later. Given the fact that in 1947 a voyage from Britain to India was still a time-consuming prospect, these plans for Lady Radcliffe's travels indicate that Radcliffe was not yet aware just how brief and busy his time in India would be.

Radcliffe was not the only person who expected a lengthy boundary-making process; the same day, Jenkins had told one of the Sikh leaders that 'the Boundary Commission might take a considerable time over its report'.[113] On 10 July, Mountbatten noted in a letter to Jenkins that the party leaders, the partition council and Radcliffe had all agreed that the boundary awards should be completed by 15 August.[114] But it is evident that even in early July, the timeline for the boundary commission's work remained somewhat ambiguous. Certainly those with the most at stake, the residents of Punjab and Bengal, did not have a clear understanding of the process that would determine where their homes fell.

As this outline of the negotiations between the British Government and the nationalist parties shows, the British skilfully incorporated nationalist suggestions in such a way that elements of the boundary commission's final shape were based on Congress or League initiatives. Congress drafted the rough terms of reference, leaving them intentionally vague, and suggested that each commission include two Congress nominees and two League nominees. Jinnah, after initially proposing that boundary-making experts be involved, requested that a lawyer chair the two boundary commissions; furthermore, all parties insisted that the chairman's decision should be final. Congress and the League also agreed that the boundary commission chair should be a man without prior experience in India. However, it was Mountbatten and the British Government who had the greatest influence over the vital factors that shaped the commission's work, particularly by suggesting Radcliffe's name first for the Arbitral Tribunal and later for the boundary commission. Mountbatten later emphasized the judicial nature of the boundary commission and the fact that it had been formed in accordance with the wishes of the party leaders in emphasizing his own lack of influence over its decision. Shortly before the award's release, he wrote, 'The Boundary Commission is a judicial body, and I have made it clear from the start that I did not frame its terms of reference, and that I should not intervene in any way in the deliberations of the Commission.'[115] The truth of this statement is examined below.

In summary, these negotiations gave Congress and League leaders a sense that they had decided the boundary commission composition; although they had certainly played a role in some areas, the British had had the greatest influence on Radcliffe's selection as chairman. It is not clear whether the party leaders realized at the time quite how much sway Radcliffe could potentially have. Since the political parties themselves apparently instructed their nominees not to negotiate, it seems reasonable that they might have foreseen that, in the event of disagreement among the commissioners, Radcliffe would have a great deal of power to shape the final decision. In the context of the harried final days of the raj, however, it is perhaps not surprising that these busy politicians failed to recognize not only the problems inherent in a format pitting political rivals against each other, but also the potential for long-term controversy over the boundary. Arson and small-scale riots had already begun in Punjab, but some leaders still hoped that partition would calm, not exacerbate, these tensions. Nehru later cited fatigue as a factor in Congress decisions, adding 'few of us could stand the prospect of going to prison again – and if we had stood out for a united India as we wished it, prison obviously awaited us. We saw the fires burning in the Punjab and heard every day of the killings. The plan for partition offered a way out and we took it.'[116] In the rush to independence, the details of that plan received short shrift.

By including Congress and League nominees, the commission's format also gave the impression that South Asians would have control over the final shape of their two new countries. It could be argued that the use of politically selected commissioners was, in part, an attempt by the British to give the Muslim League and Congress a stake in the outcome of the boundary-making effort. South Asians were allowed to testify before the commissions during their public hearings, and the judges on the commissions advised Radcliffe on the implications of various boundary decisions. But in Punjab, ironically enough, the system established by the nationalist leaders, along with the British, reduced the amount of direct South Asian influence on the shape of the border.[117] The administrative design left the British chairman with the final authority to make all decisions, authority which would be particularly important in case of wide disparity between the parties' boundary proposals. But this reality was not immediately apparent. As a result, the responsibility for the commission's decision seemed, at least briefly, to rest not just with the British, but with all the parties that had participated in the negotiations to form the boundary commission.

Notes

1 The exception, of course, is Wavell, whose boundary proposal was all but ignored by officials in London.
2 In late 1946, the British Cabinet had considered the possibility of leaving India piecemeal, transferring power to individual provinces as they withdrew, but discarded the idea as impractical: 'The Committee considered whether it was right to hand over authority to Provinces separately ... To whom would sovereignty in fact legally be surrendered? It would not be practicable for it to be renounced without being transferred to some clearly defined body' (*TP* IX p. 336).
3 *TP* X pp. 540 and 625. Emphasis added.
4 As Joya Chatterji has shown, the Congress-nominated judges of the Bengal boundary commission, arguing successfully on behalf of the Congress case, had a greater effect on the boundary line there (*Spoils*, pp. 19–60).

5   *TP* XII pp. 744–5.
6   Stephen B. Jones, *Boundary-Making: A Handbook for Statesmen, Treaty Editors and Boundary Commissioners* (Washington, DC: Carnegie Endowment for International Peace, 1945).
7   *TP* XI pp. 69–71.
8   *TP* XI p. 73.
9   *TP* XI p. 112.
10 *TP* XI p. 112.
11 *TP* XI pp. 112–13.
12 The designation 'master' dated from Tara Singh's years as a schoolteacher at Khalsa High School, Lyallpur (Singh, *History*, p. 200 n. 12).
13 *Times of India* (5 June 1947), p. 7, col. 2, cited in *TP* XI p. 136.
14 *TP* XI p. 140. Emphasis in original.
15 *TP* XI p. 259.
16 *TP* XI p. 141.
17 *TP* XI p. 190–1.
18 *TP* XI p. 226.
19 *TP* XI p. 234.
20 *TP* XI p. 240.
21 *TP* XI p. 242.
22 *TP* XI p. 242.
23 The Lord Chancellor is responsible for the administration of justice in England and Wales.
24 *TP* XI p. 258.
25 *TP* XI p. 292.
26 *TP* XI p. 293.
27 *TP* XI p. 292.
28 *TP* XI p. 328.
29 *TP* XI p. 336.
30 *TP* XI p. 336.
31 *TP* XI p. 336.
32 *TP* XI pp. 341–2.
33 *TP* XI p. 380.
34 *TP* XI pp. 506–7.
35 *TP* XI p. 539.
36 *TP* XI pp. 581, 588.
37 *TP* XI pp. 655–6.
38 *TP* XI p. 678.
39 *TP* XI p. 678.
40 *Partition Council Proceedings*, cited in *TP* XI p. 683 fn. 10.
41 *TP* XI p. 685.
42 *TP* XI p. 708.
43 *TP* XI p. 708.
44 *TP* XI p. 709.
45 *TP* XI p. 709 fn. 2.
46 *TP* XI pp. 736–7.
47 *TP* XI pp. 735–6.
48 *TP* XI p. 756.
49 H. V. Hodson, *The Great Divide: Britain – India – Pakistan*, Jubilee Series ed. (Karachi: Oxford University Press, 1997), p. 347.
50 *TP* XI p. 91.
51 *TP* XII p. 758. Emphasis added.
52 Jones, p. 57. The demarcation of the line between India and Pakistan has taken decades; in contested areas of Kashmir, it is still incomplete. B. L. Sukhwal, *India: A Political Geography* (Bombay: Allied Publishers, 1971), pp. 219–22.
53 O. H. K. Spate, *On the Margins of History: From the Punjab to Fiji* (Canberra: National Centre for Development Studies, Australian National University, 1991),

p. 54. Spate seems to have his Indian clothing confused; a laborer might wear a *dhoti*, a draped garment for the lower body, but it is unlikely he would wear the formal *sherwani*, a long coat with a high collar.

54 *TP* XI p. 756.
55 Peter Hennessy, 'The eternal fireman', *The Times* (London) (30 January 1976), p. 16.
56 Christopher Beaumont, 'The partition of India', unpublished manuscript, n.d., p. 1.
57 *TP* XI p. 342.
58 Cyril Radcliffe, 'Censors', in *Not in Feather Beds: Some Collected Papers* (London: Hamish Hamilton, 1968), p. 175.
59 Mark Tennant, personal interview, 9 February 2000.
60 *Government by Contempt* (London: Chatto and Windus, 1967); *The Law and Its Compass* (London: Faber & Faber, 1960); *Not in Feather Beds*; *The Problem of Power: The Reith Memorial Lectures 1951* (London: Secker and Warburg, 1952).
61 Radcliffe, 'Elphinstone', in *Not in Feather Beds*, p. 184.
62 This paragraph is based on Edmund Heward, *The Great and the Good: A Life of Lord Radcliffe* (Chichester: Barry Rose Publishers, 1994), pp. 4–6.
63 See R. L. Ashcroft, *Haileybury, 1908–1961* (n.p.: The Haileybury Society; Frome: Butler & Tanner, 1961), p. 181 on Haileybury's connection with India.
64 Ashcroft, p. 175.
65 Heward, p. 38.
66 Cyril Radcliffe, [no title], *The Haileyburian Centenary Magazine* (1962), p. 59.
67 Ashcroft, p. 62.
68 Ashcroft, p. 178.
69 Ashcroft, p. 187.
70 Radcliffe, 'Introduction', in *Not in Feather Beds*, p. xvi.
71 Radcliffe, 'Introduction', pp. xvi–xvii.
72 Heward, p. 12.
73 J. Cumming Morgan, 'A labour company at Ypres', in *Everyman at War: Sixty Personal Narratives of the War*, ed. C. B. Purdom (New York: E. P. Dutton, 1930), pp. 130–5.
74 For a full analysis of Radcliffe's boundary award, see Chapter 5.
75 C. M. Bowra, *Memories 1898–1939* (London: Weidenfeld and Nicolson, 1966), p. 115.
76 Bowra, p. 113.
77 Heward, pp. 15–18.
78 Radcliffe, 'Censors', pp. 176–7.
79 Heward, pp. 12–19.
80 Heward, p. 6.
81 Radcliffe, 'Thoughts on India as "The page is turned"', in *Not in Feather Beds*, p. 1.
82 Mark Tennant, personal interview, 9 February 2000.
83 Heward, p. 24.
84 Asa Briggs, *History of Broadcasting in the United Kingdom*, vol. 2, *The War of Words* (London: Oxford University Press, 1970), p. 34.
85 Charles Lysaght, *Brendan Bracken* (London: Allen Lane, 1979), p. 215.
86 Frederick Birkenhead, *Walter Monckton: The Life of Viscount Monckton of Brenchley* (London: Weidenfeld & Nicolson, 1969), p. 183.
87 Radcliffe and Monckton, undated memo, Monckton Papers, cited in Birkenhead, p. 185.
88 Birkenhead, p. 186.
89 Monckton, letter to Bracken, 22 July 1941, cited in Lysaght, p. 192.
90 Andrew Boyle, *Poor, Dear Brendan: The Quest for Brendan Bracken* (London: Hutchinson, 1974), p. 266.
91 Boyle, p. 307; Lysaght, p. 231.
92 Lysaght, p. 215.
93 Lysaght, p. 216.

94 Lysaght, p. 217.
95 Radcliffe, 'Viscount Bracken (an appreciation)', in *Not in Feather Beds*, p. 109.
96 Cited in Lysaght, p. 217.
97 Lysaght, p. 217.
98 Lysaght, p. 217.
99 Lysaght, p. 216.
100 M. S. Venkataramani and B. K. Shrivastava, *Roosevelt–Gandhi–Churchill: America and the Last Phase of India's Freedom Struggle* (New Delhi: Radiant Publishers, 1983), p. 223.
101 Lysaght, p. 197.
102 Treasury Report, 28 March 1944, cited in Lysaght, p. 231.
103 Lysaght, p. 231.
104 Kenneth Young, ed., *The Diaries of Sir Robert Bruce Lockhart*, vol. 2 (London: Macmillan London Limited, 1980), p. 466.
105 *TP* XI p. 342.
106 Briggs, p. 654.
107 Birkenhead, p. 178.
108 For a discussion of the lasting effect of youthful influences on adult decision-making, see Michael Blackwell's study of the attitudes of postwar Foreign Office officials: *Clinging to Grandeur: British Attitudes and Foreign Policy in the Aftermath of the Second World War* (Westport, CT: Greenwood Press, 1993).
109 *TP* XI p. 859.
110 *TP* XI p. 865.
111 *TP* XI pp. 783–4.
112 *TP* XI p. 903.
113 *TP* XI p. 890.
114 *TP* XI p. 891.
115 *TP* XII p. 680.
116 Mosley, p. 248.
117 Circumstances in Bengal were somewhat different; see Chatterji, *Spoils*, pp. 19–60.

CHAPTER THREE

'Nobody had been paying any attention to the case': the boundary commission at work

Arriving in South Asia on 8 July, less than six weeks before the 15 August deadline for Britain's withdrawal, Cyril Radcliffe set to work clarifying the outlines of his task. Soon after his arrival, he met with the Congress and League nominees who would serve with him as boundary commissioners. Unfortunately, it soon became clear that each party had instructed its nominees not to compromise on any important point. Radcliffe told a friend that 'he found it quite impossible to persuade either side to make any modification of their views. His chief Moslem colleague told him quite frankly: "It is not that I do not wish to make modifications, but I dare not. If I did my life would be in instant danger."'[1] Radcliffe made another unpleasant discovery shortly after his arrival in Delhi; rather than the six months he had anticipated, he would be required to produce a new boundary in only a few weeks.[2] The brevity of his stay meant that he saw little of the country beyond the cities of Calcutta, in Bengal, and Lahore, in Punjab, where the commissions held their public hearings, as well as Simla, where the commissioners deliberated, and Delhi, where he made his final decisions. His knowledge of the rest of Punjab and Bengal remained second-hand.

During his first few days in South Asia, Radcliffe began to take the measure of his task. He started by asking for clarification of his terms of reference. On 10 July, at the viceroy's Partition Council meeting, Mountbatten presented a message from Radcliffe, asking whether 'in the decisions of the Boundary Commissions account should be taken of natural features, providing defensible boundaries and markings for general administrative convenience'. Field Marshal Sir Claude John Eyre Auchinleck, the Commander in Chief of the Indian Army, pointed out that 'rivers, which might appear to form suitable natural boundaries, in India frequently changed their courses and would not therefore provide a fixed boundary' but also added that 'considerations of defence could be ignored'.[3] The Council concluded it should not give any directive to the boundary commission on its terms of reference. Despite this agreement, Mountbatten arranged for the minutes of this meeting, including Auchinleck's advice to disregard questions of defence, to be sent to the commission. In fact, according to Mountbatten's later recollections, he had already counselled Radcliffe 'not to take defence considerations under judgment in making the award'.[4] Auchinleck's advice was based on careful consideration; in a May 1946 memo, he had analyzed the repercussions of partition for both imperial and Indo-Pakistani defence. He concluded that without a united India, the British military position in South Asia would be irreparably damaged. Furthermore, although he considered the possibility of Indo-Pakistani conflict, he saw no way to define a defensible frontier.[5] Radcliffe himself seems to have consistently operated on the assumption that India and Pakistan would have good relations after independence. Other decision-makers – and many of those affected by the division – took this view as well. Mountbatten seemed optimistic that inclusion in the Commonwealth would keep India and Pakistan on mutually friendly terms, emphasizing that dominion status meant membership in a community of cooperative nations.

In mid-July, a minor crisis arose when Arthur Henderson, Under-Secretary of State for India, stated in Parliament that the provision for 'other factors' was intended primarily to allow the boundary commission to address Sikh concerns, including, for example, the location of Sikh shrines.[6] Mountbatten leapt into damage-control mode, emphasizing that the boundary commission was independent and would interpret the mandate to consider 'other factors' on its own.[7]

It was in this increasingly tense atmosphere that the members of the Punjab commission met in Lahore. The negotiations over the commission structure brought together a carefully selected British chairman with four equally carefully picked political nominees: Muhammad Munir and Din Muhammad of the Muslim League and Mehr Chand Mahajan and Teja Singh of the Indian National Congress. Like Radcliffe, the South Asian members of the commission had no background in boundary-making. Far from being independent and objective, they were closely involved in each party's preparation of the case it presented before the commission. They freely involved themselves in debates over the problematic demographic and cartographic data available to the commission, following their party lines. Their ties to the interests of their parties were so strong that they were unable to reach any consensus on the path of the new boundary. Although Radcliffe had the most influence over the commission's award, because his decision was final, an overview of the judges' background deepens our understanding of the boundary commission process.

Of the four judges on the Punjab boundary commission, Muhammad Munir went on to make the greatest, if most dubious, mark on his country's history. Born in 1895, he was appointed to the Lahore High Court in 1942. After partition, he served as Chief Justice of the Lahore High Court from 1949 to 1954, before attaining the post of Chief Justice of the Supreme Court of Pakistan.[8] His lasting contribution to the turbulent history of Pakistani governance consisted of what came to be known as the Munir Doctrine. This doctrine was based on Munir's 1954 ruling that Governor General Ghulam Muhammad's dissolution of Pakistan's Constituent Assembly was justified by 'necessity'. He reinforced this decision the following year, when he wrote, 'where civil authority is paralysed by tumult, all acts done by the military which were dictated by necessity and done in good faith will be protected'.[9] The doctrine of necessity has allowed subsequent Pakistani military leaders, including Field Marshal Ayub Khan in 1958, General Zia ul-Haq in 1977 and General Pervez Musharraf in 1999, to justify their overthrow of civilian regimes.

Din Muhammad was perhaps the most disillusioned with the boundary-making process. Born in 1886, he graduated from Gordon College in Lahore and served on the Lahore High Court from 1936 to 1946. In 1937, he was involved in another case of communal significance. That year, the High Court heard arguments on the Shahidganj Mosque, which had been demolished by Sikhs seeking to build a gurudwara (Sikh temple). The majority ruling allowed the construction of the gurudwara on the site of the demolished mosque; Din Muhammad dissented.[10] In 1947, even before deliberations began, he complained that the line had already been decided and that the commission itself was 'a farce'.[11]

Mehr Chand Mahajan (1889–1967), the most distinguished of the Congress nominees, was born in eastern Punjab and joined the High Court at Lahore in 1943. In 1945, he served on the commission appointed to investigate the Royal Indian Navy mutiny, alongside Major-General Thomas 'Pete' Rees, who would later command the ill-fated Punjab Boundary Force.[12] In 1947, Rees congratulated Mahajan on his appointment to the Punjab boundary commission.[13] Mahajan, like so many others, did not anticipate the seriousness of post-partition animosity. Like a number of well-off Hindus, he kept his house in Lahore, where he had served on the Lahore High Court. In September, however, Mahajan encountered post-partition difficulties first-hand, when Pakistani police searched the house.[14] In October 1947, Mahajan was appointed Prime Minister of Jammu and Kashmir state, but his tenure was brief, for Indo-Pakistani conflict broke out shortly thereafter. In a press conference shortly after his appointment, he said, 'I would like to mention that in the discharge of my duties as Prime Minister, I shall not be guided by any communal considerations whatsoever. I feel that religion and politics are dangerous bedfellows. That it is so has been proved by the events of the last few months across the borders of the State.'[15] This stance suggests that, although he loyally represented Congress during its efforts to carve out as much of Punjab as it could, and although those efforts were based largely on arguments about the religion of Punjab's inhabitants, Mahajan was disillusioned by the results. He went on to a distinguished career in Indian jurisprudence, serving as Chief Justice of the Supreme Court of India in 1954.[16] In 1967, he was involved in another controversial boundary issue when he chaired the commission that realigned the boundary between the states of Maharashtra and Mysore.[17]

The judges were not immune from the violence that swirled around them, and the final Congress nominee, Teja Singh (1889–1965), was the most deeply affected. Born in Rawalpindi, now in Pakistan, and appointed to the Lahore High Court in 1943, he was the first Sikh to hold that position. In March 1947, a number of his relatives were murdered in the first wave of partition violence to strike Punjab.[18] Teja Singh toured Rawalpindi in the aftermath of the violence, an experience which, combined with his personal losses, must have made a lasting impression. After serving on the Punjab boundary commission, he continued as a High Court judge in East Punjab, then served as the first Chief Justice of the Supreme Court of the newly formed Patiala and East Punjab States Union (PEPSU).[19]

All of the judges came from backgrounds in criminal law and lacked any expertise in boundary-making. One knowledgeable South Asian observer describes the use of judges as 'absolutely inappropriate', asking 'how can such people know what effects mountains and rivers have on the well-being of a country?'[20] As it was, however, the judges' background had less influence than their party loyalties, for each advanced his own party's position without negotiation or compromise.

With Radcliffe and the judges assembled, the boundary commissions for Punjab and Bengal embarked on a peculiar procedure. A number of groups submitted proposals to each commission, which then selected a subset who were allowed to argue their case during a brief public sitting. Congress and the Muslim League had the opportunity to present their case in both Bengal and Punjab, while smaller and less influential groups, like the untouchables, were allowed to state their position only in writing.[21] However, due to the mid-August deadline, the two commissions were forced to hold their hearings concurrently. Radcliffe did not attend. The Punjab commission's superintendent, Mian Muhammad Sadullah, oversaw the production of transcripts, which he sent daily by air to Radcliffe.

As Radcliffe and his colleagues gathered, Congress, the League and other organizations were also scrambling to prepare their cases for presentation at the boundary commission hearings. Both Congress and the League had recruited distinguished lawyers to present their cases. Sir Zafrullah Khan (1893–1985), the Muslim League's eminent lead counsel, was born in Sialkot (now a border town in Pakistani Punjab).[22] Although his family belonged to the Ahmadiyyas, an Islamic community considered heretical by some Muslims, he became well respected within League circles for his leadership skills and diplomatic nature. Zafrullah read law at King's College London, became a member of Lincoln's Inn and was called to the bar in 1914. Returning home in 1915, he began practising law with his father and quickly rose to prominence. In 1931 he was elected president of the Muslim League but recalled later that the League 'was not a very active or effective organization in those days'.[23] He was a judge on the Federal Court of India from 1941 to 1947, then served as constitutional advisor to several princely states. In 1947, Zafrullah accepted Jinnah's request to argue the Muslim League case before the Punjab boundary commission. After partition, Zafrullah went on to a distinguished international career. He was the first Foreign Minister of Pakistan from 1947 to 1954. During the same period he led Pakistan's delegation to the UN, where he argued Pakistan's case for Kashmir and supported Arab claims in Palestine. He was a judge on the International Court of Justice (ICJ) at the Hague from 1954 to 1961 and from 1964 to 1973, with an interlude to preside over the UN General Assembly in 1962. From 1970 to 1973 he was president of the ICJ.[24]

Zafrullah therefore provided high-powered leadership for the League's legal team. Unfortunately, he found that team completely unprepared. When Zafrullah travelled to Lahore to take up the case, he was met by a prominent League figure, the Nawab of Mamdot. Zafrullah recalled,

> I presumed that I would be meeting the lawyers who had been engaged in the preparation of the case, for I had been assured by Mr Jinnah that by the time I arrived at Lahore I would find the whole case ready and I would only have to take on its presentation on the basis of the brief prepared by the lawyers.
>
> So, under that impression, at 2.30 I presented myself at Mamdot Villa, the residence of the Nawab of Mamdot. I found there a large number of lawyers most of whom I knew very well as personal friends and

[59]

colleagues. Earlier, during our meeting with Sir Cyril in the morning he had fixed Friday noon as the deadline for filing written cases. So after the usual hand-shakes and greetings we sat down and I enquired which of them were working with me on the case. Khalifa Shuja-ud-Din, a senior lawyer, smiled and said, 'Which case'? 'The boundary case, of course. I was asked to meet the lawyers working on the boundary case this afternoon here.' Khalifa Shuja-ud-Din replied that he knew nothing at all about the boundary case. He was at a loss to understand what I was talking about, the lawyers were there only to welcome me back to Lahore and to wish me success in the case.

To say the least, I was stunned not only to learn that nobody had been paying any attention to the case, much less preparing it, but at the alarm that within less than three days – it was already the afternoon of Tuesday – I would have to present a case in writing, on the partition of this part of the country. I did not know which way to turn for statistics or any other relevant materials to ascertain the principles on which the line should be drawn or on what ground to prepare the case.

Within a few minutes I said good bye to the assembled lawyers and asked the Nawab of Mamdot, whether the Muslim League Organization had prepared any plan or collected any material or done anything in this direction. He uttered a laconic No.[25]

With luck, Zafrullah located some population statistics and found four other volunteer lawyers who had travelled to Lahore in hopes of assisting the League case. Setting to work in an atmosphere of tension and violence, he found it difficult to arrange for even the most basic services. He laboured late into the night, then rose early the next morning: 'at 7.30 I inquired whether the stenographer had arrived. There was nobody; eight o'clock, nobody. Not a pencil, not a sheet of paper, not a typewriter or a stenographer!'[26] Rush and lack of preparation characterized both the preparations and the commission itself.[27]

The Congress delegation was led by the well-known lawyer Motilal C. Setalvad. M. C. Setalvad (1884–1974) was born in Ahmedabad (now in Gujarat), where his father was an eminent lawyer. A staunch Congress supporter, he was appointed Advocate-General for Bombay in 1937, with the support of Sardar Patel. He resigned this post in 1942, after Congress issued its Quit India resolution. During the war years, his professional practice brought him into contact with Zafrullah, then a judge, whom Setalvad found 'a pleasant man and very intelligent'.[28] In July 1947, he accepted an invitation to represent Congress before the Punjab boundary commission, where he found himself working in opposition to Zafrullah. The boundary commission process left him disillusioned, however, and Setalvad reportedly refused to accept his Rs. 50,000 counsel's fee.[29] After completing his work in Lahore, he was a member of several Indian delegations to the UN from 1947 to

1949, dealing with the Kashmir question and the position of Indians in South Africa. He served as Attorney General of independent India from 1950 to 1962. After retiring as Attorney General, he became a member of the Rajya Sabha, the upper house of the Indian Parliament, from 1966 to 1972. But he did not enjoy his time as a parliamentarian; disenchanted by their 'frequent rows and disorders', he lamented his colleagues' lack of accountability.[30]

Although Congress representatives were better prepared than their League counterparts, they too had to assemble their case very quickly. Setalvad arrived in Lahore in early July and with his guidance, 'a dozen or more lawyers under the leadership of Bakshi Tek Chand set to work'. They set a hard pace but worked less frantically than the Muslim Leaguers:

> We worked at Tek Chand's house from morning till evening collecting information about Lahore and the surrounding areas to prepare a memorandum embodying the case for the inclusion of Lahore and the surrounding areas in India. We met at Bakshiji's house at about 8 in the morning and continued our labours right till late in the evening. I used to have my lunch and tea generally at Bakshiji's house. When information was collected and discussed, it would be put down on paper and a final draft would be dictated by me with suggestions made to me by my colleagues.[31]

One of the Congress-nominated judges, M. C. Mahajan, came to see the Congress delegation on several occasions during this time. There was no pretence at impartiality – the Congress-nominated commissioners worked closely with the lawyers who would be arguing Congress's case before them. By the end of their preparations, Setalvad writes, many of the Congressmen felt they had a strong case for the allotment of Lahore to India, 'but those who thought that way forgot that this was not to be a judicial award, but a political one'.[32] When the hearings began, the courtroom was packed with armed guards and Setalvad found that 'the atmosphere at the Court was the very antithesis of a judicial atmosphere'.[33] Although Setalvad had earlier admired Zafrullah for the 'clarity of his mind' and his 'strong commonsense',[34] here he concluded that 'he was not half so able an advocate as he had been a Judge'.[35] The League's lack of preparation had taken its toll.

The party leaders in Delhi, like their representatives in Lahore, were still coming to grips with the boundary question. On 21 July, Nehru wrote to Mountbatten to raise again the question of 'natural' boundaries and, somewhat oddly, to protest against a boundary-making process that concentrated too much on religious interests. Although Nehru noted that he had been considering the question for some time, his letter makes clear that he had not yet recognized the import of the commission's terms of reference, with their emphasis on 'contiguous majority areas' of religious groups. Nehru wrote, 'At present this question of a boundary is thought of far too much in terms of Sikh, Hindu or Muslim interests. I suppose every party will produce arguments for the inclusion of a little bit of territory here or there. The result might well be a very curious frontier line with numerous curves and enclaves.' Far preferable, Nehru opined, would be a 'simpler' frontier, consisting of 'a natural barrier like a river or some special kind of terrain'. Nehru concluded that some small movement of people might be necessary to make such a boundary workable, but that 'this need not involve any major transfers of population'.[36] In mid-July, therefore, Nehru, who was admittedly deluged by other cares and responsibilities, was just beginning to appreciate that the terms of reference guaranteed a division based primarily on religious grounds, making communal resentments difficult to avoid.

The next day, Baldev Singh wrote to Mountbatten to express his support for Nehru's position. A 'zig-zag' boundary running through 'numerous interlocked villages', he asserted, should be avoided in favour of a 'natural boundary line'.[37] Disregarding the complexities of the problem and the time required to prepare such arguments, he suggested that Army officers representing both sides should be deputed to argue for natural boundaries on the basis of defence requirements. He noted that the Punjab commission had begun hearing arguments the previous day and concluded, 'as the time is short these Officers should get their orders today in order to enable them to prepare the cases'. Mountbatten dissuaded Baldev Singh, reminding him of the Partition Council's earlier decision to disregard defensible boundaries.[38] Despite Congress concerns, the boundary process carried on unaltered, with the British successfully fending off nationalist efforts to play a greater role in the shaping of their own future borders.

The only professional geographer known to have taken part in the Punjab proceedings was Oskar Spate, a respected Australian geographer hired by the Ahmadiyya community, which keenly felt the risks inherent in its northern Punjabi location.[39] As a participant in the larger Muslim effort, Spate had an inside view of the Muslim League preparations and advised Zafrullah on key points. Spate's contemporary diary provides a vivid record of the public hearings and the behind-the-scenes chaos that accompanied them, as well as an expert's view of the boundary commission's methods, which Spate regarded as peculiar. On 19 July, he wrote, 'the procedure of the Commission is odd: the two Muslim and two non-Muslim judges will hear counsel for ten days, then the Chairman, Sir Cyril Radcliffe, who will receive verbatim reports but will NOT be present will go into a huddle with them and they will in effect issue an award'.[40] Spate astutely observed the political reasons that might have driven the choice of this procedure, particularly the desire to avoid lengthy negotiations. However, he also noted the potential drawbacks of such an arrangement: 'Presumably this [procedure was] adopted in order to avoid continual bargaining and to get a quick decision; but obviously the counsel must put forward maximum demands and are precluded from offering compromises as plenipotentiaries would. Presumably the judges will do this.'[41] Spate could not know at this juncture what Radcliffe had discovered: that the judges themselves apparently had been instructed not to give an inch on their parties' demands.

Radcliffe lacked the personal knowledge necessary to evaluate the conflicting claims presented at these hearings, and he noted in his decision that he found the counsel of his fellow commissioners helpful, despite the fact that their partisan bias soon became clear. The commissioners' reports reveal that they took different views of the same testimony and evidence, particularly on questions involving factors other than religious majorities. Radcliffe politely but tellingly expressed his gratitude for the 'indispensable assistance' of his fellow judges in 'the clarification of the issues and the marshalling of the arguments for different views'.[42] In private, however, Radcliffe later observed that he had not received 'the sort of judicial support one would expect from a tribunal'.[43] He was unable, in other words, to thank the other commissioners for assisting with the final result, because they did not in fact offer that assistance; he could only thank them for arguing the viewpoints of their own parties. This aspect of the commission apparently surprised him; Zafrullah recorded in his memoir that during the Punjab commission's initial meeting with the parties planning to give evidence, Radcliffe stated that 'he was not sure whether at all his function as umpire would come into play. It was only after the Commission had made its report that he would come to know whether he would be called upon to function at all.'[44] Zafrullah's account – which is far from an apologia for Radcliffe – suggests that the boundary chair was surprised to find himself in the position of making so many key decisions.

Munir offered a somewhat different recollection in his later memoir. He recalled that during the commissioners' initial meeting with their chairman, Radcliffe 'informed us that the report which would be submitted to the Governor-General would be his own report, and that no report by a member would be sent up'. Munir objected to this procedure, which, he felt, reduced the commissioners' position 'to that of the spokesmen of the parties'.[45] Whatever the initial assumptions of Radcliffe, Munir and their colleagues, these two versions of the commission's early meetings agree on several points: first, it quickly became clear that the final decision would be Radcliffe's alone; second, the judges had little influence over that final decision; and third, the judges in the end took or were forced to take the position of party advocates rather than adjudicators.

In any case, Radcliffe's colleagues did provide assistance in mastering some of the basic details that he, as a newcomer to South Asia, found unfamiliar. During the Muslim League presentation, for example, Justice Din Muhammad commented, 'The Chairman may not know what a *zail* or a thana is. While speaking of *zails* and thanas, will you just describe what they mean?' The Muslim League lawyer obliged, defining a *zail* as a collection of villages under a *zaildar*, or rural leader, who assists the administrative authorities. A *thana* is a police station, whose jurisdiction varies in range.[46] Above the *thana*, the other British Indian divisions, in increasing size, were the *tehsil*, the district and the province.[47]

The public hearings were heavily guarded, and when Spate attended for the first time he 'found [the] right court-room by observing [the] concentration of armed police'.[48] At Zafrullah Khan's headquarters, the earlier bedlam persisted. When Spate met with Zafrullah one evening, the situation reminded him of his wartime experiences as a geographer with the Inter-Services Topographic Department (ISTD), part of Mountbatten's South East Asia Command (SEAC). He found 'a great flap on for all the world as in ISTD (SEAC) when the great ones wanted to know all about some wretched island forthwith – exactly the same, railway man called in, roads man, canal expert'.[49] When he joined Zafrullah for dinner later that week, the scene was more frantic than before: 'The place is more like an ISTD shambles than ever. Sixteen people in a room with only one or two tables, and they covered up with books and dossiers, all frantically looking things up & writing notes in Urdu – quite a secretariat!'[50] Spate's Ahmadiyya employers, by contrast, were resourceful and efficient, and they worked closely with the larger Muslim League effort. Spate described the Ahmadiyya as a 'wonderful organization – they had 2 or 3 copies each of the latest American books on boundaries flown out and brought by special messenger from Bombay; arrived yesterday, in time for the commissioners' use at least'.[51] The Muslim League and the rest of Punjab's Muslim community had mustered their best lawyers, who were hard at work, despite the party's earlier lack of attention to the boundary problem. It remained to be seen whether this effort had came in time.

Spate also paid attention to the human side of the commission, both in terms of its human qualities and of its failings. He described Din

Muhammad as 'foppish, glasses with broad black ribbon, tall, far more personality than other three judges, and aware of it'.[52] The hearing room was hot and crowded and the action not always stimulating, even for the commission members. Towards the end of the hearings, he confessed of the courtroom, 'keeping awake there was hard work (too hard for Moh[amme]d Munir at one point!)'.[53] Mountbatten's aggressive timetable meant that exhaustion took a toll on everyone involved in the boundary-creation process.

Because the commission's terms of reference emphasized the importance of contiguous religious majorities, the existing census data were central to each party's argument. Unfortunately, the data themselves were highly problematic, as the census had become increasingly politicized in the preceding decades. Setalvad, for example, vehemently asserted that the census data were unreliable. The 1921 and 1931 censuses, he argued, had been disrupted by Gandhi's non-cooperation campaigns, resulting in Hindu and Sikh totals lower than they should have been. The 1941 census, by contrast, had been conducted at a time when more populous communal groups received more representation and thus more political power; in other words, a larger showing in the census brought political rewards. The result, he maintained, was that Muslims had misrepresented their numbers, skewing the census results in their favour. Setalvad asserted that the true number of Muslims in a number of Punjabi districts was much lower than reported.[54] In fact, as Spate noted, the true figures were impossible to determine with any accuracy, since this was 'a Census in which all communities did some hard lying'.[55] Spate's appraisal, harsh though it may be, captured the unreliability of the available demographic data.

Since census data showing Muslim majorities were favourable to the Muslim League case, the Muslim League defended the accuracy of the 1941 census. League lawyers even tried to argue that the commission was bound by its terms of reference to consider the 1941 census as authoritative.[56] The 'notional boundary' governing the June partition vote was based on the 1941 census figures, but Congress lawyers successfully argued that these conditions did not apply to the boundary commission. In any case, it was clear that the available census data were highly problematic. As a result, the obsession with religious categories that drove much of the partition was based on imperfect information. A façade of order, control and scientific knowledge hid the reality of flawed data, discord and chaos.

Maps submitted to the boundary commission

Maps were a key element of each party's presentation to the commission. They also provide invaluable evidence not only about the kinds of arguments each side expected to be most compelling, but also about the resources available to them and the time strain they were working under. The surviving maps, which are analysed here, were submitted by Congress, League and Sikh representatives (for the party claims, see maps 4a–b and 5c). Before and during its public hearings in July 1947, the commission received numerous maps from the various groups that submitted proposals. These maps ranged from conflicting representations of habitation by religious group to documents on canals to information on railway lines. The Punjab commission also considered preparing its own map, presumably with the idea of having an objective standard of comparison, but was unable to do so in the timeframe allotted.

At a meeting on 14 July, the boundary commission members decided that groups wishing to submit memoranda should do so by 18 July.[57] The commission directed that these memoranda 'should be accompanied by such maps as may indicate the proposed line of demarcation between the two new Provinces'.[58] On 20 July, the commission's secretaries sent Radcliffe all submitted memoranda, with maps included, by special messenger.[59] The maps analysed here are the primary maps submitted with each party's written memorandum.[60] These maps highlighted each community's territorial claims, which were generally as extensive as possible. There was less attention to the damage that would be done to existing socio-economic networks by a line drawn in any one place. Each party apparently drew up its own maps, for none of them was based on Survey of India maps. Because Survey maps were limited to 'official use only', a restriction enforced even more stringently during World War II, the lawyers arguing before the commission lacked easy access to them. As a result, the parties were somewhat handicapped in terms of the cartographic resources at their disposal. Radcliffe himself found it difficult to locate maps on the scale he required; it seems likely that the nationalist parties encountered even more severe difficulties.

Two Congress maps

Like most of the maps presented to the commission, Congress's maps emphasized the distribution of population; based on census figures, creatively interpreted, as well as certain elements of infrastructure, they argued that all of central Punjab and even areas of western Punjab should go to India. The map attached to the Congress memorandum, which had a scale of one inch to sixteen miles, contains little detail, showing only rivers, *tehsil*-level divisions, and a small number of cities in central Punjab.[61] It offers no legend. Central Punjab and salients reaching nearly as far west as the Chenab River are shaded with red lines, presumably to indicate that these are the 'non-Muslim contiguous areas' to which the map title refers.[62] The other primary feature of this map is a series of green lines radiating outwards from Lahore and Amritsar throughout central Punjab. These presumably mark 'hydro-electric transmission lines'. This map seems to be primarily intended to establish a Congress/Sikh claim to those areas of central Punjab that included the cities of Lahore and Amritsar and the area's valuable electrical power lines. (For the Congress claim, see discussion in Chapter 7 and map 4b.)

Another Congress map came in for particular criticism when Zafrullah argued that it was a visually deceiving representation of the already problematic census data.[63] This document exemplifies the controversial nature of social maps; the Muslim parties objected to it strongly, arguing that it claimed areas that actually had a Muslim majority. Purporting to show 'contiguous non-Muslim majority areas', apparently at a higher level of detail than the primary Congress map discussed above, it laid claim to large areas of Punjab. Oskar Spate, the Australian geographer hired by a Muslim group, derisively described this map, with its Hindu/Sikh majority areas 'marked in rusty red', as looking like 'a piece of streaky bacon'.[64] The Muslim representatives took great satisfaction in Judge Muhammad Munir's close cross-examination of the Congress counsel on the subject of this map. As Spate described the lawyer's admissions, 'the Muslim "pockets" have whacking great majorities and the big red areas [denoting non-Muslim majorities] very thin ones. The best example is Chunian tehsil which is coloured about half red; in the Muslim half the majority is 85,706, in the non-Muslim majority half it is just 1,100.'[65] The hearing transcripts record the dogged attempts of Setalvad, the Congress lawyer, to defend the map. Eventually, he did concede, when asked what unit had been adopted as the basis for calculation, that Congress had used 'anything from a district to a village'.[66] Spate rejoiced at Setalvad's misstep but noted that Radcliffe had not been there to witness it in person; he would rely on the daily transcript. Spate wrote in his diary, 'This [admission] was a major tactical error: if Radcliffe has enough stamina to read thus far (and Z[afrullah] K[han] laboured the point that they had gerrymandered, using no ascertainable unit, so perhaps he will), then they'll never get away with it and have effectively sabotaged this part of their case.'[67] Spate's enthusiasm seems a trifle premature, however. Radcliffe did not record his reaction to the party maps, but given the earlier discussion of flaws in the census statistics, it seems unlikely that he regarded the demographic information on any of them as authoritative.

A Sikh map

When reading the map submitted by the Sikhs, one is immediately struck by the somewhat sloppy hand lettering, which seems to indicate that it was drawn under time pressure, and by the clear visual presentation of the extent of the Sikh claim.[68] This map uses blocks of colour to differentiate Muslim from Hindu/Sikh majority areas. It claims an even larger section of Punjab than does the Congress map, with all of central Punjab and significant portions of western Punjab shaded blue, meaning Hindu/Sikh majorities. (For the Sikh claim, see discussion in Chapter 7 and map 4a.) The choice of green for Muslim areas is a visual nod to the Muslim League's party colour. Yellow marks princely states (which were ostensibly entitled to choose for themselves whether to join India or Pakistan, although in general their rulers had little real choice). This map, unlike the Congress map, includes a legend, which offers symbols for district, *tehsil* and state boundaries, as well as principal towns and rivers. Its scale is one inch to twenty-four miles. Through the use of colour, this map powerfully and clearly conveys the Sikh demand for a division along the Chenab River in western Punjab. However, it also conveys just how extreme this demand was. This map represented an ultimatum, not a bargaining position calculated to lead to negotiation and compromise.

A Muslim League map

The Muslim League submission, while almost as striking as the Sikh map, conveys a very different image: one of Punjab as a Muslim sea surrounding the Sikh island of Amritsar. This map, which concentrated on showing Muslim majority areas, is again on the relatively small scale of one inch to sixteen miles.[69] Like the other maps, this map shows provincial, state and *tehsil* boundaries, as well as rivers. It also shows additional cities and roads, railways and canals. Again, the use of colour makes this map's territorial claims dramatically clear. Nearly all of central Punjab is green, indicating Muslim majorities. (The Muslim League argued that the *tehsil* should be the unit used to determine majority areas. They claimed all *tehsils* with a Muslim majority, as well as a few additional areas in Pathankot and Hoshiarpur that were claimed under 'other factors'.[70]) In the middle of the map, however, a bright yellow segment, surrounding Amritsar, indicates 'a non-Muslim pocket'. In other words, the Muslim demand would have left the holy city of the Sikhs in an Indian enclave some ten to twenty miles inside Pakistan. In addition, two salients of land extend into eastern Punjab in the Ludhiana and Hoshiarpur areas. (For the Muslim League claim, see discussion in Chapter 7 and map 5c.) Ludhiana is shaded with green horizontal stripes, to indicate 'contiguous Muslim majority areas'. An island of land around the city of Ferozepur, some ten miles inside the Hindu/Sikh area, and a small area south of Delhi, perhaps a hundred miles from the rest of Muslim-majority Punjab, are also labelled as Muslim-majority territory. Congress lawyers criticized this map, particularly the fingers of land that stretched into Hindu/ Sikh territory. They asserted, 'you cannot have, while drawing international boundaries, salients of this character with territory eight or ten miles wide penetrating into the other state'.[71] It is not clear how they distinguished the League's salients from their own larger projections into Muslim-majority territory.

Having completed their public hearings in ten days, the commissioners moved to the cooler climate of Simla and deliberated through the early days of August. Rumours began to fly fast and furious. The commission's deliberations, although theoretically private, were the subject of widespread and often well-informed speculation. Spate recorded that the commission's Hindu member thought Congress's preparations inadequate, describing Mahajan as 'furious with Congress for giving him such a lousy case to present'.[72] Whatever the origins of the judges' position as *de facto* party spokesmen, by this stage in the process at least one of them regretted his inability to play the role more effectively.

One crucial theme, Radcliffe's concern with maintaining working infrastructure, was already emerging during these early August deliberations. In fact, at one point Radcliffe proposed to his fellow commissioners that India and Pakistan operate the Punjabi headworks jointly. Upon hearing of this idea, A. N. Khosla, Chairman of the Central Waterways, Irrigation and Navigation Commission, sent Nehru an agitated note, which Nehru passed on to Mountbatten. Khosla wrote, 'it is gathered that at the luncheon at Simla Sir Cyril Radcliffe suggested to the four Judges the desirability of recommending joint control of the canal system and electricity (presumably over the areas where this distribution is common to Pakistan and India)'.[73] Khosla objected to this notion on the grounds that it was outside the boundary commission's terms of reference. In his covering letter, Nehru diplomatically suggested to Mountbatten that Khosla's 'views have a certain value and importance. I am, therefore, sending this note to you. If you feel that this might be sent on to Sir Cyril Radcliffe, perhaps this might be done.'[74] Mountbatten refused, but Nehru's attitude was made clear. And yet this episode marks yet another example of Mountbatten undercutting nationalist attempts to shape the boundary-making process. The Muslim League was equally unenthusiastic about Radcliffe's suggestion.[75] Despite its failure, this proposal reveals not only Radcliffe's efforts to safeguard the Punjabi irrigation system, but also his expectation that the two new nations would coexist peacefully and even form cooperative relationships. In his award, he expressed the hope that 'arrangements can be made and maintained between the two States that will minimize the consequences of this interruption as far as possible'.[76] Unfortunately, this proposal's initial reception foreshadowed later difficulties between the two new states.

Perhaps indicating the commission's carefully constructed judicial façade was beginning to disintegrate, rumours were flying faster than ever by 7 August, when Radcliffe and Beaumont left for Delhi. It was already alleged that Beaumont had accepted Sikh bribes 'to give Radcliffe false figures'.[77] Spate encountered the chairman and his secretary on the train as they travelled south to Delhi, and added his own views: 'Radcliffe and Beaumont in rail car – don't like the latter's look (nor did I when I first saw him). Radcliffe looks OK. I said, "It's all over bar the shouting?" But he said there was much to do yet at Delhi. This may be hopeful: Louis [Mountbatten] may be G[overnor]-G[eneral] of India but not such a fool surely as to jeopardize lasting cooperation for three additional districts and a month's peace now.'[78] In other words, fearing that Radcliffe had in mind a line favourable to India, Spate hoped that Mountbatten would change his mind. In fact, allegations that Mountbatten had interfered with Radcliffe's deliberations over the Punjab boundary would soon arise.

Notes

1   Young, p. 624.
2   Mosley, p. 195.
3   *TP* XII p. 64.
4   Collins and Lapierre, *Mountbatten and Partition*, p. 102.
5   *TP* XII pp. 800–6.
6   Great Britain, House of Commons. Parliamentary Debates (Hansard). 5th series, vol. 440 (London: HMSO, 1947).
7   *TP* XII pp. 202, 311.
8   From 29 June 1954 to 2 May 1960.
9   Nazir Hussain Chaudhri, *Chief Justice Muhammad Munir: His Life, Writings and Judgments* (Lahore: Research Society of Pakistan, University of the Punjab, 1973), p. 416.
10 A. G. Noorani, 'Ayodhya in reverse', *Frontline* 18:3 (3–16 February 2001), www.flonnet.com/fl1803/18030890.htm, accessed 3 March 2008.
11 A. H. Batalvi, ed., *The Forgotten Years: Memoirs of Muhammad Zafrullah Khan* (Lahore: Vanguard, 1991), p. 149.
12 Mehr Chand Mahajan, *Looking Back: The Autobiography of Mehr Chand Mahajan,*

Former Chief Justice of India (London: Asia Publishing House, 1963), pp. 108–10.

13   Pete Rees, letter to M. C. Mahajan, 13 July 1947, Mahajan Papers, NMML, 1–2.

14   Unidentified correspondent, letter to Governor Chandulal Trivedi, 15 September 1947, Mahajan Papers, NMML, 2.

15   Mahajan, speech at Srinagar Press Conference, 15 October 1947, Mahajan Papers, NMML, 3.

16   From 4 January 1954 to 23 December 1954. Vidya Dhar Mahajan, *Chief Justice Mehr Chand Mahajan (The Biography of the Great Jurist)* (Lucknow: Eastern Book Company, 1969), pp. 42–50.

17   Vidya Dhar Mahajan, pp. 66–76.

18   Teja Singh did not, as has been reported, lose his wife to partition violence; she died in 1942.

19   This paragraph draws on Darbara Singh, 'Justice Teja Singh', in *Ten Eminent Sikhs* (Amritsar: Literature House, 1982), pp. 41–9.

20   Personal interview.

21   See Ishtiaq Ahmed, 'The 1947 partition of Punjab: Arguments put forth before the Punjab Boundary Commission by the parties involved', in *Region and Partition: Bengal, Punjab and the Partition of the Subcontinent*, ed. Ian Talbot and Gurharpal Singh (Oxford: Oxford University Press, 1999), pp. 116–67.

22   This paragraph draws on Batalvi.

23   Batalvi, p. 38.

24   Zafrullah's memoirs, edited by Batalvi, provide an overview of his professional accomplishments to 1962.

25   Batalvi, pp. 151–2.

26   Batalvi, p. 153.

27   Zafrullah offers no explanation for the League's lack of organization; it may be that its historical weakness in Punjab impeded the party's efforts to gather its resources for the Lahore hearings.

28   Motilal C. Setalvad, *My Life: Law and Other Things* (London: Sweet & Maxwell, 1971), p. 86.

29   *The Tribune*, 2 August 1947, cited in Raghuvendra Tanwar, *Reporting the Partition: Press, Public, and Other Opinions* (New Delhi: Manohar, 2006), p. 281.

30   Setalvad, pp. 599–600.

31   Setalvad, pp. 109–10.

32   Setalvad, p. 110.

33   Setalvad, p. 112.

34   Setalvad, p. 82.

35   Setalvad, p. 112.

36   *TP* XII pp. 285–6.

37   *TP* XII p. 290.

38   *TP* XII p. 304.

39   In Bengal, S. P. Chatterjee, head of the Department of Geography at Calcutta University, assisted Congress (Chatterji, *Spoils*, pp. 30 n. 28, 55–6).

40   O. H. K. Spate Diary, 19 July 1947, photocopy, Spate Papers, South Asian Archive, Cambridge University. Emphasis in source.

41   Spate Diary, 19 July 1947.

42   *TP* XII p. 745.

43   Mark Tennant, personal interview, 9 February 2000.

44   Batalvi, p. 149.

45   Munir, *From Jinnah to Zia*, p. 12.

46   Mian Muhammad Sadullah et al., eds, *The Partition of the Punjab – 1947*, 4 vols (Lahore: Sang-e-Meel Publications, 1993), vol. 2, p. 286.

47   Contemporary documents transliterate this term as either 'tehsil' or 'tahsil' (or occasionally 'tasil'). Throughout this book, I employ the more commonly used 'tehsil'.

48   Spate Diary, 21 July 1947.

49   Spate Diary, 22 July 1947.

50 Spate Diary, 25 July 1947.
51 Spate Diary, 31 July 1947.
52 Spate Diary, 21 July 1947.
53 Spate Diary, 31 July 1947.
54 Sadullah, vol. 2, pp. 17–27.
55 O. H. K. Spate, *On the Margins of History: From the Punjab to Fiji* (Canberra: National Centre for Development Studies, Australian National University, 1991), p. 55.
56 Sadullah, vol. 2, pp. 361–7.
57 We have already seen the difficulties that this tight timeframe caused for the Muslim League team led by Zafrullah Khan.
58 Sadullah, vol. 1, No. 141.
59 Sadullah, vol. 1, No. 243.
60 The records of the hearings show that each party employed numerous different maps, but Sadullah reproduces only the three primary maps discussed here.
61 'Index plan of the Punjab, showing non-Muslim contiguous areas & hydro-electric transmission lines' [facsimile], 1947, as reproduced in Sadullah, vol. 4, Map 3.
62 In geographical terms, a salient is a spur of land that projects out from a larger feature.
63 This map has not been traced.
64 Spate Diary, 25 July 1947.
65 Spate Diary, 31 July 1947.
66 Sadullah, vol. 2, p. 212.
67 Spate Diary, 31 July 1947.
68 'Map of the Punjab showing the proposed boundary line' [facsimile], 1947, as reproduced in Sadullah, vol. 4, Map 4.
69 'Map of the Punjab, Muslim majority tehsils and contiguous majority areas of Muslims' [facsimile], 1947, as reproduced in Sadullah, vol. 4, Map 5.
70 Sadullah, vol. 2, pp. 293–4.
71 Sadullah, vol. 2, p. 35.
72 Spate Diary, 4 August 1947.
73 *TP* XII p. 619.
74 *TP* XII pp. 618–19.
75 Sadullah, vol. 1, p. xiv.
76 *TP* XII p. 752.
77 Spate Diary, 7 August 1947.
78 Spate Diary, 7 August 1947. Emphasis in original.

CHAPTER FOUR

'Water was the key':
Radcliffe's private deliberations

An air of mystery surrounds the final phase of the boundary-creation process, in which Radcliffe, leaving his fellow commissioners behind, retreated to New Delhi to draw his line alone. Radcliffe's destruction of almost all the papers related to his private deliberations on the boundary line has heightened this sense of enigma. Among the few surviving documents is a sketch map of the line as he apparently expected to draw it only a few days before his deadline (for the line appearing in the sketch map, see map 5a). The final award differed significantly, however, from this sketch map. This apparent last-minute alteration has given rise to a great deal of speculation over why Radcliffe changed his line so late in the process. The fact that Radcliffe's award has become linked to the ongoing controversy over Kashmir further complicates efforts to analyse the reasoning behind his decision, and the seriousness of the Kashmir problem raises the stakes of such an assessment tremendously. A cloud of accusations, counter-accusations and angry defences has therefore accumulated over the years since 1947.

If the partition process had followed established best practices for boundary-making, Radcliffe's line would have had less long-term signif-icance. Contemporary texts on boundary-making allowed commis-sions a great deal of flexibility in making their awards. Commissioners did not have to make their decisions final; doing so involved providing a 'complete definition'. Indeed, attempting a complete definition ran counter to the realities of delimitation, as problems on the ground might necessitate changes in the original line. In *Boundary-Making: A Handbook for Statesmen, Treaty Editors and Boundary Commis-sioners*, regarded by contemporary geographers as authoritative, Stephen Jones warned that although making a final definition is possible, 'there is no assurance that the line so defined is the most suitable one or even that it is feasible to demarcate all parts of it'.[1] On the other hand, allowing demarcators to make necessary adjustments, an option known as 'complete definition with power to deviate', was acceptable, even common, practice.[2] But Radcliffe, by and large, approached his task as a mandate to produce a complete definition.

Because Radcliffe left so few records of his work, the testimony of his private secretary, Christopher Beaumont, provides invaluable insight into the boundary commission's workings and the rationale behind some of Radcliffe's decisions. Extended interviews with Beaumont, combined with analysis of the text of Radcliffe's award and of his surviving maps, demonstrate that Radcliffe's line was based primarily on the need to balance the division of religious majorities with the preservation of Punjab's life-giving irrigation systems. In Radcliffe's last days in New Delhi, however, it seems likely that Mountbatten did pressure him to alter his boundary in Punjab.

The primary factor Radcliffe weighed as he neared his final decision was the separation of 'contiguous majority areas', as dictated by the boundary commission's terms of reference. This priority led him to sever the cities of Lahore and Amritsar, the two primary urban areas of Punjab, which are relatively near neighbours only twenty-five miles apart. Radcliffe did award India two areas with small Muslim majorities, in Ferozepur and Gurdaspur Districts, partly because of security concerns that arose out of the division of Lahore and Amritsar. Although he attempted to limit the inevitable disruption to Punjabi infrastructure, particularly the irrigation system, these efforts were largely unsuccessful.[3]

After he returned to London, Radcliffe discussed his awards and the reasons behind them with several officials at the Commonwealth Relations Office (the India Office having ceased to exist on 15 August). Unfortunately, these officials, all former India Office staffers, were extremely discreet. Sir Paul Patrick, former Assistant Under-Secretary of State in the India Office, noted on 1 September, 'Sir C. Radcliffe when he visited this office and saw Mr Rumbold, Mr Lumby and myself explained one or two features of the award. But I do not think it profitable to record his explanations – which are mainly on certain geographical points.'[4] It is not clear whether Patrick simply found these 'geographical points' uninteresting or whether they were too sensitive for circulation. In any case, his notes reveal little.

More enlightening are records of Radcliffe's earlier visit, on 19 August, with Arthur Henderson, the former Parliamentary Under-Secretary of State for India. In a secret memo the following day, Henderson reported that, in contrast to the notional boundary (the working line based solely on census statistics), Radcliffe's line gave sections of Gurdaspur District to India: 'the reason for this change [from the notional line] is understood to be that the headwaters of the canals which irrigate the Amritsar District lie in the Gurdaspur District and it is important to keep as much as possible of these canals under one administration. The Moslems are 51% of the population of the area affected.'[5] Henderson also noted, 'to the South West of the Amritsar District the boundary has been brought forward so as to give East Punjab the eastern corner of the Lahore District, which is largely inhabited by Sikhs'.[6] Although one might wish for a fuller description of Radcliffe's explanation than these scraps of information provide, two central themes emerge. The first is the importance of infrastructure; the second is sensitivity to the needs of Sikhs living near the city of Amritsar.

In a letter written nearly two decades later, Radcliffe again expressed, albeit guardedly, his appreciation of Punjab's irrigation network and the need to maintain it. He wrote, 'In general terms it would be true to say that, when I was working on the Punjab line, I was deeply impressed – as anyone concerned would be – by the great importance of not allowing the physical division of territory to sterilize the working of the interrelated irrigation systems.'[7] Irrigation was vital because it made Punjab the breadbasket of South Asia. Punjabi grains were an important part of the subcontinental food supply, and the productivity of Punjabi agriculture depended heavily on the region's elaborate irrigation.

In his award, Radcliffe cited 'the fundamental basis of contiguous majority areas' as the primary reason for his decisions.[8] Interviews with Christopher Beaumont confirm that these demographic considerations were Radcliffe's top priority. According to Beaumont's recollections, Radcliffe's first decision was to divide the cities of Lahore and Amritsar. Beaumont observed, 'starting from the Pathankot and the beginnings of the mountains [in the north], he had to draw his line so that it bisected Lahore and Amritsar and he did the best he could with that'.[9] The rest of the line followed from that decision, driven by the need to preserve Amritsar's economic and strategic position to the limited extent possible. This need dictated the fate of Gurdaspur. Although Beaumont had served in Gurdaspur for a year as a member of the Indian Civil Service, Radcliffe did not ask him for detailed information about Gurdaspur. Beaumont recalled, 'we did discuss it from time to time, but the line was really inevitable there. You had to separate Lahore from Amritsar, and that rather tied one's hands.'[10] Neither party was prepared to openly concede Lahore or Amritsar, however; nor were local residents. As Mehr Chand Mahajan, one of the Congress judges, recalled, 'Most of the Hindus and Sikhs in the Punjab had hypnotized themselves into the belief that Lahore would remain in India, though the terms of reference of the Boundary Commission – as I read them now – seemed to exclude any such possibility.'[11] The flexibility written into the terms of reference, allowing the commission to consider 'other factors', extended only so far.

One historian has argued that Radcliffe's award was largely based on a border proposal drawn up by Wavell the previous year. He asserts, 'it is apparent that the basis for his [Radcliffe's] border line was the "detailed demarcation" produced by Wavell in February 1946'.[12] There is no evidence for or against this theory, other than the fact that Radcliffe's line is strikingly similar to Wavell's proposal – as is the notional boundary. It is entirely plausible that India Office officials showed Radcliffe maps based on Wavell's proposal; there are reports that Radcliffe was given a briefing before he went out to India, 'a thirty-minute session over a large-scale map with the Permanent Under-secretary at the India Office'.[13] If such a meeting occurred, Radcliffe did not mention it to Beaumont. In any case, it is unlikely that Radcliffe took Wavell's plan as a required blueprint. Beaumont maintained,

> I'm quite certain he [Radcliffe] was given no briefing as to where the line should run. It has been said by the Pakistanis that he was, but I don't believe it. Otherwise, I mean, drawing the line through Gurdaspur District, which we did together, the whole thing would have been a charade on his part if he'd been told what to do beforehand. Furthermore, he was a very strong character. He wouldn't have liked to be told in advance where his line was to be.[14]

The similarity between Radcliffe's line and Wavell's proposal may simply be due to the fact that both were based primarily on a division of Muslim majority and Hindu/Sikh majority territories, or to the fact that both Radcliffe and Wavell concluded, independently, that this particular line would make the best of a bad situation. In other words, the general line that Radcliffe and Wavell selected may simply have been the most logical, given the circumstances.

Those who insist that Radcliffe neither acted independently nor cared for South Asian interests will no doubt criticize this appraisal of his reasoning as overly sympathetic. As I have made clear, I do not regard Radcliffe as an altruistic imperialist whose primary interest was the good of the raj's colonial subjects. Neither do I regard him as Mountbatten's pawn, complicit in a plot to destabilize post-independence South Asia. Rather, a careful consideration of accusations against Radcliffe, as well as his own writings and other available evidence, shows that Radcliffe was aligned with the British Government to the extent that he felt it his duty to assist the government with a task it regarded as crucial. At the same time, Radcliffe was an independent thinker who carefully contemplated the practical problems that his boundary would cause. As we will see, the existence of the 'sketch map' shows that Radcliffe considered an alternate line, most likely in an attempt to prevent or diminish disruptions to Punjabi irrigation.

The role of 'other factors'

One of the most difficult questions facing the commissions was the respective significance to assign to various 'other factors'. In his awards, Radcliffe himself noted that 'differences of opinion as to the significance of the term "other factors" and as to the weight and value to be attached to these factors, made it impossible to arrive at any agreed line'.[15] Over the years, observers have speculated on various considerations that may have motivated Radcliffe, including defence needs, existing infrastructure, communal bias and pressure from Mountbatten. The role of infrastructure is discussed in detail below, as are allegations of improper pressure.

Of the many considerations potentially included in the broad category of 'other factors', we have seen that Auchinleck and Mountbatten advised Radcliffe not to place any emphasis on constructing a defensible boundary. Radcliffe obliged. He also seems to have taken to heart Auchinleck's advice that South Asian rivers often altered course. In his award, he made it very clear that, even when the boundary ran near a river, it was the nearby administrative boundary that actually marked the international line.

Radcliffe did not seriously consider 'natural' boundaries, either, despite the fact that party leaders on all sides had pushed for their use. In fact, Radcliffe conformed to the boundary-making wisdom of the time by avoiding the use of rivers as boundaries, with two exceptions where he did use river channels as boundary lines for short distances. In most cases Radcliffe indicated a preference for administrative over 'natural' boundaries. His insistence on this point is all the more striking given the fact that both Congress and the Muslim League had argued that rivers provided defensible natural barriers, which could prove vital, given the international character of the new border.[16]

Although there was much public debate over the question of sacred sites, particularly after Henderson's ill-considered Parliamentary remarks about Sikh shrines, the question of religious shrines was a relatively minor consideration for Radcliffe. After his return to London, Radcliffe reported that the flap sparked by Henderson's statement had not perturbed his fellow commissioners: 'the Commissions were not at all embarrassed by the reference in Parliament to shrines'.[17] Beaumont recalled that Radcliffe was indeed 'very worried because he had to put this Sikh holy place into Pakistan – at Sheikhupura … Guru Nanak's birthplace'.[18] But there was no real choice; its location, to the west of Lahore, made the shrine impossible to include in India without untenable geographical contortions. In the end, the location of holy places was a tertiary consideration, well behind the Muslim/non-Muslim divide and infrastructure factors. As Beaumont noted, shrines 'didn't play a part – well, apart from Amritsar, the Golden Temple, that did [play a part]. But that was the only one.'[19] The issue of pilgrimage sites carried little weight in Radcliffe's thinking.

Radcliffe's line itself demonstrates that yet another factor played a major part in his boundary delineation: existing administrative divisions. Whenever possible, Radcliffe used the prevailing administrative borders defined by British officials. The commission's terms of reference directed it to draw its lines within the two provinces of Bengal and Punjab, so the existing provincial boundaries were not an option. Within provinces, however, Radcliffe preferred district and *tehsil* boundaries. Even in Kasur *tehsil*, where he departed from this general rule, he followed village boundaries.[20] The text of Radcliffe's award makes it clear throughout that existing administrative boundaries, rather than nearby rivers or any other 'natural boundary', marked the new line.[21] It is entirely possible that Radcliffe made this choice in an effort to ease the administrative transition. As Jenkins wrote the following year, 'the Boundary, if it did not follow existing district boundaries, would inevitably leave certain areas "in the air", severed from their old districts and not yet absorbed by their new ones'.[22] However, it seems likely that this choice carried a deeper significance as well. Although Radcliffe did not state explicitly his reasons for making this choice, the delineation of a completely new boundary, one that did not follow existing colonial divisions, might have been perceived as a rejection of British rule.[23] The existing boundaries were, after all, symbols of British rule.

Radcliffe's use of administrative boundaries reinforced the impact of imperial rule. The territory of the raj was honeycombed with boundaries of all kinds, which had been maintained partly as a means of perpetuating British imperial control, although many had Mughal origins.[24] Radcliffe's award retained for the postcolonial states of India and Pakistan (whether they wanted it or not) a central element of the legacy of imperial rule; the raj's political boundaries marked the (ostensible) stability of its rule.

When appraising their imperial legacy, British officials emphasized their impact on everyday life and the improvements they had made in the average peasant's lot. One staunchly imperialist former Indian

Army officer asserted that the British 'brought peace to the land, albeit the peace of an alien hand. By this means, and while they were there, India became politically and administratively one.'[25] British administrative boundaries were markers of that impact, a striking cartographic sign of the primary achievements of British rule. As such, their retention was an imperial priority. This priority was never articulated; rather, it was taken for granted that decolonization would retain these local boundaries. The question of changing them may never have entered Radcliffe's mind, and it is possible the decision to follow them wherever possible was unconscious.[26]

In the context of existing boundaries, it is also important to look more closely at the reasons why Radcliffe could not follow existing provincial lines. The commission's terms of reference instructed it to divide Punjab, making it clear that simply allotting the province in its entirety to either side was not an option. (The same was true for Bengal.) The League had hoped for Punjab and Bengal in their entirety to join Pakistan, but Congress demanded that they be divided. It seems likely that this demand was rooted in Nehru's desire for a strong central government, rather than a federal arrangement that gave more power to the provinces. This desire, a reflection of Nehru's fear of the 'Balkanization' of India, drove his rejection of the 1946 Cabinet Mission plan, which involved groups of provinces with divisions based on existing provincial boundaries, and his criticism of the May 1947 handover plan.[27] It seems likely that it also guided Congress's call in April 1947 for the Punjabi and Bengali partitions.[28]

Years later, Mountbatten offered this curious appraisal of Radcliffe's reasoning: 'I'll tell you something ghastly. The reasons behind his award weren't very deep-seated at all. I am quite certain they were based on some rule of thumb about the proportion of population.'[29] Given the fact that Mountbatten's government gave Radcliffe the mandate to focus on religious demographics, it seems odd that the former viceroy thought it 'ghastly' that Radcliffe had not come up with 'deeper' reasons for drawing his lines. Mountbatten's sentiment may indicate an awareness among British officials that the categories they themselves had established were inadequate for the job at hand.

Even by Mountbatten's standards, this statement about Radcliffe's 'rule of thumb' is peculiar. Perhaps by the time Mountbatten gave this interview, in the early 1970s, he had developed reservations about the partition process. Until his death, Mountbatten staunchly defended his actions in 1947, making it unlikely that he would openly question himself.[30] However, Mountbatten had a great capacity for remembering history differently from other observers, invariably along the lines most flattering to himself. Given the fact that, as we shall see, it was the viceroy himself who brought up the notion of 'balance', one wonders whether Mountbatten subconsciously transferred responsibility for his own idea onto Radcliffe's shoulders, before criticizing it. Such speculation may seem convoluted, but Mountbatten was notable for his sometimes contorted recollections of events. A colleague once told him, 'Dickie, you're so crooked that if you swallowed a nail you'd shit a corkscrew!' Mountbatten's biographer records that this was 'a remark which Mountbatten remembered and repeated, though characteristically changing the recipient of the insult'.[31] Mountbatten's memory of this and other conversations, therefore, was not always to be trusted.

Mountbatten apparently failed to recognize that Radcliffe's line was the product of his struggle to balance the overriding mandate to divide territory along religious lines with the need to minimize the damage to Punjabi infrastructure. In his award, Radcliffe wrote, 'I have made small adjustments of the Lahore-Amritsar district boundary to mitigate some of the consequences of this severance [of the Upper Bari Doab Canal].'[32] This passage demonstrates that Radcliffe diverged from administrative boundaries, the unspoken priority discussed above, only when he felt compelled to do so. It also shows that he felt no need to explain his decision to use these divisions as a base, only a need to explain his divergence from them. But it also highlights the fact that, of all the other factors he might have considered, Radcliffe placed the most importance on preserving the Punjabi canal network.

The importance of infrastructure

In both the Punjab and Bengal awards, Radcliffe discussed canals, canal headworks, roads, railways and ports before turning to population factors. In the Punjab award, he explicitly stated that 'there are factors such as the disruption of railway communications and water systems that ought in this instance to displace the primary claim of contiguous majorities',[33] and the Bengal award demonstrated similar concerns with maintaining 'railway communications and river systems', as well as preserving the relationship of the Nadia and Kulti river systems with the port of Calcutta.[34] Beaumont confirmed this point, recalling that, after contiguous majority areas, 'water was the key. And railways would come second, and electricity would run third.'[35] Muhammad Munir, one of the Muslim League judges on the commission, independently recalled that 'the preservation of the present [1947] irrigation system was an obsession with Sir Cyril'.[36] Radcliffe's interest in Punjabi irrigation was second only to his determination to divide the province along religious lines.

[80]

Despite his attention to this question, Radcliffe found that any line would inevitably disrupt the water supply to one side or the other. In an effort to solve this problem, he proposed that India and Pakistan operate the irrigation system together, including a tactfully worded recommendation in his award. In reference to the Dipalpur canal and the Ferozepur headworks, he wrote, 'I find it difficult to envisage a satisfactory demarcation of boundary at this point that is not accompanied by some arrangement for joint control of the intake of the different canals dependent on these headworks.'[37] Reportedly, both Jinnah and Nehru summarily rejected this proposal: Jinnah replied that 'he would rather have Pakistan deserts than fertile fields watered by the courtesy of Hindus', while Nehru 'curtly informed [Radcliffe] that what India did with India's rivers was India's affair'.[38] Neither side embraced Radcliffe's suggestion.

The irrigation systems and other infrastructure of Punjab and Bengal had been built to function under a single administration. They were never intended to be divided. No partition line Radcliffe could have concocted would have allowed Pakistan and India to operate their infrastructure separately, without cross-border interference. In the few weeks he had, Radcliffe tried to minimize infrastructure disruptions, but he was well aware that his proposal was flawed. In his attempt to draw the boundary near the Sulemanke canal headworks in Punjab, for example, he emphasized that his intention was to award this equipment to Pakistan and acknowledged that the reality of the terrain might necessitate later adjustments to the boundary.[39]

To the British and to most Indian leaders of the 1940s, religious categories were a primary consideration, within the larger context of their desire for a speedy British withdrawal. Indeed, religion was the only consideration explicitly recommended to the boundary commissions in their terms of reference. However, when British officials were confronted with the reality of partitioning India, it became clear that infrastructure questions were a close second. In some cases, as explicitly stated in his award, Radcliffe gave these considerations more weight than he gave to the determination of contiguous religious majorities.[40]

The emphasis on infrastructure can be traced to Britons' own conception of their task in India and of the legacy of their imperial rule. In the Indian case, British imperialism was inextricably related to the concept of stewardship: the idea that the British had an obligation to educate Indians so that, at some future date, they would be able to take on self-government. This undeniably paternalistic concept may sound implausible to twenty-first-century ears, but many Britons took this 'duty' seriously. When Ismay, one of Mountbatten's top aides, described his sadness over leaving India, his regret was prompted at least in part by the thought that the British empire's accomplishments in India – roads, railways and irrigation canals – might be threatened by partition. By the early twentieth century, he wrote, 'law and order prevailed throughout the land. Roads, railways, canals and harbours had been built, and vast areas of hitherto waterless desert had been brought under irrigation.'[41] Radcliffe's own comments reflect the same notion of Britain's imperial legacy. In a BBC address on 2 October 1947, he said, 'The gifts we brought were Roman ... Like the Romans, we built our roads, bridges and canals and we have marked the land as engineers if we have not improved it as architects.'[42] This comment places the raj squarely in the ranks of the world's great empires, emphasizing the value of the material improvements it bestowed upon its subjects. Here we see Radcliffe operating as an imperial apologist *par excellence*.

The irony of such statements was that the canal system had in fact originated with the Mughals.[43] The Mughal appreciation of the importance of water remains visible in the channels that brought cooling water into their forts at Agra and Delhi. Also, many of the Punjab's canals, particularly those in the 'canal colonies' of western Punjab, were built by Sikh labour.[44] The British, in other words, felt great pride in a system originated by the empire they displaced and enlarged and maintained by indigenous workers.

The haste of the 1947 partition drastically reduced the efficiency and economic independence of Pakistan, parts of northern India and what is now Bangladesh. Radcliffe strove to preserve what he saw as imperialism's legacy of modern infrastructure for the two new nations. However, there was no practical way to divide between two states – hostile states, as it soon became clear – a unified system of infrastructure.

In summary, Radcliffe's award was deeply controversial, involving as it did a number of conflicting factors. Radcliffe himself remained keenly aware of this fact, as he would demonstrate in a letter written in the mid-1960s, when he had had the benefit of nearly two decades to consider his award:

> The many factors that bore upon each problem were not ponderable in their effect upon each other. The effective weight given to each was a matter of judgment, which the circumstances threw it upon me to form; each decision at each point was debatable and formed of necessity under great pressure of time, conditions and with knowledge that, in any ideal sense, was deficient. I decided therefore that it was in the best interests of everyone that I should leave the matter as an Award, conditioned by the terms of reference that were set me, instead of trying to argue it or elaborate upon it further.[45]

[82]

Knowing that any explanation he might offer would be unsatisfactory to one side or the other, Radcliffe chose to offer no explanation at all, but simply to leave his award unadorned.

What maps reveal about the Radcliffe award

The major primary sources Radcliffe did leave – the maps he used in drawing his line and the maps he attached to his award – have been dismissed by many scholars as outdated, inaccurate or insufficiently detailed.[46] Although these statements, particularly the intriguing assertion that the boundary commission's maps were outdated, appear to offer a potential explanation for the problems associated with the Radcliffe award, they have not been seriously examined. In fact, an analysis of the pre-partition history of the Survey of India and the relevant cartographic material available to the boundary commission in 1947 provides new information on the maps that guided the boundary award. These maps certainly did not represent terrain as it was at that moment, but this failure was due to other shortfalls in raj cartography. These inadequacies point in turn to larger flaws in the overall partition process. In short, an examination of the cartographic material Radcliffe used illuminates the patterns of thought that shaped the decolonization of the subcontinent.

The primary resources in this area are Pakistani reproductions of selected maps submitted during the boundary commission hearings, of a 'sketch map' showing an early version of Radcliffe's line and of the maps Radcliffe attached to his award.[47] The India Office Library also holds a copy of one map attached to the Radcliffe decision. It has so far proved impossible to trace any original boundary commission maps in the British, Indian or Pakistani archives.[48] Fortunately the available reproductions, although limited in number,[49] allow a rich analysis of the cartographic information available to Radcliffe and of its effects on his work.

The history of the Survey of India (see Chapter 1), which provided the official maps used by the boundary commission, reveals these maps' origins as tools for imperial control. Here, we turn to the impact of map use on the final boundary award. This combination of close analysis and contextual study provides the foundation necessary to address the following questions. What was the nature of the maps available to the boundary commission? How did the boundary commission use these maps? Given the long history of British attempts to control South Asia by mapping it, what was the role of imperial cartography in relinquishing that control? The answers are somewhat surprising. Political priorities shaped the commission in such a way that conventional boundary-making data and procedures were neglected. As a result, I argue, citing 'outdated maps' as an explanation for the boundary's failings is inadequate.

Maps are problematic sources. They may appear authoritative, but by their very nature they display only selected, and sometimes distorted, aspects of reality. Noting that 'the neat boundaries and striking colors of many maps conceal the fundamental inaccuracy of the basic data and the subjective decisions made by the cartographer', the contemporary boundary expert Stephen Jones emphasized the fact that maps of religions, in particular, are less precise than they seem.[50] Aside from the problem of inaccuracy, even precise maps can be misleading if the scale is too small. Citing historical precedents, Jones recommended the use of a 1:250,000 scale for partitioning districts. Most of the maps submitted to the commission by interested parties did not meet this standard of precision, using scales of 1:1,000,000 to 1:1,500,000. The primary map Radcliffe annexed to his final award did use a larger scale, 1:253,440, while another map of a smaller section of the boundary was roughly 1:127,000. However, some of the evidence Radcliffe viewed in making his decision represented information on a scale that may have been too small to be useful.

After returning to England, Radcliffe spoke very little about his experiences in India, but he did grant an interview to the war correspondent and author Leonard Mosley, which shed further light on his use of maps.[51] Mosley's account is a problematic source, not only for its journalistic approach and sometimes unreliable use of material, but also for its anti-Mountbatten bias; Mosley's book was clearly intended to discredit the viceroy's handling of the British withdrawal. In the early 1970s, Radcliffe also spoke with Larry Collins and Dominique Lapierre, as they conducted research for their book *Freedom at Midnight*. Lapierre has subsequently published a narrative account of that interview, but this source too is problematic. It quotes Radcliffe as saying that he was 'completely ignorant of India', a statement which cannot be supported in light of Radcliffe's knowledge of Indian politics from his time at the Ministry of Information; it also quotes him as asserting that he 'had no contact with the outside world', which we will see was inaccurate.[52] Despite these drawbacks, the fact remains that Radcliffe did speak directly with Mosley, Collins and Lapierre about his experiences in India, providing the careful historian with clues to his map use, among other issues.

First of all, Radcliffe was undoubtedly confronted with conflicting cartographic information. In describing the commission's public hearings, Mosley writes, 'The delegations arrived armed with their maps, and it was from these that he must make his decisions. The only trouble was that the maps of each side were different. They had "doctored" them according to their arguments and petitions.'[53] Mosley also notes that when Sikh leaders realized how deeply the boundary commission decision could damage their community, 'they descended upon Sir Cyril Radcliffe with petitions, maps, arguments, threats and bribes. The Muslims in turn began to harry him.'[54] Mosley's language, with its reference to delegates '*armed* with their maps' (emphasis added), depicts a situation in which maps are not mere tools to present an argument, and certainly not collections of neutral scientific data, but weapons to bludgeon that argument home.

In response to the many conflicting maps offered to him, Radcliffe apparently sought the refuge of an official – and therefore ostensibly objective and unbiased – map, in order to evaluate the reliability of the others. 'One of his principal worries', Mosley writes, 'was to obtain a big enough ordnance map upon which he could work and use as a master map – because the two sides were always up to their tricks.'[55] The phrase 'big enough' here presumably refers to the scale of the map (rather than its paper dimensions). The larger its scale, the more detail the map could provide, and the more useful it might be in familiarizing a stranger with the details of Punjabi terrain. Overall, it seems that Radcliffe regarded a map produced by the (British) Government of India as more authoritative than any map submitted to him by the other parties. We have no indication that he considered the possibility that Survey of India maps might have biases of their own.

According to both Mosley and Lapierre, Radcliffe was not provided with adequate official maps. After noting that one of Radcliffe's 'principal worries' was locating a map on a suitable scale, Mosley writes, 'It seem extraordinary that when you have to decide the fate of 28,000,000 people you are not even given the right map to do it with.'[56] This passage, with its use of the second person, seems a little out of place in Mosley's otherwise third-person account, and it may reflect a question Mosley asked of Radcliffe rather than a statement Radcliffe himself made. 'With the slings and arrows of importunate Muslims, Hindus and Sikhs whistling about his ears', Mosley picturesquely narrates, Radcliffe 'took up the largest contour map he could find and began to draw'. This passage again emphasizes the scale of the maps available to Radcliffe. Lapierre too quotes him as saying, 'The equipment I had at my disposal was totally inadequate. I had no very large-scale maps.'[57] Eventually, Radcliffe presumably obtained maps of the scale he desired, for he attached to his award a map of the Kasur *tehsil* with a scale of one inch to two miles, in order to clarify a particularly tortuous section of the boundary. However, Radcliffe also found problems with official maps: he told Collins and Lapierre that 'the information provided on those [official maps] I did have sometimes proved to be wrong. I noticed the Punjab's five rivers had an awkward tendency to run several miles away from the beds officially assigned to them by the survey department.'[58] Radcliffe had encountered one of the more problematic features of monsoon-fed rivers: a yearly tendency to alter course. Overall, Mosley and Lapierre's accounts portray the maps given to the boundary commission as thoroughly inadequate, either because they were biased creations produced by the various parties, or because they were small-scale government maps unsuited to Radcliffe's purposes or inaccurately representing natural features.

Contemporary texts warn against relying solely on maps and stress the importance of field surveys. The belief that maps and documents alone are sufficient for delimitation, Jones writes, 'is unfounded in many cases. Field observations have a definite and important place in the pre-delimitation stage of boundary-making. Ideally, there should be a complete field study of the border region. At the very least, there should be a careful reconnaissance of the boundary site before the line is defined irrevocably in a treaty.'[59] The strict 15 August deadline allowed the commission no time to conduct any kind of local survey. The desire of all parties for a hasty withdrawal interfered with the substantive needs of the boundary-making process.

Radcliffe's award indicates his awareness of the problems inherent in using maps. By design or not, he followed established procedure in attaching both a written and a graphic description of his boundary line and indicating that the written description took precedence in case of any discrepancy: 'the map is annexed for purposes of illustration, and if there should be any divergence between the boundary as described in Annexure A [the text of the boundary award] and as delineated on the map in Annexure B, the description in Annexure A is to prevail'.[60] In this description, he wrote out each district, *tehsil*, *thana* or village that the border would touch. Merely drawing a boundary line on a map is inadequate because such a line can never be as precise as a line demarcated on the ground by surveyors. For example, a line on a map may correspond to a swathe of land several miles across, depending on the map's scale. In addition, awards described solely by reference to maps are tied to that particular document. This approach is dangerous not only because the map may be inaccurate or out of date, but also because it may be lost or may not be included every time the text is reproduced. Radcliffe was apparently aware that a line drawn on a map could be deceiving and that written definitions were less open to misinterpretation.

This decision was an important element in avoiding potential misunderstandings that might arise from linking the award with any particular map.[61] The history of boundary commissions is replete with examples of such confusions.[62] Privileging textual descriptions over visual representations is therefore a basic tenet of boundary-making practice. Given his ignorance of those procedures, it is curious that Radcliffe chose this route. It may simply have been due to his legal background, for Radcliffe was presumably accustomed to evaluating precise written decisions; this experience would have sensitized him to potential misunderstandings of such work and may have alerted him to the perils associated with map use.

If Radcliffe had chosen to make the visual depiction of his line authoritative, the line on the overall map attached to his award could have exacerbated the confusion of partition. It is roughly a quarter of an inch thick, which, on a map with a scale of one inch to four miles, translates to a line one mile wide on the ground. The line was undoubtedly drawn so thick in order that it would be the prominent feature on the map. However, when it came to actually demarcating the boundary (which, like all boundaries, would be in theory a line with no width), a mile-wide line could have created a great deal of trouble. As an indicator of where to place boundary pillars, this map would have been inadequate.

If the commission had followed established procedures for boundary-making, which called for a new survey to be made of the area to be divided, the question of 'outdated maps' would have been rendered moot.[63] However, the extremely aggressive timetable for the transfer of power meant that there was no possibility of conducting a new survey, and indeed the boundary commission structure did not allow any such survey. Nor did the boundary commission format provide for expert advice from Survey of India officials or Indian Civil Service officers familiar with the area to be divided. Even if the boundary commission had called upon the Survey of India to provide expertise, they would have found that the Department was still in disarray, hampered by the effects of World War II.

The Survey of India's wartime difficulties by themselves do not, however, explain the deficiencies in the maps available to Radcliffe. In the late 1940s, the Survey of India returned to the work the war had interrupted, but as late as 1949, the effects of the war and of the subsequent focus on surveys for development projects still took a toll. The Surveyor-General wrote in April of that year, 'Owing to the urgent need for surveys for development projects, nearly all resources were concentrated on these; and practically no progress was made on the programme of topographical surveys begun in 1905 and as yet not nearly finished.'[64] The urgency of this civil work, combined with the Department's extensive wartime experience with air surveys (and the concomitant lapse in ground-survey training and research), resulted in the increased use of air-survey techniques. As a former Surveyor-General wrote, 'Experience with modern air methods, greatly developed during the war, and the acquisition of aircraft under our own control (charter with Messrs. Indian Air Survey and Transport Company Ltd., from 1942 onwards) gave great impetus to the use of air survey not only for the revision of existing out-of-date maps but also for the preparation of new maps at prices competitive with ground survey.'[65] Most of the territory through which Radcliffe drew his boundary had been subject to land surveys in the mid-1930s or late 1920s.[66] Some sections of Punjab had not been surveyed since before World War I, and more remote areas had last been surveyed in the 1890s. However, it remains unclear when the *latest* pre-partition survey information about Punjab was gathered. It seems likely that the Department updated pre-war land surveys with air surveys and limited land surveys during the war years.

Given the conditions under which the Survey of India worked, particularly its nearly complete suspension of land surveys from 1939 onwards, Punjabi maps were, compared to Survey maps as a whole, relatively up to date. Within the context of British information about the region, it was fairly well covered, although in absolute terms, of course, this land had not been surveyed for over a decade. The evidence indicates, however, that Radcliffe most likely used maps that displayed more recent information than the pre-war maps listed in the 1951 catalogue. The maps he attached to his award are gridded, meaning that they were published during World War II. The vast majority of pre-war maps of British India did not have an overlying grid, required for military use; the Department added grids to maps printed during the war. In other words, the maps Radcliffe saw may well have been updated during the war, probably with information gathered from air surveys.

All in all, the evidence suggests that the information available to Radcliffe was not significantly out of date. The Punjab was fairly well covered, within the constraints imposed by the Survey of India's wartime circumstances and by fundamental flaws in the colonial state's attempts to understand Indian space and society. The cartographic information most relevant to Radcliffe's work, particularly the location of infrastructure links and administrative boundaries, would likely have been adequately represented on the maps available to him.[67] More importantly, the facts suggest that the limitations of the boundary commission and the Radcliffe award cannot be attributed primarily to the 'out-of-date' condition of available maps. Whether Radcliffe's maps were up to date mattered relatively little compared to the fundamental problems with the cartographic presentation of data amassed by British institutions of colonial control.

Requests for advance notice of the boundary award

As Independence Day drew near, all of Punjab and Bengal waited for the release of the boundary commission award. Not only residents of the provinces to be divided but also South Asian leaders and British officials were eager to hear the contents of the award. From Lahore, Governor Evan Jenkins made numerous pleas for advance information on the location of the new boundary. Earlier, his private secretary had written to George Abell: 'H.E. [His Excellency the Governor] has asked me to make a special request for as much advance intimation not only of the date of the award but also of its contents as can be given. Whatever the date and whatever Government will be in power when the award is announced, it will be necessary to take precautions, especially in those districts which are likely to be affected, particularly those in the Central Punjab.'[68] When Mountbatten visited Lahore a few days later, Jenkins made this point to him in person. Mountbatten's private secretary passed on the request for an early award to Radcliffe's private secretary, writing that Jenkins had told Mountbatten 'that it would be of great practical advantage if he could be given advance information of the general purport of the Award of the Boundary Commission when the time comes. Even a few hours warning would be better than none, as the nature of the Award would affect the distribution of police and troops.' He concluded with a proposal that led directly to the controversy over the sketch map: 'If it is possible to give us an abstract here in advance we could telegraph it in secret cipher to the Governor.'[69] As we will see, this practical suggestion provided fuel for allegations that Mountbatten had changed the award at the last minute.

Mountbatten himself wrote to Radcliffe the next day to say, 'We should all be grateful for every extra day earlier that you could manage to get the award announced. I wonder if there is any chance of getting it out by the 10th?'[70] Radcliffe replied that he would bear in mind the importance of an early announcement. He reminded Mountbatten of the 'fine' time schedule dictated by the requirement that he hold public hearings in both Punjab and Bengal and then confer with both sets of judges, and concluded, 'Unless the Punjab judges agree with each other more than I have reason to expect, I do not think that I could manage the 10th: but I think that I can promise the 12th, and I will do the earlier date if I possibly can.'[71] Radcliffe's time limit was growing even tighter.

Mountbatten continued his efforts to obtain early notice for the Governor of Punjab, writing to Jenkins on 6 August, 'I have not forgotten your request that you should be given advance warning of the nature of the Boundary Commission's award, and I will try to secure this.'[72] Two days later, Jenkins again cabled Mountbatten to say that, in addition to military and police reinforcements, he required 'earliest possible advance information of Boundary Commission's award'.[73] In fact, this telegram crossed with a note from Abell, which included a sketch map giving advance information on the award, sent to Lahore the same day.[74] At noon the following day, 9 August, Jenkins's private secretary cabled Abell to acknowledge receipt of these documents, noting, 'Governor is taking law and order action on preliminary information given. He trusts final version will be very precise and will be related as far as possible to existing administrative units and boundaries. To enable us to arrange publicity and to make administrative arrangements he would like the document in final form 24 hours before its release.'[75] This note shows that British-established administrative boundaries were still central to provincial government and provided the foundation for Jenkins's planning.

In addition to British requests for advance notice, many South Asians pleaded for the boundary decision to be announced well in advance of the British withdrawal. In a 13 July letter to Mountbatten, Jenkins noted that Hindu and Sikh representatives in Punjab insisted that the boundary commission award should be announced by 7 August. Furthermore, they maintained, 'if this is impossible the date of the transfer of power must be postponed'.[76] In other words, local politicians, if not the leaders in New Delhi, believed that the partition process was moving too fast. Their demands for advance notice were ignored. But the reply to Jenkins's request, sent by Mountbatten's staff on 8 August, fed later controversies over the viceroy's role in the division.

The sketch map

The 'sketch map' sent by Mountbatten's office is one of the most controversial elements of this story.[77] Mountbatten's private secretary, George Abell, sent it to Stuart Abbott, Governor Jenkins's private secretary, on 8 August, in response to the governor's request for early information about where the boundary was likely to fall. The final boundary, however, differed from the line represented on this map, and Pakistanis later alleged that Radcliffe and/or Mountbatten had unfairly changed the award.

The map was a small-scale depiction of Punjab, with a red line indicating where the new boundary would fall. Abell's covering note, labelled 'Top Secret', stated,

> I enclose a map showing roughly the boundary which Sir Cyril Radcliffe proposes to demarcate in his award, and a note by Christopher Beaumont describing it. There will not be any great changes from this boundary,

but it will have to be accurately defined with reference to village and zail boundaries in Lahore district. The award itself is expected within the next 48 hours, and I will let you know later about the probable time of announcement. Perhaps you would ring me up if H.E. the Governor has any views on this point?[78]

Abell's information came from Beaumont, who did not consult Radcliffe about sending the map. He recalled, 'I never asked Radcliffe if I should send the map or not, so I'm not sure he knew that I had, even. Because it was so obvious that it had to be done – and then the governor had to know where to send the police and the troops. Radcliffe was very busy working on the line, and I don't think I asked him.'[79] Abell had passed Jenkins's repeated requests for advance information to Beaumont, offering to convey any such reports to Jenkins. Given the emphasis that Mountbatten had placed on providing Jenkins with advance warning, it is not surprising that Beaumont and Abell proceeded without explicit confirmation from Radcliffe or, apparently, Mountbatten. Mountbatten always insisted that he had no knowledge of the sketch map, which is plausible. It is much less likely that, as he implied, he had no knowledge of the contents of Radcliffe's award until after independence.

The note accompanying the sketch map is worth reading carefully. Although it clearly indicates that Radcliffe's intention, as of 8 August, was to award the Ferozepur salient to Pakistan, Abell wrote, 'The *award itself* [emphasis added] is expected within the next 48 hours.' This sentence could be read as distinguishing the 8 August documents from Radcliffe's final award. On this interpretation, this phrase would release Mountbatten from any serious suspicion of having altered the award after it was officially submitted, although it certainly does not disprove the allegations that he persuaded Radcliffe to change his thinking before submitting the award. In any case, Abell wrote, 'there will not be any great changes from this boundary',[80] indicating that he regarded this line as very nearly final.

In fact, the line was soon changed. As Jenkins later recalled, on 10 or 11 August, he received a message that said, in its entirety, 'Eliminate salient.' Jenkins interpreted this communication to mean that the Ferozepur salient would go to India, not Pakistan. He recalled later, 'The change caused some surprise, not because the Ferozepore salient had been regarded as inevitable or even probable, but because it seemed odd that any advance information had been given by the commission if the award was not substantially complete.'[81] Providing a line that might be changed later would defeat the purpose of the advance information, which was to enable Jenkins to strengthen the military and administrative presence in areas likely to be divided.

Information about the contents of the sketch map seems to have leaked almost immediately. As rumours – some remarkably accurate – about the boundary's location began to circulate, all sides bombarded the viceroy with objections. As discussed in Chapter 3, on 9 August, Nehru forwarded to Mountbatten A. N. Khosla's note objecting to Radcliffe's suggestion that India and Pakistan assume joint control of Punjabi irrigation and electricity. The following day, Mountbatten received a similar complaint from the Maharajah of Bikaner, leader of a princely state that relied heavily on canal waters. The maharajah had clearly been informed of the sketch-map line. Noting that 'it is strongly rumoured that the Boundary Commission is likely to award Ferozepur Tehsil to Western Punjab', he argued that such an arrangement 'may gravely prejudice [the] interest of Bikaner State'.[82]

On 11 August, Liaquat Ali Khan sent Ismay a message saying that he knew that the boundary commission had given most or all of Gurdaspur to India, in what was 'a political decision, and not a judicial one'.[83] Liaquat implied that Pakistan might not accept such an award. Ismay, somewhat disingenuously, since he must have known that rumours about the boundary award were flying, responded, 'I am told that the final report of Sir Cyril Radcliffe is not yet ready, and therefore I do not know what grounds you have for saying that Gurdaspur *has been* allotted to the East Punjab.' He emphasized the independent nature of the commission and reminded Liaquat that the party leaders themselves had agreed to the commission's format and procedure: 'The [British] Indian leaders themselves selected all the Boundary Commissions, drafted their terms of reference and undertook to implement the award, what ever it might be.'[84] Confronted with exactly the situation they had feared – nationalist leaders threatening to reject the boundary decision – British officials fell back on the effective defence that the entire process was in fact a joint responsibility.

Over the next few days, Mountbatten and his aides struggled to combat the widely held perception that the viceroy had dictated the award according to his own preferences. On 12 August, for example, Mountbatten responded to a thinly veiled request from the Maharajah of Patiala, who asked that the viceroy engineer a certain boundary line in Punjab. He wrote,

> There seems to be widespread belief that the boundary line on which the Boundary Commission decides will, in some way, have been approved by myself, that I can interfere with the Boundary Commission, and that I shall be responsible for the result. Nothing can be further from the truth. The Boundary Commission is a judicial body, and I have made it clear from the start that I did not frame its terms of reference, and that I should not intervene in any way in the deliberations of the Commission.[85]

Next was Sardar Patel, who sent Mountbatten a strongly worded objection on 13 August. This protest referred to the Chittagong Hill Tracts in Bengal; Patel termed the possibility of this area going to Pakistan 'monstrous' and stated openly that armed resistance, supported by Congress, would result. Sardar Patel acknowledged that Congress had pledged to accept the award but warned that the party might repudiate it. He admitted that the party leaders had participated in the boundary commission formation, noting, 'I make this statement with a full sense of responsibility as one who was party to the setting up of the Commission,' but asserted that such an award would be 'unjust'.[86] The commission's carefully crafted judicial façade was fast disintegrating. At the same time, however, the British effort to portray the partition process as a joint effort continued to pay dividends. Even Patel, Congress's famously hard-nosed strongman, seemed to accept the notion of his full responsibility for the boundary decision.

In his final Viceroy's Report to London, Mountbatten complained of Patel: 'the one man I had regarded as a real statesman with both feet firmly on the ground, and a man of honour whose word was his bond, had turned out to be as hysterical as the rest'.[87] Mountbatten's use of the words 'as hysterical as the rest' belies the great respect he claimed to have for the Indian leaders, particularly Nehru, and suggests that he was not impervious to racialist ideas about the emotional, irrational nature of the average Indian.

As Jenkins and Abbott prepared to leave Lahore prior to independence, Abbott sorted through various confidential papers in the governor's safe. Upon finding the sketch map, he asked Jenkins whether or not he should destroy it. Recalling that Francis Mudie, the incoming Governor of West (Pakistani) Punjab, had been staying with him and had seen the map when it arrived, Jenkins decided that destroying the map would be 'discourteous'.[88] Accordingly, Abbott replaced the map in the safe, where Mudie found it again after independence.

Reading Radcliffe's maps

A close reading of Radcliffe's maps reveals the extent to which imperial attitudes pervaded these documents, as well as gaps in the kinds of information they provided; it also demonstrates the haste with which he drew his final line. All of the Survey of India maps examined here are much more heavily detailed than the Congress and Muslim League maps submitted to the commission (which were designed to emphasize territorial claims rather than local details). The general patterns discussed above are visible in the specific maps Radcliffe used. We begin with the smallest-scale map, the 'sketch map'. Then we examine the group of degree sheets (maps on the scale of one inch to four miles) that showed the line announced on 17 August. Finally, we analyse the largest-scale map Radcliffe attached to his award, a settlement map of one area of central Punjab.[89]

The sketch map

This analysis focuses primarily on the 1:1 million scale map of the Punjab used as a base map for the sketch, rather than on the line drawn on it. Although there are conflicting reports as to whether Radcliffe saw the line drawn on this map before Abell sent it to Lahore, it seems highly probable that the map itself was among the many he perused in making his award. If the viceroy's staff had access to this map, there is every reason to suppose that they would have given Radcliffe, whose need for maps was evident, use of it as well.

One of the most striking features of this map is the inclusion of numerous small icons, showing two crossed sabres, with a date above them. The crossed sabres mark the site of East India Company (EIC) battles against Sikh resistance. These symbols are particularly intriguing because they do not appear in the map legend, suggesting that the mapmakers assumed that the map's readers would automatically understand their meaning. These symbols celebrate past British victories and express British domination.

The battles featured on this map include nearly all the major clashes of the First and Second Anglo-Sikh wars. Somewhat surprisingly, one EIC defeat is included (although the map does not differentiate it from other, victorious, encounters); another significant setback is not. For the First Anglo-Sikh War, these battles include: Mudki (18 December 1845), a Sikh defeat in which both sides lost large numbers of men; Ferozeshah (21 December 1845), a near loss for the EIC troops, who were saved by treacherous assistance from the Sikh leader Tej Singh; Aliwal (28 January 1846), another victory for the regrouping EIC army; and Sabraon (10 February 1846),[90] a crushing defeat for the Sikh armies.[91] The victorious British military leader, Lord Gough, described the battle at Sabraon as the Waterloo of India.[92] The map does not, however, show the Company's close shave at Buddowal, on 21 January 1846, which severely damaged its supplies. From the Second Anglo-Sikh War, which was both shorter and more decisive, the map shows the battle of Chillianwala (13 January 1849), which was actually a dangerous defeat for the British, who suffered heavy losses. After this encounter, the EIC army retreated but rejected the Sikh offer of a truce. Having regrouped, the British overwhelmed the Sikhs at the battle of Gujrat (22 February 1849) and ended organized resistance.

[94]

The following month, Maharajah Dalip Singh gave up his throne (and the magnificent Koh-i-Noor diamond, which is now among the British crown jewels). The Company began to consolidate its power in Punjab, and later British maps commemorated the military foundation of that power.[93]

The map legend focuses on administrative boundaries and transportation links, as well as elevation information. It also provides hierarchical symbols for urban areas and villages. These emphasize the 'country capital' at Delhi and the provincial capital at Lahore, in large bold capital letters, as well as the headquarters of districts and *tehsils*, in smaller bold lettering. Towns and villages are printed in standard text. However, the map itself includes a number of infrastructure-related features that are not listed in its legend. Among them are an underground oil pipeline, many canals, a number of canal headworks, multiple ferry crossings, and power lines radiating outward from Lahore and Amritsar. Although railway lines are represented in the legend, their names are not; the map's casual use of 'NWR' indicates an expectation that readers would know that this abbreviation stood for the 'North Western Railway'. As a vital means of transportation for large numbers of civilians, as well as military troops, the railways of British India were a key element not only of British claims to have improved the country but also of British plans to hold it militarily.

The quarter-inch maps

The maps Radcliffe used for the overview of his line provide further insight into the British vision of Punjab primarily as a theatre of battle, a sphere of colonial administration and a showcase of British engineering achievement, rather than the complex and heterogeneous society it was. At one inch to four miles, these maps are on a larger scale than the sketch map. In order to obtain a map large enough to cover the necessary area, Radcliffe actually taped seven different degree sheets together.[94] These maps, with their prominently displayed administrative boundaries, implied that the Punjab could be divided along clear administrative lines. Such a division would, presumably, minimize administrative disruption. These maps also displayed other information, such as the location of roads, railways and canals, that showed that any line drawn through Punjab would disrupt infrastructure significantly. But they did not display the sort of information that would have allowed Radcliffe to judge the social disruptions that might result.

Degree sheets did not display information such as trading patterns between Amritsar and Lahore or kinship links between western and eastern Punjab. This omission is not, perhaps, surprising; such documents often originated in military maps and therefore emphasized strategic features over cultural information.[95] Patterns of local social interaction throughout Punjab were of relatively little significance for British administration – the purpose for which these maps were originally made – but their disruption was vitally important for the people affected by partition. Maps are not, of course, incompatible with social information. However, there are fundamental difficulties inherent in mapping social patterns, which are often controversial.[96] As we have seen, census information on the size and distribution of population groups in 1940s Punjab was unreliable and hotly debated.

Maps sometimes functioned as imperial 'weapons', supporting and legitimizing empire and communicating imperial messages.[97] By the middle of the twentieth century, Survey of India maps were not intended as tools for imperial pacification to the degree that they had been in the days of the EIC.[98] They were still instruments for imperial defence, however, and became particularly important after the humiliating February 1942 surrender of British troops at Singapore exposed India's eastern flank. In civilian terms, however, these maps portrayed India as a land already pacified and controlled, a land that produced revenue. It was also, crucially, a landscape that had been improved by the British, through the construction of public works such as roads, railroads and canals.

The features included on these quarter-inch maps demonstrate their military and strategic origins, as well as the way that they portrayed this imperial realm as one of order and productivity. Like the sketch map, these maps include the crossed-sabres sign indicating past colonial battles. (Here, this symbol is glossed in the legend as 'battle-field', but its imperial significance is again left unexplained.) These maps also include more detailed information on contemporary military installations, including troop barracks and training areas. For example, one map identifies Amritsar's cantonment (in capital letters) and rifle range (as well as its 'reformatory settlement', another institution of state control). There is no indication that the city is also the site of the Sikh holy of holies, the Golden Temple. This map emphasizes the city's military status, not its religious significance. The maps also include information on elevation, another factor in planning military manoeuvres.

The legend includes roads and tracks of varying types, three kinds of railways, canals and administrative boundaries on seven levels. Transportation networks are of obvious importance to a government desirous to deploy troops on short notice, but the Punjabi irrigation system was also vital. Not only would canal sabotage have severe long-term effects, damaging north India's food supply, but canal cuts and subsequent flooding could also impede troop movements in the short term.[99] Overall, these maps portray Punjab in terms of its suitability for military action, its organization for administrative control, and its complex network of British-built and maintained infrastructure systems, rather than in terms of its complex social fabric.

Because roads and railways are prominent features here, these maps clearly show the transportation links between Lahore and Amritsar that the Radcliffe line would affect. These links include the fabled Grand Trunk Road, which ran through Punjab on its way from Kabul, in Afghanistan, to Calcutta, on India's eastern shores. The degree sheets also foreshadow some of the boundary disputes that would arise after partition: the Radcliffe line snakes back and forth across the Ravi River (following colonial administrative boundaries), never following the river's path exactly. As a result, India and Pakistan would each find themselves in control of territory on the opposite side of the river. Towards the bottom of the map, in clear and decorative handwriting, is the following inscription: 'Certified as Annexure B to my Report dated 12 August 1947/Cyril Radcliffe Chairman Punjab Boundary Commission.'

If these maps had provided Radcliffe with more information on potential social disruptions, would partition have turned out differently? Given the power of graphic representations to convey information, perhaps confronting the leaders in Delhi with a map showing Lahore cut off from Amritsar, with all the infrastructural and economic difficulties that separation entailed, might have impelled them to act sooner to ameliorate these problems. But such speculation assumes that decision-makers understood that the new boundary would soon become hostile and eventually a tightly controlled barrier.[100] An additional reason to doubt that better cartographic representations might have improved the partition process is the inherent tendency of maps to distance the map reader from the social reality of the terrain portrayed. As a prominent cartographic historian has written,

> maps as an impersonal type of knowledge tend to 'desocialize' the territory they represent. They foster the notion of a socially empty space. The abstract quality of the map, embodied as much in the line of a fifteenth-century Ptolemaic projection as in the contemporary images of computer cartography, lessens the burden of conscience about people in the landscape. Decisions about the exercise of power are removed from the realm of immediate face-to-face contacts.[101]

Even with graphic representations about the effects that the new boundary would have, British and nationalist leaders might have continued to deny the likelihood of negative repercussions.

Intriguingly, the seven maps required to show the full extent of the line, from the Kashmir border, north of Punjab, to the tip of Bahawalpur, were assembled imprecisely. Someone in Radcliffe's office, perhaps Beaumont or even Radcliffe himself, used tape to anchor the maps together. As they are taped, however, none of these maps matches up exactly. The grid lines on the different maps do not align, although Radcliffe's line runs smoothly across the edges of the map, indicating the line was drawn after the maps were taped together. Furthermore, the point where the boundary crosses the edge of the map is not always the point of best fit between these misaligned maps. These facts underline the great hurry in which Radcliffe and his aide assembled this essential visual representation of the Indo-Pakistani boundary.[102] It is no surprise to find that the tight deadline imposed on the boundary-making process created pressure on Radcliffe and his colleagues, but these maps provide particularly striking visual evidence of their haste.

The Kasur tehsil *map*

The base map Radcliffe used to delineate his boundary in Kasur *tehsil* focuses on one particular means of British administrative control: the collection of taxes.[103] The most detailed of Radcliffe's maps, the 'Map of Kasur Tahsil' (see map 3) was very large scale, at one inch to two miles. Radcliffe annexed this map to his award to clarify the boundary's path between villages in Kasur, where the line diverged from administrative boundaries. Village boundaries are the most prominent feature on the map, for it was intended as a guide to revenue collection. The revenue system was based at the local level, where authorities collected taxes from peasants in accordance with their agricultural production. The base map carries the name of 'G. E. B. Abell, I.C.S./Settlement Office/ Lahore District', who was Mountbatten's private secretary in 1947.

This map describes selected villages, primarily in terms of which government buildings (police stations, telegraph offices, schools, etc.) are present where, as well as the population of 'principal places'. The legend includes district, *tehsil*, village and assessment (taxation) boundaries, roads (metalled – that is, surfaced with broken stone – and unmetalled), canals, railway lines and stations, elevated ridges known as *dhayas*, and police headquarters and outposts. As with the other Survey of India maps discussed, this map portrays the land primarily in terms of British administration and police control, with attention to infrastructure links with neighbouring areas. The map also provides a detailed view of the Sutlej River, vividly demonstrating the way that

British administrative boundaries wandered back and forth across the water. As we will see in Chapter 7, disputes arose from these intertwining boundaries and rivers.

Finally, scrawled on the map are the following words: 'Attached to my Report d. 12 August 1947 for reference. Cyril Radcliffe Chairman Punjab Boundary Commission.' This hasty handwriting, a marked contrast to the neat script Radcliffe used on the quarter-inch map, provides another indication of his last-minute rush. It is unclear why the writing on the quarter-inch maps is so much clearer. Perhaps the Kasur map was an afterthought, attached at the last minute when Radcliffe realized the need to clarify this particularly tricky part of the line.

Taken as a group, the maps available to Radcliffe did not provide the information necessary to minimize the disruptions inherent in the boundary-making project. Given the difficulties involved in dividing intermingled religious communities, however, it seems likely that even perfect information, if such a thing existed, would not have guaranteed a nonviolent outcome. Still, the question remains: how might the Radcliffe award have been different if it was based on improved maps? The following chapter addresses the boundary decision in detail, but some comment on the influence of map use is appropriate here. It is unlikely that maps with more detail of, for example, the organization of Punjabi society, would have changed Radcliffe's final decision significantly. The one possible exception is the irrigation network of central Punjab. In the case of the Sulemanke headworks, which Radcliffe indicated might require boundary adjustment, more detailed maps – or adequate local knowledge – might have prevented not only post-partition confusion but also the resulting military clashes over the area.[104] But overall, better cartographic information would not have dramatically altered the fundamental considerations guiding Radcliffe's decisions. If the problems connected with Radcliffe's line are not attributable to faults in the maps on which the decision was based, what caused them? Although maps appear at first glance to provide a convenient scapegoat on which to blame the boundary commission's flaws, the evidence does not support such an interpretation. The real failure here was attributable not to any one set of data, or any one individual, but to the deeply problematic partition process, which combined pell-mell hurry with a fragile façade of order.

Conflicting and inaccessible evidence makes the picture of Radcliffe's map use difficult to clarify. What is clear is that partition historiography has repeatedly used maps as markers of chaos. Whether they are 'out-dated',[105] on too small a scale,[106] wildly conflicting[107] or flapping in the breeze from the ever-turning overhead fan that cooled Radcliffe's sweltering office,[108] the maps provided to Radcliffe are consistently described as deficient and/or disorganized. These assertions may not be entirely factually correct, but they do highlight the larger truth that the partition process was deeply political, disordered and inadequate. Survey of India maps were not the scientific, rationally constructed documents they seemed; neither was the boundary commission the judicial, rationally constructed entity it appeared to be. These maps, like the larger process of partition, were not adequately connected to the reality of what was happening on the ground. The maps Radcliffe used, with their crossed sabres indicating past battles, were clearly marked by colonial violence; as decolonization progressed, the real landscape that those maps sought to portray was again marked by bloodshed.

The final days before independence

By the time Radcliffe had submitted his award, he was eager to leave South Asia. He was exhausted by the pace of work and by the South Asian summer, which he reported to a friend was 'the hottest in India for seventy years'.[109] The heat seems to have made a great impression on Radcliffe, who frequently visited the pool at Viceroy's House.[110] We find another lament about the Indian heat in a letter Radcliffe wrote to his stepson, Mark, as he prepared to leave India. This note reveals both the fatigue that followed on weeks of difficult labour and Radcliffe's early regrets about the results of his work. Of his plans for the following morning Radcliffe wrote, 'I station myself firmly on the Delhi airport until an aeroplane from England comes along. Nobody in India will love me for my award about the Punjab and Bengal and there will be roughly 80 million people with a grievance who will begin looking for me. I do not want them to find me. I have worked and travelled and sweated – oh I have sweated the whole time.'[111] These are not the words of a man satisfied with a job well done. Radcliffe himself understood clearly that his award would anger many people, as demonstrated by his reference to 'roughly 80 million people with a grievance'.[112] It seems that Radcliffe expected not only that the award would render him personally unpopular, but also that violent repercussions were a possibility. He was far from the only one to express a growing sense of unease.

Oskar Spate, the Australian geographer who assisted the Muslim preparations, had privately expressed similar fears a few weeks earlier. In keeping with his belief in the validity of the Muslim claim, he recorded in his diary, 'I think it is essential that Pakistan keeps Amritsar, but I want to have one foot on the running-board of the Karachi mail [train] when the announcement is made.'[113] Having witnessed first-hand Sikh preparations for battle, Spate was eager to get out of town before the imminent explosion.[114] Many British officials and South Asians shared this distinct sense of a gathering storm.

By mid-August, Spate was even more uneasy. By now he had moved to Karachi, in order to attend Pakistan's independence celebrations. While there he wrote, 'I feel now that the whole procedure was a mistake. It is axiomatic that satisfaction could <u>not</u> be given to the Sikhs consistently with justice to say 15 times the number of Muslims, and with economic fairness to Pakistan. It ought to have been negotiated at the highest level, and imposed by fiat.'[115] The next day, he encountered an unnamed aide to Evan Jenkins, who outlined the final award and said that it had been altered: '<u>it has been changed at least once:</u> he wouldn't tell me in w[hi]ch direction, but later let slip that the first one, would have annoyed the Sikhs, second Sikhs <u>and</u> Muslims. Could folly go further?'[116] Having heard of the award's postponement, he concluded bitterly, 'Apart from the last minute jiggery pokery[, the] idea seems to be to get the celebrations over and then have the shooting.'[117] Spate was not alone in anticipating a violent reaction.

The party leaders shared this apprehension, a feeling that a storm was about to break. On 13 August, for example, even the phlegmatic Patel wrote to Mountbatten to protest a rumored element of the Bengal award. He concluded, 'if the award confirms the worst fears entertained by the public, it is impossible for me to predict the volume of bitterness and rancour which would be let loose and I am certain that this will create a situation which both you and I may have to regret'.[118] For many people, this sense of unease was, of course, combined with feelings of national joy as the moment of independence approached. But for inhabitants of the areas whose fate was uncertain – localities that might end up in either India or Pakistan – apprehension and mortal fear overwhelmed the joy.

Notes

1 Jones, p. 58.
2 In fact, Jones offers 'seven main methods of boundary definition'. These range from 'complete definition' to 'definition in principle', with five variations of 'complete definition with power to deviate' in between. In these five variants, deviation can be unrestricted, restricted by major turning points, restricted by courses and distances, restricted by a zone or restricted by natural features. Jones, pp. 59–63.
3 The notable exception was the vital Triple Canal Project in northern Punjab, which Radcliffe preserved intact and awarded to Pakistan (Aloys Michel, *The Indus Rivers: A Study of the Effects of Partition* (New Haven: Yale University Press, 1967), p. 176). However, the Mangla headworks that feed this system are located just inside what is now Pakistan-occupied Kashmir (O. H. K. Spate, 'The partition of India and

the prospects of Pakistan', *Geographical Review* 38 (1948), p. 29).

4   IOR/L/P&J/10/117, p. 28.
5   IOR/L/P&J/10/117, pp. 69–70.
6   IOR/L/P&J/10/117, p. 70.
7   Radcliffe, letter to Aloys Michel, 28 March 1965, cited in Michel, p. 164 n. 47.
8   *TP* XII p. 746.
9   Beaumont, personal interview, 8 February 2000.
10 Beaumont, personal interview, 8 February 2000.
11 Mehr Chand Mahajan, p. 117.
12 French, p. 324.
13 Mosley, p. 194. See also Dominique Lapierre, *A Thousand Suns: Witness to History* (New York: Warner Boolis, 1999), p. 372.
14 Beaumont, personal interview, 8 February 2000.
15 *TP* XII p. 745.
16 Sadullah, vol. 2, p. 34.
17 To his summary of their 1 September meeting, Sir Paul Patrick added, 'What was difficult for them, particularly the Pakistani members, was that they were acting under orders' (IOR/L/P&J/10/117, p. 28).
18 Guru Nanak was the founder of Sikhism. Beaumont, personal interview, 29 February 2000.
19 Beaumont, personal interview, 8 February 2000.
20 Beaumont emphasized that Radcliffe took special care over this area because it had a particularly difficult mix of Muslims, Hindus and Sikhs and his 'prime concern was to get people the right side of the line'. Beaumont, personal interview, 29 February 2000.
21 *TP* XII pp. 747–9.
22 IOR/L/P&J/10/119, p. 104.
23 I am grateful to Marjorie McIntosh for raising this point.
24 Edney, p. 333.
25 Tuker, *While Memory Serves*, p. 524.
26 After independence, however, the Indian Government soon altered those boundaries significantly. In 1956, Punjab was reorganized to include a number of former princely states, which had been amalgamated as the Patiala and East Punjab States Union (PEPSU). In 1966, linguistic reorganization altered Punjab still further, as the Government of India split off Hindi-speaking areas to join Himachal Pradesh and to form the new state of Haryana, while the central Punjabi-speaking areas remained the rump state of Punjab. Surya Kant, *Administrative Geography of India* (Jaipur: Rawat Publications, 1988), pp. 61–2.
27 *TP* X p. 768.
28 I am grateful to David Gilmartin for bringing this point to my attention.
29 Collins and Lapierre, *Mountbatten and Partition*, p. 103.
30 Mountbatten insisted that later historians would vindicate all of his decisions and disprove his critics (Andrew Roberts, 'Lord Mountbatten and the perils of adrenalin', in *Eminent Churchillians* (London: Phoenix, 1994), p. 125).
31 Field Marshal Sir Gerald Templer delivered the insult. Philip Ziegler, *Mountbatten: The Official Biography* (New York: Harper & Row, 1985), p. 528.
32 *TP* XII p. 747.
33 *TP* XII pp. 746–7.
34 *TP* XII pp. 751–2.
35 Beaumont, personal interview, 8 February 2000.
36 Chaudhri, p. 53.
37 *TP* XII p. 747.
38 Mosley, p. 199.
39 *TP* XII p. 749. In this area, therefore, Radcliffe varied from the concept of 'complete definition'.
40 *TP* XII pp. 746–7.
41 Hastings Lionel Ismay, *The Memoirs of General Lord Ismay* (London: Heinemann,

1960), p. 411.

42 Radcliffe, 'Thoughts on India', in *Not in Feather Beds*, p. 5.

43 And in some cases even earlier. Michel, pp. 49–51.

44 M. Mufakharul Islam, *Irrigation, Agriculture and the Raj: Punjab, 1887–1947* (New Delhi: Manohar, 1997), p. 26.

45 Radcliffe, letter to Michel, 28 March 1965, quoted in Michel, p. 194.

46 Stanley Wolpert, *A New History of India*, 3rd ed. (New York: Oxford University Press, 1989), p. 348; Hugh Tinker, *Experiment with Freedom: India and Pakistan, 1947* (London: Oxford University Press, 1967), p. 141; Reg Herschy, *Disputed Frontiers* (Lewes, Sussex: Book Guild, 1993), p. 72; Michael Edwardes, *The Last Years of British India* (Cleveland: World Publishing Company, 1963), p. 209; Collins and Lapierre, *Freedom at Midnight*, p. 248. Sugata Bose and Ayesha Jalal quote W. H. Auden's poem 'Partition', which says of Radcliffe, 'The maps at his disposal were out of date' (*Modern South Asia* (London: Routledge, 1998), p. 189).

47 Sadullah, vol. 4.

48 In Britain, neither the India Office Library nor The National Archives possess Radcliffe's map of his boundary decision; Indian and Pakistani governmental security concerns continue to block any access to relevant cartographic material in South Asian archives.

49 Sadullah lists the location of a number of the maps reproduced in his vol. 4 as 'Punjab Archives' or, in the case of the 'sketch map', 'Foreign Office, Government of Pakistan'; attempts to locate the originals in any Pakistani archive have been unsuccessful thus far. It is instructive that the sketch map, at the time of *Partition of the Punjab*'s publication in 1983, had not yet been deposited in an archive but was still held by the Pakistani Foreign Office. Presumably it was considered to be of continuing relevance to Pakistan's foreign affairs, a fact that emphasizes the role of maps as instruments of strategic power, as well as the continuing sensitivity of border maps in both India and Pakistan.

50 Jones, p. 86.

51 Mosley worked as a foreign correspondent and later a film and theatre critic for the *Daily Express*, a London newspaper controlled by the Conservative William Maxwell Aitken, Lord Beaverbrook ('Leonard Mosley', *The Times* (London) (22 June 1992), p. 17, col. 1). Despite their early friendship, Beaverbrook and Mountbatten grew to dislike each other heartily after disagreements over Mountbatten's actions in South East Asia and India. Beaverbrook regarded Mountbatten as 'the biggest menace to the Empire' (Ziegler, *Mountbatten: The Official Biography*, pp. 488–9).

52 Lapierre, pp. 371, 373.

53 Mosley, p. 198.

54 Mosley, p. 197.

55 Mosley, p. 198.

56 Mosley, p. 198.

57 Lapierre, p. 372.

58 Lapierre, p. 372.

59 Jones, p. 6.

60 *TP* XII p. 746.

61 Confusions arose in any case; see Chatterji, 'Fashioning', pp. 216–31.

62 For example, the authors of the 1915 Treaty of Sofia relied too heavily on their map in declaring that 'from the letter č of the word Karagač, a town assigned to Bulgaria, the frontier ... continues in a straight line to the letter š of the word Demirdeš'. Jones, p. 64.

63 See especially Jones on the need for fresh surveys.

64 G. F. Heaney, 'Preface', in *Survey of India Technical Report 1947* (Dehra Dun: Survey of India, 1949), p. iii.

65 Wheeler, p. 82.

66 *Survey of India Map Catalogue*, corrected up to 1.5.51 (Dehra Dun: Surveyor General of India, 1950), G. F. Heaney Papers, Box 5, Book 3, South Asian Archive, Cambridge University.

67 For other information crucial to his work, such as demographic information, Radcliffe would have been obliged to turn to non-cartographic materials like the Indian census, which were problematic in their own right. Although this aspect of the boundary commission's work cannot be adequately discussed here, materials like the census may have created, as well as reflected, divisions between social groups. Radcliffe's maps, based on an understanding of those divisions as irreconcilable, in turn created a new reality of divided countries.

68 *TP* XII p. 191.

69 *TP* XII p. 279.

70 *TP* XII p. 291.

71 *TP* XII p. 305. Emphasis in original.

72 *TP* XII p. 557.

73 *TP* XII p. 584.

74 Sadullah, vol. 1, pp. 245–6.

75 *TP* XII p. 615. On 10 August, the Governor of Bengal cabled Mountbatten with a similar request, noting that 'it is essential that we should have at least 24 hours notice for putting on the ground effectively our internal security arrangements in Calcutta on publication of award' (*TP* XII p. 646).

76 *TP* XII p. 133.

77 'Map of the Punjab, Punjab states and Delhi' [facsimile], 1947, with a line forecasting Radcliffe's division of Punjab, as reproduced in Sadullah, vol. 4, Map 2. The debate over this map is examined in Chapter 5.

78 *TP* XII p. 579.

79 Beaumont, personal interview, 29 February 2000.

80 *TP* XII p. 579.

81 IOR/L/P&J/10/119, p. 105.

82 *TP* XII p. 638.

83 *TP* XII p. 662.

84 *TP* XII p. 663. Emphasis in original.

85 *TP* XII p. 680.

86 *TP* XII p. 692.

87 *TP* XII p. 761.

88 IOR Mss Eur D 807/3, p. 178.

89 The evidence indicates that Radcliffe saw large-scale, district-level maps as well, certainly for Bengal and presumably for Punjab. On 11 August 1947, the secretary of the Governor of Bengal cabled Beaumont to request the return of maps loaned by the Governor's Office: 'Please arrange for return of our eight District Maps and 1941 census report in due course.' IOR/R/3/1/157, p. 276.

90 The map gives the wrong year for this battle, showing the date as '10-2–1840.'

91 For the First Anglo-Sikh War, see Singh, *History*, pp. 40–54.

92 Singh, *History*, p. 53.

93 For the Second Anglo-Sikh War, see Singh, *History*, pp. 66–82.

94 The specific maps used were 'Lahore', 44I; 'Jammu', 43L; 'Gurdaspur', 43P; 'Jullundur', 44M; ['Lyallpur'?], 44E; 'Montgomery', 44F; and 'Ferozepore', 44J. With the guidance of the India Office Library's invaluable Andrew Cook, I have identified the specific edition used for the following maps: 44I, 'Lahore', 1943 interim edition; 43L, 'Jammu', 1944 interim edition; 44F, 'Montgomery', 1944 reprint of 1941 interim edition (with minor corrections) and 44J, 'Ferozepore', 1943 interim edition. All maps are from the Survey of India's 'India and Adjacent Countries' quarter inch topographic series.

95 'Text and contexts', in Harley, pp. 39–40.

96 For a discussion of the problems associated with social mapping, see Jeremy Black, *Maps and Politics* (London: Reaktion Books, 1997), pp. 65–78.

97 'Maps, knowledge, and power', in Harley, pp. 57–8.

98 See Chester, 'The mapping of empire', pp. 256–75 and 'Mapping imperial expansion: Colonial cartography in North America and South Asia', *The Portolan* 45 (Fall 1999), pp. 9–24.

99   During partition, canals were occasionally cut with the express purpose of slowing refugees and rendering them more vulnerable to attack. See S. Wajahat Husain, 'The evacuation of Kapurthala state Muslims', *Dawn* (14 August 1992), p. VII.

100 At the time, many leaders assumed that travel and commerce between India and Pakistan would continue normally after the division. Jinnah, for example, famously kept his house in Bombay.

101 'Maps, knowledge, and power', in Harley, p. 81.

102 I am grateful to Andrew Cook for bringing these points to my attention.

103 IOR/L/P&J/10/117, Map 1. The version reprinted in Sadullah, vol. 4, Map 6, bears additional marks (certain villages underlined and marked with checks) indicating post-partition use, perhaps by the Government of Pakistan.

104 *TP* XII p. 749.

105 Wolpert, *A New History of India*, p. 348.

106 Mosley, p. 198.

107 Spate, *Margins*, p. 54; Sadullah, vol. 4.

108 Sunil Khilnani, 'India's mapmaker', *Observer* (London), Review (22 June 1997), p. 7.

109 Young, p. 624.

110 As recalled by one of Mountbatten's aides-de-camp (Suzanne Goldenberg, 'Memories of Mountbatten', *Guardian* (7 August 1997), p. 3).

111 Radcliffe, letter to Mark Tennant, 13 August 1947, cited in Heward, p. 42. This letter remains in the possession of Mark Tennant, who prefers to keep it private but has confirmed the section reprinted in Heward. He states that the rest of the letter does not relate to India, with the exception of an additional line reading, 'Do not ask me about India because I haven't seen anything of it' (personal interview, 9 February 2000).

112 Radcliffe, letter to Mark Tennant, cited in Heward, p. 42.

113 Spate Diary, 19 July 1947.

114 Spate Diary, 3 August 1947.

115 Spate Diary, 14 August 1947. Emphasis in original.

116 Spate Diary, 15 August 1947. Emphasis in original.

117 Spate Diary, 15 August 1947.

118 *TP* XII p. 692.

CHAPTER FIVE

'A political decision, and not a judicial one': the Radcliffe award

Independence Day saw the inhabitants of Punjab in limbo, without any official information as to the location of their new boundary. Radcliffe had prepared his decision before 15 August, as the various parties, including Mountbatten, had insisted. With the transfer of power approaching, however, the viceroy chose to delay the boundary announcement. In public statements, he insisted that he simply wished to avoid spoiling the joyous celebration of independence by announcing news that would undoubtedly distress all parties. However, private government communications and the minutes of the 9 August staff meeting at which he took this decision make clear that Mountbatten's primary goal was avoiding the appearance of British responsibility for the disorder that inevitably would follow the announcement. The meeting minutes record Mountbatten's views on the subject: 'without question, the earlier it [the award] was published, the more the British would have to bear the responsibility for the disturbances which would undoubtedly result'. Abell pointed out that publishing the decision sooner rather than later would bring 'administrative advantages', but the viceroy overruled him.[1]

John Christie, joint private secretary to the viceroy, recorded in his diary that at another staff meeting, on 12 August, Mountbatten was again adamant that the boundary announcement must be postponed. Christie wrote,

> H[is] E[xcellency, Mountbatten] most anxious to postpone publication till after 15th. Pug [Ismay] and George [Abell] against this for adminis-trative reasons. H.E. adamant: sent Alan [Campbell-Johnson, Mountbat-ten's press secretary] and me to Sir C[yril] R[adcliffe] to arrange the dates. C.R. refused flat – too many people know it's ready. Stretched a point to redate 13th; will arrive complete after H.E. has gone to Karachi. Back to H.E. who had had a couple. Didn't like it but swallowed it.[2]

In fact, the Bengal and Punjab awards were dated 12 August; the award for Sylhet, a small locality adjoining Bengal, was dated 13 August, which allowed Mountbatten to claim that he had not been able to see the complete award before leaving on 13 August for Karachi and the Pakistani independence ceremonies. Christie makes no mention of Mountbatten's concern for Indian feelings.

When Jenkins later read a description of this meeting that cited 'psychology' and a reluctance to 'mar independence day' as reasons for the award's delay, his reaction consisted of three eloquent exclamation points in the margin.[3] Combined with his pre-independence pleas for an early release of the boundary decision, Jenkins's incredulity was presumably due either to a conviction that Mountbatten could not believe such a ridiculous thing or to an assumption that the viceroy had other reasons in mind when he made this decision.

It is difficult to see how these considerations, either for Indian or Pakistani national joy or for the evasion of British national responsibility, could outweigh the potential benefits of making administrative, military and police arrangements before the actual transfer of power took place. As we have seen, Jenkins had begged Mountbatten repeatedly for advance notice of the award. As it was, many administrators joined the last-minute flow of refugees themselves, as 15 August drew closer, causing disruptions across India by leaving their posts empty. Punjab's government had in any case been limited by months of Section 93 administration; as Ismay later described the impact of governor's rule, 'when the time came, neither the East nor the West Punjab had any Government worthy of the name'.[4] And yet some areas had too many administrators rather than too few: in parts of Gurdaspur District, Pakistani officials began to set up shop and even raised the Pakistani flag. When the award announcement made it clear that these *tehsils* had gone to India, the Pakistanis had to scramble across the line.[5] In short, the moment of independence found Punjab in administrative chaos, ill prepared to deal with the impact of partition. The lack of a firm announcement of the boundary award, combined with speculation about its contents, aggravated the tension. On 15 August, Auchinleck reported, 'The delay in announcing the award of the Boundary Commission is having a most disturbing and harmful effect. It is realised of course that the announcement may add fresh fuel to the fire, but lacking an announcement, the wildest rumours are current, and are being spread by mischief makers of whom there is no lack.'[6] Even at the time, Mountbatten's senior aides were convinced that the announcement's delay was causing more harm than good.

When Mountbatten released the award to the Indian and Pakistani leaders on 16 August, both sides objected furiously to various aspects

[107]

of the boundary. In the end, however, they agreed to issue the decision as it stood, with no public statement of their disappointment. When the award was finally announced, on 17 August, the border forces in place were inadequate to stop the communal massacres. Rumour played a central role in provoking these massacres by sparking retaliatory killings.[7] Given the fact that postponing the announcement triggered a flood of speculation about the location of the boundary and the reasons for its delay, it is possible that earlier notice would have reduced provocative rumours about the boundary location, thereby diminishing local anxieties about where the line would fall. In doing so, the earlier release of information might have reduced the level of violence. On the other hand, an earlier announcement might have given troublemakers more time to plan their attacks; but since the delay does not seem to have hampered raiders' preparations, and since contemporary observers called for earlier information rather than later notice, this argument seems less convincing.

Years later, Governor Jenkins's secretary Stuart Abbott recalled his disapproval of Mountbatten's tardy announcement: 'I remember very vividly the first news we had about the actual boundaries of the two Punjabs, as we went aboard our flying boat in Karachi at 5 am on Sunday August 17th. I once silenced Ismay's encomium of Mountbatten by asking what sort of administration it was to establish two dominions two days before the boundaries were even settled, adding that no Punjabi would ever forgive this and I doubted if history would either.'[8] Abbott's remarks highlight the absurdity of two nation-states coming into existence without clear boundaries. Legally speaking, the 'notional boundary' would serve as a temporary line until the boundary commission's decision was announced, but in reality it meant little. The Radcliffe line was what mattered.

In any case, it is clear that Mountbatten's decision to delay the announcement had more to do with British interests than with the Indian or Pakistani public good. The priority accorded to avoiding the appearance of British responsibility does not mesh well with claims that the partition was designed to satisfy nationalist desires and goals, or that the division's failings were due to South Asian squabbling. When it came down to it, partition was (from the British perspective) a means of avoiding British responsibility while shedding the economic burden that India had become. This fact is not surprising – it simply reflects political realities – but it does not jibe with imperialist propaganda about empire's benefits for subject peoples or about partition as the natural result of steady progress towards self-rule.

Reception of the boundary decision

Radcliffe's line allotted 64 per cent of the area of undivided Punjab to Pakistan, with slightly less than 60 per cent of the populace. By and large, the new boundary followed major administrative divisions, although it did meander between villages in the Kasur region south-east of Lahore. The boundary ran from the border of Kashmir state in the north to the border of Bahawalpur state in the south; Bahawalpur was a princely state whose ruler, like the Maharajah of Kashmir, had (in theory) the choice of acceding to Pakistan or India. Further south, the existing boundary between the province of Sindh and the region of Rajputana (now the Indian states of Rajasthan and Gujarat) became the international boundary (see map 1 for a British representation of these provincial boundaries; note the imperial spelling of Sind).

The Radcliffe award gave Pakistan 63,800 square miles of Punjabi territory, while India received 35,300 square miles. The 1941 census figures showed the seventeen districts that went to Pakistan to have a population of 16.8 million, or 59.2 per cent of the undivided province's total population, compared to the 11.6 million who went to India. This left Pakistani Punjab with a minority population of 26.8 per cent. Indian Punjab had an even larger minority population of about 35 per cent,[9] but neither side would retain these minorities long.

The primary feature of Radcliffe's line was that it divided Amritsar, now in India, from Lahore, which went to Pakistan. The two most controversial elements of this line involved parts of Gurdaspur and Ferozepur Districts. Pakistani critics interpreted Radcliffe's decision to grant most of Gurdaspur District to India as an attempt to provide India with a land link to Kashmir. As one element of the beginning of the Kashmir conflict, this allegation remains controversial. It is worth noting that no all-weather road linked Kashmir and India in 1947; when conflict began in late 1947, India airlifted troops and supplies into Kashmir rather than take an overland route.[10] The so-called land link between India and Kashmir was therefore of little value in the initial stages of the conflict. Confusion has arisen over Gurdaspur; even some prominent scholars have stated that 'Radcliffe awarded the Ferozepur subdistricts and Gurdaspur to Pakistan in his initial maps.'[11] In fact, there was no change in Gurdaspur's assignment; as Beaumont made clear, Radcliffe intended to award Gurdaspur to India from the beginning. The other controversy was over Ferozepur's allocation to India. This decision came as a surprise in the wake of early August leaks indicating that Radcliffe would allot a section of Ferozepur to Pakistan.

At his gloomy 16 August meeting with the Indian and Pakistani leaders, Mountbatten did raise the notion of deviation from Radcliffe's line. But both sides reluctantly agreed, despite their bitter complaints about specific elements of the award, with League representative Liaquat Ali Khan, who announced that he was opposed to any 'adjustments between representatives of the two Governments' at that time. Liaquat advocated publishing the awards as they stood, without any mention of governmental dissatisfaction.[12]

After Radcliffe's award was published and it became clear that both India and Pakistan were unhappy with it, the language used to describe the decision changed significantly. Before 15 August, it was known as the 'boundary commission award'. After its release, when the other commission members had presumably made clear their relative lack of influence over the decision-making process, the decision began to be cited as the 'Radcliffe award'. It is this phrase that is commonly used to this day, reflecting not only attempts by the Indian and Pakistani governments to distance themselves from the decisions, but also the idea that the line was a British creation. It may also signify a willingness on the part of the British Government to have the line associated with Radcliffe the individual rather than with Mountbatten, the British Indian Government he headed, or the British Government as a whole. Radcliffe served as a convenient scapegoat for problems associated with the British retreat.

When the award was finally made public, the reaction was violent. Major-General Thomas 'Pete' Rees, the head of the Punjab Boundary Force, reported that 'the publication of the Boundary Award on 17th August added fuel to the flames'.[13] In an editorial a few days after the division, the Pakistani newspaper *Dawn* labelled the Radcliffe award 'territorial murder'. The unexpectedly non-judicial nature of the award was a recurring theme. *Dawn*'s editors wrote, 'To describe the three reports [for Punjab, Bengal and Sylhet] which Sir Cyril Radcliffe has submitted as judicial awards is to insult the very name of justice.' Outraged because Radcliffe 'had been trusted to be fair', because he was 'neutral' and because this was 'an unjust award', the editors displayed a somewhat surprising sense of surprise that Radcliffe's decision had turned out to have political elements. They concluded that the decision was 'miscalled a judicial award'.[14] In this they were quite correct. It seems unlikely that informed observers could really have expected that the boundary-making process, surrounded as it was by political wrangling and staffed by political nominees, would be free of politics. Expressing outrage at the revelation of this fact, however, proved politically useful. The commission's judicial façade was breaking down in public.

The Radcliffe commission, and Radcliffe in particular, served as a useful scapegoat not only for the British, but also for the Pakistani and Indian governments. British leaders originally hoped to shift the blame for problems with partition to the nationalist leaders,[15] but even after it became clear that the line was largely Radcliffe's creation, they still had an external scapegoat who could take the blame. Ever dutiful, Radcliffe cooperated in this process. He staunchly denied that Mountbatten had had any influence on the award, insisting that it was entirely his own creation. The Indian and Pakistani governments, for their part, found it convenient to blame the violence and dislocation of partition, as well as the economic woes that followed, on the perfidious drawing of the line. Many Indians and, in particular, Pakistanis, did not believe that Radcliffe had acted alone. In Pakistan, Mountbatten is still regarded as a villain who attempted to the bitter end to foil Jinnah, the heroic *Quaid-i-Azam*. But Radcliffe too is often cited as a key factor in the unfair treatment that, it is alleged, Pakistan received at the time of partition. In a radio broadcast on 31 August, Jinnah said: 'The latest blow that we have received was the Award of the Boundary Commission. It is an unjust, incomprehensible, and even perverse award. It may be wrong, unjust and perverse; and it may not be a judicial but political award, but we had agreed to abide by it, and it is binding upon us. As honourable people we must abide by it.'[16] Pakistani newspapers elaborated upon the theme of Radcliffe's treachery with articles like 'Punjab Boundary Commission Held Responsible for Riots', which reported:

'The responsibility of the massacre of Muslims in the East Punjab is on the shoulders of the Chairman, Punjab Boundary Commission' says Qaid Majlis Khuddam-ul-Ahmeddiya, Delhi, in the cours[e] of a telegram to Qaid-e-Azam, M.A. Jinnah, Governor-General of Pakistan. The telegram adds, the transference of predominantly Muslim majority areas into Hindustan was a direct hint to the non-Muslims in the East Punjab to launch their attack against the Muslims who had been the spear-head in the struggle for the attainment of Pakistan.[17]

To this day, Radcliffe's name and his alleged misdeeds (particularly the 'theft' of Ferozepur and Gurdaspur) are a standard part of the Pakistani history curriculum.[18]

Rhetoric aside, however, it proved difficult to establish the Radcliffe award's illegitimacy. After independence, the Government of India explored the possibility of mounting a legal challenge to the Radcliffe decision. It formed a Cabinet committee to consider the boundary commission awards for both Bengal and Punjab, but government lawyers concluded that the award was invulnerable to legal challenge. The possibility of effective protest was limited by the Indian Independence Act of 1947, which stipulated that 'the boundaries of the said new Provinces shall be such as may be determined, whether before or after the appointed day, by the award of a boundary commission appointed or to be appointed by the Governor-General in that behalf'.[19] In fact, Radcliffe himself had ensured that his award would be legally unassailable. Immediately after his arrival in India, he wrote to Mountbatten to suggest that a new clause be added to the Indian Independence Bill, in order to make certain that, in case of disagreement between members of the boundary commission, the chairman's decision would be final.[20] Mountbatten presented this proposal to the party leaders, who agreed to the inclusion of the following sub-clause: 'the expression "award," means, in relation to a boundary commission, the decisions of the chairman of that commission contained in his report to the Governor-General at the conclusion of the commission's proceedings'.[21] Thus the nationalist leaders had once again been party to a decision they later regretted.

As the Legal Advisor to the Government of India noted later in 1947, 'the award was given under the provisions of the Indian Independence Act. This Act was passed by the British Parliament which, at that time, certainly had power to legislate on any question relating to the Indian Empire. It made the decision on boundaries final.'[22] Any challenge to the award would be 'based on the assumption that the award was the award of an arbitrator. This might be so in fact, but it may also be considered that the whole proceeding was under an Act of the then Supreme Legislature and that therefore there is really no legal remedy at all.'[23] In any case, the terms of reference had been so vaguely worded as to make nearly any decision valid: 'Since the reference includes "other factors" – a very vague term – it is difficult to say that the principles have been departed from.'[24] The Special Committee, noting that 'the partition council had agreed to accept the decisions of the Chairman of the Boundary Commission, and we cannot therefore openly challenge the award', was forced to recommend that 'the Boundary Commission's award should be treated as final in regard to the Punjab'.[25]

Allegations against Mountbatten of improper influence

In early 1948, members of the British Parliament questioned Mountbatten's influence on Radcliffe's award. The British Government also faced the prospect that Pakistan might raise the sketch map question in the UN (for the line appearing in the sketch map, see map 5a). As a result, the Commonwealth Office consulted with Radcliffe and those who had spoken with him in order to gather material to exonerate

Mountbatten. On 26 February 1948, an official reported on a conversation with Arthur Henderson, previously Parliamentary Under-Secretary of State for India:

> I asked Mr Henderson if he could say what passed between him and Sir Cyril Radcliffe about the alleged last minute alteration in the Radcliffe Award. Mr Henderson said that Sir Cyril Radcliffe had merely told him that he showed the first draft of the proposed award to the authorities in Delhi (he did not specify if the draft had been shown to Lord Mountbatten), that the contents of this draft were telegraphed to the authorities at Lahore and Calcutta from Delhi, presumably with a view to enabling advance security precautions to be taken, that on further consideration he, Sir Cyril Radcliffe, made the Award in terms which departed from the first draft.[26]

Sir Archibald Carter of the Commonwealth Relations Office consulted Radcliffe himself shortly thereafter, and on 13 April 1948, Radcliffe replied with thanks for showing him the draft statement on the Punjab award. Radcliffe noted, 'I do not think that it is quite correct to speak of provisional and final awards. There could be no award until I had decided to make a report to the viceroy, and only the document which contained that report could be called an award. All the earlier drafts – and there were quite a few – were drafts and no more.'[27] This somewhat legalistic response does not directly address the question of whether Radcliffe consulted Mountbatten in the final stages of his decision-making. Legally speaking, Radcliffe was quite right to point out that Mountbatten could not be said to have tampered with the award, as the award did not exist until Radcliffe officially submitted it. However, the real question was whether Mountbatten had played any role in Radcliffe's deliberations.

Later that month, in a letter to the United Kingdom's High Commissioner to India, Carter observed, 'It is, of course, true that no improper attempts were made to influence Radcliffe's decision, but he tells me that he did quite deliberately seek the views of all sorts of people including British officials and some of these conversations took place at a late stage. There is, therefore, a certain awkwardness in any wording that suggests that Radcliffe was absolutely aloof.'[28] Radcliffe's biographer also records that while in India, Radcliffe had lunch with Auchinleck and with Sir Patrick Spens, the Chief Justice of India, as well as visiting his old friend Sir Walter Monckton, who was in Delhi at the time.[29] In other words, Radcliffe was not a completely isolated, independent arbiter. However, Beaumont, who accompanied Radcliffe nearly everywhere, described these engagements as purely social and insisted that Radcliffe avoided any discussion of the boundary. He recalled, for example, Monckton's frequent visits: 'Monckton used to come along quite a lot in the evening, and we'd all drink whiskey outside [on the verandah]. I think they used to talk about the Temple and the Bar in the UK, mostly. Monckton asked no questions about the boundary at all.'[30] Even with Evan Jenkins, an experienced Punjab hand who could have advised him astutely, Radcliffe confined his conversation to 'trivialities, the weather'.[31]

Mountbatten was a prime mover in the portrayal of Radcliffe as a completely independent figure. One historian, who had close ties to the viceroy, wrote, 'Indeed Lord Mountbatten was careful to keep personal contacts with Sir Cyril to a minimum, and to decline either to offer any interpretation of the terms of reference – which Sir Cyril certainly did not invite from anyone – or to make any third-party representations to the Commissions.'[32] This statement is most likely based on Mountbatten's own assertion, in his 14 August report to Listowel, that 'I personally have scrupulously avoided all connection with Boundary Commissions, including interpretation of their terms of reference and putting before them the various points of view forwarded to me.'[33] None of these assertions was entirely accurate. In fact, Mountbatten met with Radcliffe as soon as he arrived and kept himself apprised of Radcliffe's progress through direct correspondence and the intermediary services of George Abell and other aides; he provided Radcliffe with at least one document that contained British views on how the terms of reference ought to be interpreted in regards to defence; and he forwarded to Radcliffe and/or Beaumont a representation from the Governor of Sylhet. Mountbatten was not as aloof as he portrayed himself to be.[34]

If Mountbatten intended to isolate himself from the commission's decision-making process, he neglected to communicate this fact to Radcliffe. Upon Radcliffe's arrival in India, Mountbatten himself reported that Radcliffe was 'staying with me for 48 hours to get into the picture'.[35] Shortly thereafter, Radcliffe made two requests of Mountbatten, both of which the viceroy shared with the nationalist leaders. As we have seen, these leaders approved Radcliffe's first suggestion, that the Indian Independence Bill be amended to state that the boundary commission chairman's decision would be final. Radcliffe also asked whether he should consider natural boundaries, including defensible terrain, a query that was met with a general decision that the commissioners could 'do what they consider[ed] best' as long as they conformed to their terms of reference. As noted above, Auchinleck stated that natural boundaries were undesirable and defence considerations irrelevant.[36] Mountbatten forwarded to Radcliffe the meeting's minutes, which included Auchinleck's remarks.[37]

At a 14 July staff meeting, Mountbatten noted that some British officials were assuming that the award of the Boundary Commission would not be available by 15th August. The assumption more likely to prove correct was that the award would be available by 15th August, but within so short a time before that date that it would not be possible to make the adjustments required before then. HIS EXCELLENCY said that he was in fact expecting to receive the awards of the Boundary Commissions on the night of 11th August.[38]

A day or so later, Mountbatten again noted, 'I have asked Sir Cyril Radcliffe to see that the report of the Boundary Commission is presented before the 15th August and he intends to do this.'[39] Both these comments indicate that Mountbatten or his staff had been in contact with Radcliffe on the question of the award's timing, and in fact this correspondence, quoted above, survives.[40]

On 15 July, when Jinnah and Liaquat protested to Mountbatten that Arthur Henderson's comments about Sikh shrines could prejudice the commission, Mountbatten noted their protest in a telegram that he copied to Radcliffe.[41] On 18 July, Mountbatten's personal report included details of Radcliffe's preliminary assessment of his fellow commissioners:

> Radcliffe came back with an optimistic report of the Bengal Boundary Commission in Calcutta. He thought all four Judges were of a higher class than he had expected and were fully determined to work as a team to a programme which would enable Radcliffe to give me his decision by the 12th August ... Radcliffe then flew on to Lahore where he had satisfactory discussions with the Punjab Boundary Commission. He says that they seemed very reasonable and were on good personal terms with one another.[42]

For a man ostensibly isolated from the boundary commission proceedings, Mountbatten had surprisingly good information on Radcliffe's thoughts and plans.

Mountbatten's aides were also in contact with Radcliffe's staff. On 21 July, Abell wrote to Beaumont to impress upon him Evan Jenkins's desire for advance warning of the award's contents.[43] Beaumont also consulted with Abell informally. He recalled,

> I occasionally asked him some very general questions, about what a suitable boundary would be; for example, whether it would be a thing called a *dhaya*, which is a bit of humpy ground here, or whether it'd be easier to follow the existing tehsil boundaries. I had asked him these questions, I think, because he was a Punjab civilian [Indian Civil Service officer] like me, and he'd been settlement officer of Lahore district. He knew every village there.[44]

Not only did Abell know the Punjab well, he was a paragon of British

Establishment accomplishment, excelling in three sports and achieving a first in classical honour moderations (as well as a second in *literae humaniores*) at Oxford.[45] It therefore seemed natural to Beaumont to ask Abell's advice. The fact that this consultation took place suggests that neither Abell nor Beaumont believed there was a need for isolation from the viceroy's staff.

On 2 August, Radcliffe again asked Mountbatten for clarification, this time of the Bengal commission's terms of reference.[46] He requested that the viceroy's private secretary or deputy private secretary convey the reply to him in person.[47] Mountbatten responded much as he had to Radcliffe's earlier request for clarification; he gave his opinion, then stated that he could not officially give his opinion. Abell noted, 'He authorized me to tell Sir Cyril Radcliffe that he agreed with his view about the meaning of the terms of reference but thought he must leave it to Sir Cyril Radcliffe to decide the matter for himself since there would be too many complications if H.E. gave a ruling.'[48] Furthermore, Radcliffe's communications with the members of the Bengal commission (who were in Calcutta, while Radcliffe remained in Delhi) passed through Abell's office.[49]

Ismay actually used this episode as ammunition for his argument that Mountbatten had removed himself from all questions relating to the boundary. In response to Liaquat Ali Khan's complaint that the award was unfair, he wrote, 'The Viceroy has always been, and is determined to keep clear of the whole business. As I told you only last week, his reply to Sir Cyril Radcliffe's enquiry about the interpretation of a certain point in his terms of reference was that the Viceroy did not feel justified in even expressing a view.'[50] This interpretation of Mountbatten's remarks is somewhat disingenuous. Although Mountbatten had stated that he could not give a 'ruling', in the very same sentence he had clearly communicated his own opinion to Radcliffe. This is not to argue that Mountbatten imposed his views on Radcliffe in this matter, but simply to reinforce the point that Mountbatten was not the disinterested observer his staff claimed he was.

It is true that Mountbatten's aides urged him to direct any boundary-related pleas to the commission itself and that he agreed.[51] However, it is also evident that, from the beginning, Mountbatten interested himself in the details of the commission's work. For example, when the Governor of Assam cabled Mountbatten to request that a certain road be awarded to India and not Pakistan, Mountbatten arranged for this document to be shown to Beaumont and replied, 'Radcliffe's Secretary has seen your telegram and it has been verified that Commission is fully seized of the point made by you on behalf of your Government.'[52] None of the examples cited here constitute open interference in Radcliffe's decision-making process, but they demonstrate that Mountbatten and Radcliffe were in communication.

Further evidence that the viceroy's staff were closely involved with the preparation of the award, at least in its final stages, come from a Royal Engineer who assisted with the mapping of the final line. In 1947, Donald Thyer was working in the Geographical Section of the General Staff in Delhi. He recalls a telephone call from one of Mountbatten's aides-de-camp during the second week of August, summoning three Royal Engineers with mapping experience for 'a highly confidential assignment'. Radcliffe had completed his work, and the new boundaries needed to be plotted. When Thyer and his colleagues arrived at the viceregal residence, they were shown to 'an air-conditioned conference chamber where a map of India and a folder containing official documents lay upon a large oval table'. A military aide explained their assignment: to plot the new boundary on the map provided, working from the details in the accompanying documents. Copies of this map would on 16 August be handed over to the new leaders of India and Pakistan. Significantly, Thyer notes that 'Lord Ismay, the Viceroy's Chief of Staff, also discussed the project with the sergeants and periodically checked on their rate of progress throughout the day.'[53] Well before the viceroy's return from Karachi, therefore, Ismay, if not Mountbatten, knew exactly where the boundary would be.

Even at the time, many observers assumed that Mountbatten and Radcliffe were in close contact and that Mountbatten had the final say over the location of the boundary. Among those who found the boundary-making process suspicious were some of the judges on the commission. Their claims tend to follow national lines, with the two Muslim League (later Pakistani) judges accusing Mountbatten and Radcliffe of misbehaviour, while a Congress (later Indian) judge was more circumspect. Of the judges on the Punjab commission, Congress nominee Teja Singh did not leave a memoir of his experiences; Din Muhammad of the Muslim League left a note. For the Punjab, therefore, we must rely primarily upon the recollections of Mehr Chand Mahajan and Muhammad Munir, Congress and League members respectively, as well as Din Muhammad's note and a passage from Zafrullah Khan's memoirs that sheds light on Din Muhammad's concerns.

Din Muhammad's 1952 note roundly criticizes Radcliffe's award as unfair to Pakistan and asserts that Radcliffe's conduct was 'unworthy' of his position as a 'leading member of the English bar'.[54] Specifically, Din Muhammad wrote that 'while on his only visit to the Punjab in the middle of July, Radcliffe was supplied by Mountbatten with his own aeroplane in order to take him over the same territory which he ultimately placed in Hindu Punjab'.[55] This planned flight, Din Muhammad noted, raised the suspicions of the Muslim judges on the commission. As further evidence that Mountbatten had a hand in the boundary, Din Muhammad concluded that 'it cannot be imagined that such an absurd and dishonest award could be the creation of an English lawyer's brain'.[56] Even after partition, respect for the British legal system coloured Din Muhammad's view of the boundary-making process.

According to Zafrullah's memoir, which fleshes out this brief account, a 'very agitated' Din Muhammad came to see him before the commission even began its public hearings, saying, 'I have a strong suspicion that the boundary line has already been decided upon and all of us are going to be engaged in a farce.'[57] Din Muhammad related that earlier in the day Radcliffe had planned to survey the disputed area in a small plane, accompanied by Munir and Teja Singh. The flight had been cancelled due to a dust storm, but Munir had obtained the slip of paper bearing the pilot's instructions and shared it with his colleague. When Din Muhammad saw this flight plan, he interpreted it as evidence that the boundary line had already been determined, and reported his suspicions first to Zafrullah and then to Jinnah himself. Jinnah, however, dismissed Din Muhammad's fears, reiterating his faith that Radcliffe was 'a responsible man'.[58] Although Jinnah found the evidence of the flight plan unconvincing at the time, this episode, particularly since it is reinforced by Zafrullah's independent recollection of Din Muhammad's reaction, suggests that even before the commission set to work some of its central actors were uneasy about the work ahead.

In his memoir, Mahajan asserted that he was suspicious of the judicial nature of the commission from the beginning. When he was invited to join the commission, he later recalled, 'I was not inclined to accept the invitation as it seemed to me then that this Commission was a farce and decisions would be taken by the Viceroy himself. Eventually I was persuaded to accept the invitation.'[59] Mahajan thought Radcliffe's conduct suspicious at times. For example, when Mahajan argued that India should retain Lahore, he found Radcliffe's response inappropriate: 'while we were discussing the award at the hotel [during deliberations in Simla], Lord Radcliffe had once exclaimed, "How can you have both Calcutta and Lahore? What can I give to Pakistan?" I protested against this non-judicial observation.'[60] But Mahajan dismissed allegations that Mountbatten had influenced Radcliffe, observing, 'I for one have no reason for believing that he could be so influenced.'[61] Given that these accusations generally involved Indian gains at Pakistani expense, Mahajan's denials are perhaps to be expected.

Writing from a Pakistani perspective, Munir was more sceptical than his former colleague from India. He rejected allegations that Radcliffe had been bribed – but remarked, 'I cannot say the same thing about his secretary Beaumont. This I.C.S. officer had distinct pro-Hindu leanings as whenever I went to his office, I found him poring over a large map and surrounded by Hindus. This suspicion of mine is founded on the ground that he had considerable influence on Sir Cyril and would not hesitate to mislead him.'[62] Beaumont dismissed Munir's accusations as 'a pack of lies, from beginning to end',[63] pointing out that Congress regarded him as pro-Muslim. Patel, for one, had complained about 'the selection, as Secretary of the Commission, of one of the European officers of the Punjab, who are generally associated in public mind with pro-League sympathies'.[64] Certainly there was plenty of suspicion to go around in the summer of 1947.

Beaumont asserted that there was never much question about Gurdaspur's fate, rejecting Munir's allegation that Mountbatten dictated the award of Gurdaspur to India. Beaumont and Munir agree on one point; both believe that Mountbatten influenced Radcliffe's decision in the area of Ferozepur. Munir recalled that when he discussed the Muslim League case with Radcliffe, Radcliffe indicated that there was no need to address the question of Ferozepur District: 'Sir Cyril asked me to leave [alone] the case of the Ferozepur tehsils and the Firozepur Head Works because he said that these tracts of which he gave me a full description must go to Pakistan.'[65] Munir was convinced that the subsequent award of Ferozepur to India was due to Mountbatten's influence. Beaumont agreed.

Beaumont believed that Mountbatten persuaded Radcliffe to alter the boundary line at a lunch held at Ismay's house, around 9 or 10 August (he was not certain of the date), from which he was 'deftly excluded'. On the previous evening, he wrote,

> towards midnight, while Radcliffe was working, V. P. Menon, the k[e] y figure after Nehru in Indian Politics at the time[,] appeared at the outside door, was let in by the Police guard on duty, and asked me if he could see Radcliffe. This was of course highly irregular. Radcliffe was supposed to be isolated from all outside contacts. He and he alone was responsible for the course of the line. I told Menon politely, but firmly, that he could not see Radcliffe. Menon then said that Mountbatten had sent him. I told him less politely that it made no difference. He departed with good grace. I think he anticipated the rebuff. He was a very able and perceptive person. But he had the Hindu axe to grind. The next morning, at breakfast, I told Radcliffe what had happened. He made no comment. Later that morning Radcliffe told me that he had been invited to lunch by Lord Ismay, Mountbatten's Chief of Staff, but he had been asked by Ismay not to bring me with him – the pretext being that there would not be enough room at the table for the extra guest. Having lived for six

months in the house occupied by Ismay, I knew this to be untrue. But my suspicions were not aroused as they should have been. I was leaving India the next week and welcomed the chance to get on with my own affairs. This was the first time, however, that Radcliffe and I had been separated at any sort of function.[66]

Although Beaumont had no first-hand knowledge of what went on at this meeting, he recalled that 'that evening the Punjab line was changed'. He believed that Mountbatten persuaded Radcliffe of the importance of the adverse irrigation effects for Bikaner state if Ferozepur went to Pakistan, as well as the possibility of civil war. He concluded that Radcliffe yielded 'to what he thought was overwhelming political expediency' and 'allowed himself to be overborne'.[67] Beaumont was convinced that Mountbatten guided the assignment of Ferozepur to India.

There is other circumstantial evidence to support Beaumont's position. At the time that Beaumont gave Abell the information on which the sketch map was based, he believed that this line was final.[68] Abell's note reflected this understanding, for he wrote, 'there will not be any great changes from this boundary'.[69] Abell went further in a note to Mountbatten on the same day, stating that Radcliffe 'has, in fact, already dictated his award'.[70] And at Mountbatten's staff meeting on 9 August, the minutes record, 'it was stated that Sir Cyril Radcliffe would be ready by that evening to announce the award of the Punjab Boundary Commission'.[71] Mountbatten's press secretary recorded in his journal that 'it is rumoured that Radcliffe will be ready by this evening to hand over the Award of the Punjab Boundary Commission to the Viceroy'.[72] More revealingly, John Christie, the viceroy's deputy private secretary, noted in his diary, 'George [Abell] tells me H.E. is in a tired flap, & is having to be strenuously dissuaded from asking Radcliffe to alter his award.'[73] In short, the documentary evidence depicts the boundary award as largely complete by 8 or 9 August; it also suggests that Mountbatten was familiar with the award's contents at this time. Of course, the award did not officially exist until Radcliffe submitted it to Mountbatten, and there is no account that he submitted anything to Mountbatten until 13 August. But Radcliffe and his staff sent numerous signals that their work was very nearly finished.

When, on 9 August, Nehru forwarded irrigation engineer Khosla's letter to Mountbatten, the letter argued that the Ferozepur salient must be awarded to India. It outlined strategic and irrigation-related reasons why it would be dangerous to allot it to Pakistan.[74] Mountbatten replied to Nehru the next day, 'I hope you will agree that it is most important that I should not do anything to prejudice the independence of the Boundary Commission, and that, therefore, it would be wrong for me even to forward any memorandum, especially at this stage.'[75] However, given the fact that Mountbatten spoke to Radcliffe about his award sometime on 9 or 10 August (that is, after Abell sent the sketch map but before the dispatch of the 'eliminate salient' message), it seems likely that Khosla's letter provided ammunition for Mountbatten's argument that Ferozepur should go to India.

Another important piece of evidence was provided in 1978 by Kanwar Sain, former chief irrigation engineer for the princely state of Bikaner, south of Punjab. On 10 August 1947, Sain recalled, he received an urgent letter telling him that key sections of Ferozepur were likely to go to Pakistan. The information came from the Chief Irrigation Engineer of Punjab; he had learned from the District Commissioner of Ferozepur that Governor Jenkins had ordered the establishment of a new headquarters for Ferozepur District outside the *tehsils* of Ferozepur, Zira and Fazilka, because those three *tehsils* were likely to be awarded to Pakistan.[76] Sain's recollection is consistent with the contents of the sketch map and with Jenkins's intention in requesting advance information, which was to facilitate administration arrangements.

Ferozepur District and Bikaner state were closely linked, because Bikaner relied upon the canal waters controlled by the Ferozepur *tehsil* headworks. Sain told the Maharajah of Bikaner that Ferozepur was likely to go to Pakistan, and the maharajah cabled Mountbatten to protest. This cable has not survived, but according to Sain it ran as follows:

> It is strongly rumoured that Boundary Commission is likely to award Ferozepur Tehsil to Western Punjab. This Tehsil contains Headworks of Bikaner Gang Canal and under existing agreement State is entitled to receive for its perennial canal specified amount of water. Fear greatly that administration and regulation of this water exclusively by Western Punjab may gravely prejudice interest of Bikaner State as its economic life is to very large extent dependent on water supply from Gang Canal. Have every confidence that your Excellency in finally arriving at decision on award of Boundary Commission will be good enough to safeguard interests of Bikaner State.[77]

Sain and the Prime Minister of Bikaner were dispatched to New Delhi posthaste in hopes of laying their case before Mountbatten. Once there, they had to argue their way past George Abell, who was obviously reluctant to allow them to see the viceroy, but after some difficulty, Sain writes, they arranged a brief meeting for the morning of 11 August.

The interview began poorly. When the Bikaner Prime Minister raised the subject of the Ferozepur headworks, Mountbatten 'shouted at him. "The Viceroy had nothing to do with the Radcliffe Commission. That Commission has been appointed by His Majesty's Government. Radcliffe is not to report to me."[78] In desperation, Sain delivered a threat from the maharajah: if the Ferozepur headworks went to Pakistan, Bikaner state would have no option but to follow. Sain knew that the viceroy had a personal interest in the future of the princely states and had devoted a great deal of energy, in the final weeks before independence, to securing their future. He records, 'As I said this, I could see a change in the colour of the face of Lord Mountbatten. He said nothing and we left His Excellency's room.'[79] Arguing that this conversation did indeed convince Mountbatten to persuade Radcliffe to change the line, Sain cites Judge Munir's statement that Radcliffe changed the Ferozepur line at the last minute – in consultation, Munir implies, with Mountbatten – as proof.[80] Mountbatten's papers contain no mention of this interview with Sain, but Mountbatten's official biographer, Philip Ziegler, believes Sain's account and is convinced by the evidence for a last-minute effort to change Radcliffe's mind. He writes, 'I must now say that I am satisfied that the Viceroy did speak to Radcliffe before the partition line was finalized and urged him to bear certain considerations in mind when reaching his conclusions.'[81] The evidence undermines Mountbatten's portrayal of himself as entirely aloof from the boundary-making process.

As the decisive piece of evidence in this matter, Ziegler cites an April 1948 letter from Mountbatten to Ismay. He notes, 'the letter ended with an injunction to Ismay to burn it after reading – as usual a guarantee that the recipient will file it with particular care'. In this letter, Mountbatten mentioned a meeting that he and Ismay had with Radcliffe. During this discussion, Radcliffe 'had spoken of the difficulties he was encountering in sorting out certain irrigation issues, Ferozepur being a particularly knotty problem. Mountbatten had said that, if favours were to be done to Pakistan, he hoped it would be in Bengal rather than the Punjab, since there was no Sikh problem in Bengal.'[82] Ziegler interprets this letter to mean that Mountbatten advised that concessions to India in Punjab could be balanced by concessions to Pakistan in Bengal.[83]

Beaumont thought that the irrigation system, particularly as it related to Bikaner, played a central role in Mountbatten's attempts to persuade Radcliffe to change his line in Ferozepur. He noted that Bikaner state depended heavily on waters from Ferozepur for its survival and surmised that the Maharajah of Bikaner bluffed Mountbatten into thinking he might join Pakistan if Ferozepur went to the west. Beaumont concluded, 'I think it's what caused Mountbatten to intervene, you see. I think what he would have said is that it's in the interests both of India and Pakistan – otherwise there may well be a civil war – and in the interests of Her [*sic*] Majesty's Government to do it this way. And therefore that Radcliffe having heard that argument put to him, on this one occasion did change the line. I think that was the pressure applied [to Radcliffe].' In short, he speculated, Bikaner 'used the threat of joining Pakistan as a lever to get the line changed, to get the headworks into Indian hands'.[84] Although there is no direct evidence on this point, Beaumont's scenario is plausible.

Despite his conviction that Mountbatten persuaded Radcliffe to change the line in Ferozepur, Beaumont was adamant that no change involving Gurdaspur was made. He asserted that the division of Lahore and Amritsar, which Radcliffe decided early on, required that part of Gurdaspur go to India. He gave no credence to suggestions that the British Government dictated the line before Radcliffe flew to India: 'Radcliffe would not have been ordered in London to do any such thing. He was far too independent-minded. The Pakistan Government, of course, were affronted [that] a Muslim-majority *tehsil* had gone to India, but as I said there is an explanation for that.'[85] Based on his knowledge of Pathankot, where he had served in 1937–38, Beaumont denied that a strategic land connection linked India and Kashmir in 1947. He pointed out that the only road leading to Kashmir was 'a track. Nothing that would take tanks or heavy vehicles. As you know, all the forces from India and Patiala went by air' when India and Pakistan began their battle over Kashmir.[86] Even Munir conceded that 'it was clear to both Mr Din Mohammed and myself from the very beginning of the discussions with Mr Radcliffe that Gurdaspur was going to India'.[87] The allegations of a change involving Gurdaspur, therefore, lack any foundation.

As for Mountbatten himself, given his strenuous denials of any participation in the boundary-making process, one might expect that he would offer no comment on the reasoning behind the award. This was not the case. In a series of interviews given in the early 1970s, Mountbatten spoke at length about his experience in India, including his contact with Radcliffe. He said, 'The only instruction he had from me was the date' but added only moments later, 'I told him he was not to take defence considerations under judgement in making the award.' He continued, 'In my original discussion with him I said, "It's up to you, but basically I hope you're going to get the right population on the right side of the line. But the line must make some sense. It is possible for people to move in small quantities to the right side of the line, but if you make it an impossible line to work along, there'll be trouble. We need the best national boundary line you can find without doing violence to the population."'[88] This version of events is somewhat confused. What is clear, however, is that even as he asserted that he gave Radcliffe no instructions other than the submission deadline, Mountbatten made plain that he had other factors in mind and that he had discussed them with Radcliffe.

Another indication of the content of the viceroy's discussions with Radcliffe comes from H. V. Hodson. Hodson's account is particularly valuable because of his access to Mountbatten, whose recollections form the basis for the following passage. Addressing allegations of improper influence, Hodson writes,

> There was, however, one conversation, undisclosed hitherto, which might have some bearing on the point. It has been mentioned above because its primary purpose was to discuss the timing and method of publication of the Chairman's reports. It took place in Lord Ismay's house on the Viceregal estate in New Delhi over an evening drink on or about 9th August 1947. There is no contemporary record of it and the recollections of the three participants differ. On the point now under discussion Lord Mountbatten recalled, a year or two later, remarks which neither Lord Ismay nor Lord Radcliffe could recollect having been made on that occasion. It seems fairly certain, however, that at some time – probably not in that conversation, as he supposed, but more likely soon after Radcliffe arrived in India – he did make the point to Sir Cyril that the fairness of the eastern and western awards to the Muslims and non-Muslims respectively should be judged as a whole, so that disgruntlement in one area might be offset by satisfaction in another.[89]

Hodson is probably correct in speculating that Mountbatten suggested balancing the awards at an earlier date. In fact, the record shows that Mountbatten openly advocated such an approach in a 26 June meeting of the Partition Committee, when he noted the desirability of Radcliffe chairing both the Punjab and Bengal commissions: 'The advantage of such a course would be that Sir Cyril Radcliffe would be enabled to adjust any slight loss one State might have to suffer in one particular area by compensating it in another and generally to see that justice was done uniformly to all claims.'[90] If, as seems likely, Mountbatten made this suggestion to Radcliffe as well, it would account for Radcliffe's question to Mahajan, 'How can you have both Calcutta and Lahore?', which implied that it would be unfair for India to have both of these important cities.[91]

On 19 March 1948, Mountbatten wrote to Jenkins to say that he had no knowledge of any changes made to the boundary line 'between 8th and 13th August. But the assumpt[io]n that can be drawn is that the line indicated in the documents attached to Abell's letter [the sketch map and its accompanying description] was only a tentative one and that it was amended subsequently to "balance" the Bengal Boundary line.'[92] It is necessary to read this passage along with Hodson's account in order to understand why Mountbatten should make this somewhat peculiar assumption about 'balance'.

Hodson went on to say that he had Radcliffe's assurance that he ignored Mountbatten's balance suggestion in making his award.[93] This assertion is not, however, incompatible with the possibility that Radcliffe did take into account other arguments advanced by Mountbatten, such as the possibility of severe irrigation problems and even civil war. Furthermore, regardless of when the notion of 'balance' was raised, Mountbatten's recollection of an 'evening drink on or about 9th August 1947' in Ismay's house reinforces Beaumont's contentions.

At the time of my interviews with him, the late Christopher Beaumont was the best positioned of any participant still alive to offer an informed judgement on these events. His opinion that Mountbatten prevailed upon Radcliffe to change his mind in the last few days is most likely correct. However, there are larger questions here, questions that are rarely asked. Was it inappropriate for Radcliffe and/or Mountbatten to alter their thinking on the award? Patrick French points out that Radcliffe 'took advice, as might be expected, from his client'.[94] As Alastair Lamb observes, 'Radcliffe was a barrister following a brief.'[95] In conclusion, the existing evidence indicates that Mountbatten may well have had a hand in the final award.[96] But such allegations miss the point profoundly; assertions that such behaviour was improper are founded on the assumption that partition was an objective, apolitical process, when in reality it was just the opposite.

In the days following partition, the geographical reality of the Radcliffe line remained as murky as the political circumstances behind it. Although the use of the national map as a logo is a key element of modern nationalism, congratulatory advertisements taken out in newspapers in the days immediately following independence did not – indeed, could not – employ maps of independent India or Pakistan as a means of rallying patriotism.[97] No one knew what a national map for India or Pakistan might look like, because of Mountbatten's decision to delay the announcement of the borders of the new states. The creators of these celebratory advertisements improvised by including maps of all of British India, or, occasionally, a map of the subcontinent that simply left north India conveniently off the map.[98] In other words, the lines that Radcliffe drew did not simply reflect pre-existing national limits – limits that any informed observer would be able to draw – but in fact shaped a new territorial reality. Not only did partition create an international boundary where none had existed previously, but it also made the perceived gulf between Muslims, Hindus and Sikhs a much starker and more violently enforced division than it had ever been before.

Notes

1 *TP* XII p. 611.
2 *TP* XII p. 674 fn. 2.
3 IOR Mss Eur A 221, pp. 228–9. The description was from Mosley, p. 229, citing Alan Campbell-Johnson, *Mission with Mountbatten* (New York: Atheneum, 1985), p. 152.
4 Liddell Hart Centre for Military Archives (hereafter LHA), King's College London, Ismay Papers, 3/7/66/3g, personal note on 'The Indian situation', 5 October 1947.
5 Michel, p. 192.
6 *TP* XII p. 736.
7 For a discussion of the role of rumour, see Gyan Pandey, *Remembering Partition: Violence, Nationalism and History in India* (Cambridge: Cambridge University Press, 2001), pp. 69–74.
8 Abbott, letter to Jenkins, n.d. [December 1967?], IOR Mss Eur D 807/3, p. 158.
9 Tan Tai Yong, '"Sir Cyril Goes to India": Partition, boundary-making and disruptions in the Punjab', *International Journal of Punjab Studies* 4:1 (1997), p. 15.
10 Lamb, *Incomplete Partition*, pp. 235–7.
11 Stanley Wolpert, *Shameful Flight: The Last Years of the British Empire in India* (Oxford: Oxford University Press, 2006), p. 167.
12 *TP* XII pp. 739–40.
13 IOR Mss Eur D 807/2, Rees Report on the Punjab Boundary Force, 15 November 1947, p. 48.
14 *Dawn* (19 August 1947), cutting in NAI 68/47–R.
15 *TP* XII p. 611.
16 Z. H. Zaidi et al., eds, *Jinnah Papers*, vol. V (Islamabad: Quaid-i-Azam Papers Project: 2000), p. 175.
17 *Pakistan Times* (4 September 1947), p. 3, col. 2.
18 Khursheed Kamal Aziz, *The Murder of History: A Critique of History Textbooks Used in Pakistan* (Lahore: Vanguard, 1993), p. 74.
19 *TP* XII p. 236.
20 *TP* XII p. 64.
21 *TP* XII p. 236.
22 NAI, MEA, File No. 3–8/47 OSV, notes 7.
23 NAI, MEA, File No. 3–8/47 OSV, notes 8–9.
24 NAI, MEA, File No. 3–8/47 OSV, notes 7.
25 NAI, MEA, File No. 3–8/47 OSV, correspondence 6. As for Bengal, Pakistan and India agreed to set up another boundary tribunal, headed by the Swedish jurist Algot Bagge, to clarify select portions of the line. Bagge issued his award on February 1950. Chatterji, 'Fashioning', p. 220.
26 IOR/L/P&J/10/119, p. 166.
27 IOR/L/P&J/10/119, p. 92.
28 IOR/L/P&J/10/119, p. 78.
29 Heward, p. 46.
30 Beaumont, personal interview, 29 February 2000.
31 Beaumont, personal interview, 8 February 2000.
32 Hodson, p. 347. Mountbatten was intimately involved in Hodson's book, which Hodson wrote at the urging of Ismay, V. P. Menon (another close aide) and Mountbatten himself (see LHA, Ismay Papers, 1/24). Hodson reports in his introduction, 'First and foremost of my thanks, therefore, are offered to Admiral of the Fleet Earl Mountbatten of Burma, who entrusted to me all the papers that he brought back from India, encouraged me, was patient with me, talked with me in complete frankness, answering my questions or volunteering recollections, and finally read my manuscript and made many valuable comments, yet without attempting to alter my conclusions or to press any amendment, save on verifiable fact' (Hodson, p. xxxviii).
33 *TP* XII p. 732.

34   It seems most unlikely, however, that Mountbatten attended a 22 July meeting of the Punjab boundary commission (as stated by Ian Scott, cited in French, p. 322), as his presence at this public meeting would certainly have been noted and reported in the press. It is true that on 20 July Mountbatten was present at a meeting of the Punjab Partition Committee, an entirely separate entity that guided the overall partition process for Punjab province.

35   *TP* XII p. 93.

36   *TP* XII p. 64.

37   *TP* XII p. 304.

38   *TP* XII p. 158.

39   *TP* XII p. 162. This note is undated but was considered by the Partition Council on 17 July.

40   *TP* XII pp. 290–1 and 305.

41   *TP* XII p. 179.

42   *TP* XII p. 226.

43   *TP* XII p. 279.

44   Beaumont, personal interview, 8 February 2000.

45   Roger Ellis, 'Abell, Sir George Edmond Brackenbury (1904–1989)', rev., *Oxford Dictionary of National Biography* (Oxford: Oxford University Press, 2004), www.oxforddnb.com/view/article/39894, accessed 29 February 2008.

46   *TP* XII pp. 483–4.

47   *TP* XII p. 484.

48   *TP* XII p. 484.

49   *TP* XII p. 484 n. 6.

50   *TP* XII p. 663.

51   See for example the 8 July note from C. P. Scott, Mountbatten's assistant private secretary, on the undesirability of entertaining representations about the boundaries (*TP* XII p. 6).

52   *TP* XII pp. 647–8.

53   Donald C. Thyer, 'The partition of India – A personal account', *Royal Engineers Journal* 111 (December 1997), p. 263.

54   Din Muhammad, 'Din Muhammad on Radcliffe's boundary award in the Punjab', in *Pakistan Resolution to Pakistan 1940–1947: A Selection of Documents Presenting the Case for Pakistan*, ed. Latif Ahmed Sherwani (Karachi: National Publishing House, 1969), p. 276.

55   Din Muhammad, p. 278.

56   Din Muhammad, p. 279.

57   Batalvi, p. 149.

58   Batalvi, p. 149.

59   Mehr Chand Mahajan, pp. 113–14.

60   Mehr Chand Mahajan, pp. 115–16.

61   Mehr Chand Mahajan, p. 115.

62   Muhammad Munir, *Highways and Bye-Ways of Life* (Lahore: Law Publishing Company, n.d. [1978]), p. 62.

63   Beaumont, personal interview, 8 February 2000.

64   *TP* XII p. 692.

65   Munir, *Highways and Bye-ways of Life*, p. 60.

66   Beaumont, 'The partition of India', pp. 3–4.

67   Beaumont, personal interviews, 8 and 29 February 2000; Simon Scott Plummer, 'How Mountbatten bent the rules and the Indian border', *Daily Telegraph* (24 February 1992), p. 10.

68   Beaumont, personal interview, 29 February 2000.

69   *TP* XII p. 579.

70   *TP* XII p. 580.

71   *TP* XII p. 611.

72   Campbell-Johnson, p. 151.

73   *TP* XII p. 611 fn. 3.

74 *TP* XII pp. 619–20.
75 *TP* XII p. 639.
76 Kanwar Sain, *Reminiscences of an Engineer* (New Delhi: Young Asia Publications, 1978), p. 117.
77 Sain, p. 119.
78 Sain, p. 121.
79 Sain, p. 122.
80 Sain, pp. 122–3.
81 Philip Ziegler, *Mountbatten Revisited* (Austin, TX: Harry Ransom Humanities Research Center, The University of Texas at Austin, 1995), p. 16.
82 LHA, Ismay Papers, 3/7/24a–d, Mountbatten letter to Ismay, 2 April 1948.
83 Ziegler, *Revisited*, p. 17.
84 Beaumont, personal interview, 8 February 2000.
85 Beaumont, personal interview, 8 February 2000.
86 Beaumont, personal interview, 8 February 2000.
87 'Munir was told Ferozepur, Fazilka will go to Pakistan?' *Tribune* (26 April 1960), reprinted in Sain, p. 86.
88 Collins and Lapierre, *Mountbatten and Partition*, pp. 102–3.
89 Hodson, p. 354. Hodson stood by this account, even after hearing Beaumont's version, on the grounds that 'no one has shown what pressure [Mountbatten] could exert' on Radcliffe (Hodson, pp. xxxv–xxxvi).
90 *TP* XI p. 656.
91 Mehr Chand Mahajan, p. 115.
92 IOR/L/P&J/10/119, pp. 102–3.
93 Hodson, p. 355.
94 French, p. 322.
95 Cited in French, p. 322.
96 Roberts, pp. 93–101.
97 Benedict Anderson, *Imagined Communities: Reflections on the Origin and Spread of Nationalism*, rev. ed. (London: Verso, 1991), p. 175.
98 For a 'logoized' version with all of South Asia, see Bata Footwear, advertisement, *Times of India* (15 August 1947), p. 4. For examples with north India unclear or left off the map, see Union Life Assurance, advertisement, *Times of India* (Bombay) (15 August 1947), p. 3; Godrej, advertisement, *Times of India*, Supplement (15 August 1947), p. 9.

CHAPTER SIX

'The stories they carried': the aftermath

Violence had been brewing in Punjab throughout 1946. In August, Governor Jenkins had warned Viceroy Wavell, 'We have here the material for a vast communal upheaval.'[1] The winter was relatively quiet, but riots began again in March 1947, shortly after the initial British Government announcement that it would hand over power in June 1948. Rawalpindi, in western Punjab, bore the brunt of the March killing, and its Sikh community was particularly hard-hit. The violence tapered off after about three weeks, although sporadic outbursts continued in April and June.[2] British reports on Punjabi casualties up to 2 August show about 4600 killed and 2600 seriously injured.[3] These numbers, though large in their own right, would soon seem small in comparison with the carnage of partition.

A few days before independence, on 9 August, a special train carrying Pakistan Government employees and their families from Delhi to Karachi was derailed by a mine laid under the tracks. Although the human damage from this attack was limited to about ten people injured and two killed by the force of the derailment itself, worse was to come. This was also the day that rumours first leaked out that Radcliffe intended to award a large section of Ferozepur to Pakistan. Ferozepur had a significant Sikh population, and the rumours that it was going to Pakistan likely convinced Sikh radicals, who had been making military preparations for the possibility of an unfavourable boundary decision, that the worst had arrived.

In the following days, violence spread with further attacks on trains, train stations, minority neighbourhoods and even entire villages.[4] In these attacks, which spread quickly from Lahore and Amritsar to adjoining districts, train stoppages or derailments were followed up by brutal attacks on passengers. Beginning in September, this pattern spread to more rural areas of Punjab. Also in September, the rail authorities began scheduling Refugee Specials, trains that usually carried all

Muslims or all Hindus and Sikhs. Normal train traffic was drastically reduced, and, as a result, nearly every train headed east across the border was packed with Hindu and Sikh refugees, while every train moving west carried Muslims – ideal targets for communal violence.[5] This period saw particularly ghastly assaults, some reportedly killing up to 1500 people on a single train.[6] One of the most potent images in the iconography of partition is a train slowly rolling into an Indian or Pakistani station, having just crossed the border; when it stops, no one emerges but the engineer, and the authorities find that the train is filled with corpses. By the third week of October, efforts to guard refugee trains more effectively and to handle their dispatch with greater secrecy reduced the violence. Refugees were able to move more safely.[7]

The image of the train filled with dead refugees is evoked in part because many discussions of partition violence have centred on attempts to lay blame on one side or the other. The existing records, such as they are, do not allow historians to draw conclusions about which side was *most* responsible or committed the *worst* atrocities, but there is clearly plenty of blame to go around. Many Hindus, Muslims and Sikhs joined in the killing, and many more members of all three communities were among the victims.

Overall, the scale of killing in Punjab was extremely large. Tallies of partition casualties are controversial and vary widely; estimates of partition deaths throughout India and Pakistan range from 180,000 to 2 million, with most scholars settling on a number between 500,000 and 1 million.[8] The migrants moving across the new borders in Punjab and Bengal probably numbered between 10 and 12 million, but again some estimates range much higher, up to 17 million.[9] In addition, tens of thousands of girls and women were raped and/or abducted.[10]

A number of factors contributed to the carnage. One of the most important, as noted above, was the boundary award, specifically the timing of its announcement and rumours about its content. In Punjab, casualty rates rose just after independence and during the following two months.[11] A second important condition was the demographic mix, particularly in the major cities of central Punjab, where many Hindus, Muslims and Sikhs lived in intermingled communities. The groups that suddenly became minorities on 15 August were therefore extremely vulnerable to militant elements in the majority community. The third central factor was the militaristic nature of contemporary Punjabi society. In the months before partition, Muslim, Sikh and Hindu groups had all built up private armies.[12] Those groups included soldiers recently demobilized from the Indian Army who were well trained and had World War II combat experience.

In the violence of August and September, marauders used both sophisticated military arms and locally produced weapons. They sometimes applied military tactics to train attacks, with covering fire from light machineguns and rifles protecting raiders who rushed the trains using spears and knives.[13] One of the few historians to offer an in-depth analysis of partition violence writes,

> 'country-made weapons, often forged from farm tools ... hatchets, battle axes of all shapes and sizes, and spears', knives and *lathis* [wooden batons], were supplemented with modern weapons ... The attacking gangs in Punjab were often armed with 'efficient hand grenades', '.303 rifles', 'shotguns', 'twelve bore guns', 'revolvers', as well as the 'most modern tommy gun and light machine-gun' ... While the country-made implements contributed to the savage nature of the killings, the modern weapons made the killings efficient and quick. Both kinds had their uses depending upon the situation the killers found themselves in.[14]

The government created a Punjab Boundary Force (PBF) to maintain law and order, but, undermanned and confronted by 'accurate sniping, bombing, and rifle and automatic fire', it was ineffective.[15]

The authoritative history of the Punjab Boundary Force notes that it numbered a mere 23,000 men at its strongest.[16] Given the fact that it was responsible for law and order in twelve districts, it could allot, on average, only four men to every three villages.[17] This weakness meant that the PBF could not protect refugees effectively. In one case, one officer and twenty men escorted a refugee column estimated at 10,000 people.[18] The PBF was also a communally divided group: its ranks included some 40 per cent Hindus, 35 per cent Muslims, 20 per cent Gurkhas and 'non-caste Hindus', as well as 5–10 per cent Sikhs.[19]

The boundaries of princely states posed another problem for the Force. The PBF's orders authorized commanders to pursue raiders across state lines. Being allowed the leeway of hot pursuit, however, did not solve other problems facing the PBF, including the fact that raiders could prepare their raids in comparative ease within state lines or simply carry out train attacks inside the princely states themselves.[20]

Confronted by insurmountable obstacles, both external and internal, the Force's morale crumbled. It was disbanded on 1 September, having been active for exactly one month.[21] The Governor of Pakistani Punjab, for one, regarded the deployment of the PBF as fundamentally misguided. As it was demobilized, Francis Mudie wrote apologetically to Rees: 'the setting up of your force was constitutionally and politically wrong. The decision to create the force was however taken at a high level and I can express my opinion only in private.'[22] Even at the time, some observers recognized the PBF as a deeply flawed effort to enforce order, one that British officials had assembled with more attention to appearances than to effectiveness.

The PBF may have been ineffective, but on a smaller scale, countless people were saved by the bravery of individuals who defied their co-religionists and sheltered, supplied or otherwise protected their neighbours. Oral histories of partition from both sides of the border invariably include stories of Muslims aiding Hindus and Sikhs, and Hindus and Sikhs protecting Muslims.[23] In addition, some members of other groups, such as Parsis and Christians, assisted refugees of all religions. One Delhi resident recalls stories told by her Christian parents, who remembered sheltering Muslims at one end of their house and Hindus at the other.[24] People like these, who at great personal risk aided the victims of partition, are the real heroes of this sad story.

By late October, the violence was dissipating relatively quickly, probably because most minorities had already fled. In other words, the fire had run out of fuel, because the ethnic cleansing campaigns on both sides of the new border had been remarkably effective. In 1950, Indian Punjab had a Muslim population of just over 1 per cent; Pakistani Punjab had a Hindu and Sikh population of less than 1 per cent.[25] The thoroughness of the ethnic cleansing was rooted in extensive preparations, both for violence and for evacuation, made by groups on both sides. In other words, a number of well-ordered organizations were operating in Punjab in the summer and autumn of 1947; unfortunately, most of them were focused on perpetrating violence rather than preventing it.

Sikh *jathas* were not the only paramilitary groups active in Punjab. Both the Muslim League National Guard (MLNG) and the Hindu nationalist Rashtriya Swayamsevak Sangh (RSS) had assembled private armies in the months preceding partition.[26] These paramilitary groups consisted, as noted above, of demobilized soldiers fresh from the battlefields of World War II. There are conflicting reports on the preparations carried out by each group, and it remains difficult to find objective appraisals of their role in the violence.[27] As early as 1946, however, Punjabi militarization had been on the rise. A British aide with the Cabinet Mission heard reports that the Muslim League was preparing for violent resistance: 'In the Punjab they are busy contacting and training demobilized soldiers and are even training women to use arms. I am told that Jinnah is getting letters from Muslim soldiers still in the Army, saying that they will fight for him.'[28] Aiyar, author of the most objective available study, points to the role of Sikh *jathas* as decisive, although she notes that all sides formed their own militias:

The growing fear of civil war over the last year before independence had led to the build up of private armies. While the Muslim League mobilized Muslim public opinion through the Muslim League National Guards (MLNG), the Hindu Mahasabha and its militant front, the Rashtriya Swayamsevak Sangh (RSS) sought to rally Hindu popular opinion. Both the MLNG and the RSS formed their own armies which were constantly being expanded and trained.[29]

In a contemporary appraisal, the PBF commander, Pete Rees, reported that the Sikhs had the upper hand, at least initially: 'In the rural areas, the Sikh jathas ... in the East Punjab were the first to take the field. Later, the Muslims started retaliation. But during the month of August, it was evident to the P.B.F. that, as opposed to their enemies, the Sikhs were thoroughly organized and prepared for such events as took place.'[30] It is certainly true that Sikh leaders made clear their displeasure with any boundary proposal that did not include the canal colonies in India, as well as their plans for resistance, in public statements and in conversations with officials such as Jenkins.[31] When the British failed to answer these preliminary probes of their determination convincingly, Sikh militants may have taken this inaction as a signal that the British would not act forcefully to stop them if they took matters into their own hands.

When the violence came, it prompted mass migration in both directions. Mountbatten's press secretary, Alan Campbell-Johnson, accompanied the viceroy on a trip taken with Nehru and Patel to view the mass migration in the border areas. In the viceroy's small plane, they flew westward from Delhi across the boundary into Pakistan, coming down to about 200 feet at key points, then turned back towards India. Campbell-Johnson's recollections are worth quoting at length, for they provide a vivid record of the scale of human misery caused by partition:

> We struck the first great caravanserai between Ferozepur and Balloki Head, and pursued it far across the Ravi. We flew, in fact, for over fifty miles against this stream of refugees without reaching its source. Every now and then the density of bullock-carts and families on foot keeping to the thin life-line of the road would tail away, only to fill out again in close columns without end.
>
> At Balloki Head, the actual boundary, the refugees waiting to cross the bridge overflowed and took on the appearance of a squatters' township. Here they had been brought to a standstill, but the general movement was very slow, and we could see men on horseback passing up and down who seemed to be giving some coherence, if not command, to the closely packed mass. At the roadside some families were flanked by their cattle, in many cases their only worldly asset, but few, if any, would be able to

pass their livestock across the bridge. Already the flow of human traffic across it was beyond any conceivable capacity for which it had been built.

As we flew back into India we came down low over the northernmost of the Moslem refugee convoys making its slow and painful way along the main Lyallpur-Lahore road. Their exodus brought them across the Beas River, and involved an elaborate detour to save them from passing through Amritsar. We estimated that it took us just over a quarter of an hour to fly from one end to the other of this particular column at a flying speed of about a hundred and eighty miles per hour. This column therefore must have been at least forty-five miles long.[32]

Campbell-Johnson concluded, 'Even our brief bird's-eye view must have revealed nearly half a million refugees on the roads. At one point during our flight Sikh and Moslem refugees were moving almost side by side in opposite directions. There was no sign of clash. As though impelled by some deeper instinct, they pushed forward obsessed only with the objective beyond the boundary.'[33] This view offers stunning testimony to the scale of the migration. However, the words Campbell-Johnson chooses to depict the crowds are also striking. From his vantage point in the skies, Campbell-Johnson describes these people as 'impelled by some deeper instinct', moving in herds like animals, with their livestock at their sides. This episode displays the changes wrought by partition – but also reveals how, in a way, little had changed. The British still occupied an almost god-like position,[34] but now the Indian leaders, sitting in the same aeroplane, had a similar vantage point. All, however, were still looking down on India's poorest and most miserable people, who had borne the brunt of partition. What was the experience of the people within these teeming masses, or of those who stayed where they were? How did the new boundary affect their lives?

The boundary as source of confusion, trigger for violence, promised land

For refugees fleeing across Punjab in the months after partition, the boundary represented safety. However, its announcement, and even, as we have seen, earlier rumours about its location, functioned as a trigger for the escalation of partition violence. And in the first few days after independence, the main characteristic of the boundary was confusion. Until the 17 August announcement, few people in Punjab knew exactly where the boundary line had fallen. Uncertainties remained even after the boundary announcement about which villages fell in which state, as communications problems limited public understanding of the new line. Many people heard about the award over the radio.[35] Those who read the textual descriptions or saw the small-scale maps that were printed in newspapers would not necessarily have been able to tell which border localities went where without a good understanding of the administrative boundaries in those areas.[36]

For those on the move, however, the boundary was defined in purely practical terms: they knew they were on the other side of the border when they were safe. Crossing the line meant entering a zone of protection – even if that protection, provided by the crumbling PBF and by state apparatuses struggling under the refugee influx, was not always reliable. The boundary announcement came late, but not, for most, too late. For those who crossed before the award's announcement, however, as well as those who did not know the exact location of the boundary line, the border was an uncertain zone rather than a fixed line. These early refugees could not know exactly where one country ended and the other began; only when they reached a place of relative safety, such as Lahore or Amritsar, could they be confident that they had crossed the line.

Many refugees had not yet grasped the enormity of the change that had come upon them. The high politics of the end of empire meant little until it impinged directly on their lives; unfortunately, that impact often came violently. In late 1948, a prominent Indian social worker described her conversations with bewildered refugees in Pakistan: '"Bibi," they asked, "how did all this happen? And why? How are we different from you? Those who came to attack us told us that we were Muslims, that Pakistan was where Muslims belonged and that we had to go away. But Bibi, why, we asked them? We had neither heard of Pakistan nor knew what it meant. Who likes to leave his 'vatan' [native land]?"'[37] For these refugees, the border between India and Pakistan meant little more than another patch of ground to be crossed in their reluctant flight.

This boundary was still poorly marked and posed no barrier to those who wished to cross. (The region's overloaded transportation facilities, as Campbell-Johnson's account shows, were another matter.) Millions of refugees flowed across the line in the first months of independence. This is not to say that they found their travels easy – far from it – but the boundary itself did not impede their movement. Once they had crossed, however, refugees wanted the boundary to close behind them, protecting them from the dangers they had escaped. Government of India situation reports from the border area show persistent public complaints about border defence.[38]

In addition to marking the transition between zones of danger and zones of safety, the boundary also played a more sinister role. Its announcement exacerbated the violence that had already roiled the Punjab throughout early August. As Aiyar notes, 'the timing of the violence – which peaked around 13 to 19 August – coincided with two major events: the advent of independence and the announcement of the Boundary Award on 16 August'.[39] Even before the division, Britons and South Asians alike assumed that the boundary award would provoke trouble. Governor Jenkins, who was well placed to evaluate the situation, had foreseen difficulties when he bluntly cabled on 6 July, 'I expect trouble when [the] Boundary Commission reports.'[40] Although these predictions do not in themselves prove that the boundary was a contributing factor in the violence, they indicate the role it played in contemporary thinking.

Rumour and reaction were also important factors in the Punjab violence. Muslims, Hindus and Sikhs sought revenge for real or rumoured outrages perpetrated across the border by inflicting their own, equivalent, atrocities. Quoting Rees's final report, which states that 'any area they [refugees] traversed or settled in was apt to be disturbed and stirred up to great communal bitterness', the authoritative appraisal of the PBF concludes, 'the number of refugees was not so important as the stories they carried'.[41] The role of rumour in the spread of mass violence offers a fruitful avenue of work for historians.[42]

Popular outrage at partition violence was directed not only against the 'enemy', but also against the country's leaders. On the eve of independence, the Hindu nationalist newspaper *The Organiser* published a front-page illustration of 'Mother India, the map of the country, with a woman lying on it, one limb cut off and severed, with Nehru holding the bloody knife responsible for doing the severing'.[43] This example demonstrates the symbolic power of maps, used here to identify women with the Indian nation, both of whom are portrayed as violently mutilated. However, maps were also being used at this time for brutally practical purposes.

The Surveyor General of India during partition, Brigadier-General G. F. Heaney, recalled one suspicious instance involving a request for maps of Punjab. In October 1947, shortly after rumours of further Sikh unrest had reached Heaney's ears, a young Sikh officer came to him with a request for a large number of maps. Heaney wrote, 'I glanced at the list and it was at once apparent to me that it included most of the Punjab, now part of Pakistan, in addition to much of northern India and the adjoining part of the UP [United Provinces, now Uttar Pradesh].' The request struck him as peculiar, so Heaney asked the officer to come back the next morning and immediately contacted his superiors in government. They advised him to release only a single copy of each map requested. The next morning, when the officer returned, Heaney gave him one copy of each map but noted that 'this did not satisfy him'. Later, Heaney heard from a colleague responsible for issuing maps from the Survey of India's Delhi stocks that 'after leaving me the Sikh officer went to him and tried, without success, to get further copies'.[44] The implication is that Heaney suspected this officer of planning cross-border raids or other forms of violence in Punjab. Government officials, particularly military officers who were intimately familiar with the value of maps during wartime, were keenly aware of the potential for militants to put maps to violent use.

Violence was the most dramatic repercussion of partition, but the boundary award contributed to other disruptions: long-term border tensions, infrastructure problems and the lasting conflict over Kashmir. First, the high casualties and tremendous population dislocation that burdened both India and Pakistan during and after partition proved awkward responsibilities for fledgling states. In Pakistan, the position of *mohajirs*, or migrants from India, remains a dangerous political problem. Second, the boundaries that Radcliffe defined turned out to be restless divisions, and in both the 1965 and 1971 wars India and Pakistan battled over their Punjabi border. Third, the Radcliffe line also cut through the Punjab's well-developed infrastructure systems, disrupting road, telephone and telegraph communications, but, most importantly, interfering with the region's vital irrigation system. These water problems were related to the final and most serious issue plaguing current Indo-Pakistani relations: Kashmir.

Because the Maharajah of Kashmir was entitled to choose for himself between India and Pakistan, Radcliffe had no responsibility for Kashmiri territory. However, the Radcliffe award and the Kashmir problem have subsequently become entwined. This connection is rooted in the fact that the water feeding the Punjabi irrigation system originates in Kashmiri rivers, as well as in allegations that Radcliffe awarded India parts of Gurdaspur as a corridor to Kashmir. In the absence of any concrete evidence, such suspicions remain speculative.

These long-term repercussions, combined with memories of the great suffering that accompanied partition, form part of the division's legacy. It is not 1947's only legacy, of course – that year also brought independence and great pride to many Indians and Pakistanis – but partition's scars remain in the minds, if no longer on the bodies, of many South Asians. It is not only the actual survivors of partition who exhibit this damage; their descendants are also marked. Pakistani bitterness against India and Indian bitterness against Pakistan are facts of life in South Asia. Many other Indians and Pakistanis long for peace, feeling that the people across the border are their kinfolk.

Unfortunately, government propaganda and certain streams of public discourse, particularly within the press and educational institutions, reinforce cross-border resentments.

Notes

1   *TP* VIII p. 372.
2   Swarna Aiyar, '"August anarchy": The partition massacres in Punjab, 1947', in *Freedom, Trauma, Continuities: Northern India and Independence*, eds D. A. Low and Howard Brasted (Walnut Creek, CA: AltaMira Press, 1998), p. 17.
3   IOR/L/P&J/8/663, Jenkins memo to Mountbatten, 4 August 1947, cited in Aiyar, n. 7.
4   Aiyar, p. 18.
5   Aiyar, p. 20.
6   Francis Tuker, *While Memory Serves* (London: Cassell, 1950), p. 486.
7   Aiyar, p. 24.
8   French, pp. 348–9. For a detailed discussion of casualty estimates (combined with vigorous criticism of Mountbatten's role), see Roberts, pp. 127–32; for a thoughtful consideration of these estimates in relation to other rumours about partition violence, see Pandey, *Remembering*, pp. 88–91.
9   French, p. 347.
10 Ritu Menon and Kamla Bhasin, *Borders and Boundaries: Women in India's Partition* (New Brunswick, NJ: Rutgers University Press, 1998), p. 70; official estimates were 50,000 Muslim women abducted in India, 33,000 Hindu and Sikh women abducted in Pakistan.
11 Aiyar, p. 17.
12 Aiyar, n. 60.
13 Tuker, pp. 485–88, cited in Aiyar, p. 21.
14 Aiyar, p. 27.
15 IOR L/MIL/17/5/4319, Rees, 'Report on the Punjab Boundary Force', p. 21, cited in Aiyar, p. 28.
16 Robin Jeffrey, 'The Punjab Boundary Force and the problem of order, August 1947', *Modern Asian Studies* 8:4 (1974), p. 498.
17 Jeffrey, p. 500.
18 *The Times* (5 September 1947 (dateline 3 September)), p. 4, cited in Jeffrey, p. 509 n. 106.
19 Jeffrey, p. 500.
20 Jeffrey, p. 505.
21 Jeffrey, p. 514.
22 Mudie, letter to Rees, 31 August 1947, Rees Papers, cited in Jeffrey, p. 497.
23 'Old journeys revisited', *The Economist* (12 February 2000), pp. 86–8.
24 Meera Chatterjee, personal communication, 18 June 2002.
25 French, p. 351.
26 Anders Bjørn Hansen, *Partition and Genocide: Manifestation of Violence in Punjab 1937–1947* (New Delhi: India Research Press, 2002), p. 135.
27 For a Pakistani view, see the report on the role of the RSS included in the Islamabad National Documentation Centre's *Disturbances in the Pubjab 1947*, comp. Rukhsana Zafar (1995), pp. 411–24. See also Indivar Kamtekar, 'The military ingredient of communal violence in Punjab, 1947', *Abstracts of Sikh Studies* 4:1 (2002), pp. 48–52.
28 *TP* VII p. 23.
29 Aiyar, p. 35 n. 60.
30 Rees Report, p. 21, quoted in Jeffrey, pp. 505–6.
31 *TP* XI p. 136 n. 1.
32 Campbell-Johnson, pp. 200–1.

33 Campbell-Johnson, p. 201.
34 Members of the Indian Civil Service were traditionally known as the 'Heaven-Born'.
35 See for example the recollections of PBF officer S. Wajahat Husain, 'Woman in the pond!: Reminiscences [of] Punjab Boundary Force operations '47', unpublished manuscript, n.d.
36 See for example 'Radcliffe award announced', *Pakistan Times* (19 August 1947), p. 1; 'Partition of the Punjab', *Times of India* (19 August 1947), p. 7.
37 Mridula Sarabhai, 'The recovery of abducted women-V', National Press Syndicate, India, n.d. [after 29 August 1948], NAI 1–G(R)/49, vol. I, p. 68.
38 NAI 10(16)-PR/47, 'Fortnightly [Situation] Reports, Punjab.'
39 Aiyar, p. 17. The Indian and Pakistani leaders learned of the new boundaries at a 5.00 pm meeting on 16 August, but radio and newspaper announcements to the public occurred on 17 August.
40 *TP* XI p. 943.
41 Jeffrey, p. 495.
42 See Pandey, *Remembering*, pp. 69–74, 79–84, 88–91 and Veena Das, 'Official narratives, rumour, and the social production of hate', *Social Identities* 4:1 (1998), pp. 109–30.
43 Urvashi Butalia, 'Muslims and Hindus, men and women: Communal stereotypes and the partition of India', in *Women and Right-Wing Movements: Indian Experiences*, eds Tanika Sarkar and Urvashi Butalia (London: Zed Books, 1995), p. 69.
44 'The winding trail: A detailed memoir of life and work in the Survey of India and Naga Hills', Box 7, p. 307, Heaney Papers, South Asian Archive, Cambridge University.

CHAPTER SEVEN

'An awful lot of thought should have gone into it': alternatives to the Radcliffe award

What was the relationship between the violence of partition and the new boundary? Certainly the boundary announcement provided additional fuel for a fire that was already burning. But how did the line's location affect the violence? In other words, would the violence have been ameliorated by a better boundary? This chapter offers a surprising answer to that question, by way of a counterfactual analysis comparing the Radcliffe line with other major proposals put forward by the nationalist parties in the summer of 1947. It is clear that Radcliffe's boundary was deeply problematic, but in terms of its effect on partition violence and on long-term resentments, it was superior to the major alternatives.

Overall, Radcliffe's Punjab award was kinder to India than to Pakistan. Two Muslim majority areas that might have gone to Pakistan – the three *tehsils* in Ferozepur District and areas of western Gurdaspur – went to India. (In Bengal, Congress complained vociferously that the award of the non-Muslim majority Chittagong Hill Tracts to Pakistan was unfair, so Mountbatten may have achieved his goal of 'balance' after all.) But beyond the claims of unfairness, the award created other difficulties.

The Radcliffe line cut through the middle of the Punjab's well-developed irrigation system. Canal headworks were left on one side of the boundary while the canals they fed fell on the other side. As Beaumont later recalled, 'it's a tremendously difficult job to partition a country, in two places. Particularly in the Punjab, where the populations were mixed up. There were Hindu villages next to Muslim villages next to Sikh villages, all being nourished by the same canals and railway systems. I mean, an awful lot of thought should have gone into it and much more expert advice should have been taken, from the canal engineers and the railway engineers and the military.'[1] Without such detailed advice, and more time to gather it, the Radcliffe line was doomed to disrupt Punjab's road, rail, telegraph, electricity and irrigations networks.

Rivers also posed a major potential problem. Radcliffe's textual description attempted to prevent any uncertainty about the path of the boundary, which on the map appeared to follow the Ravi and Sutlej Rivers, by stating that the existing administrative boundary, not the river, was the actual international boundary line. This effort was unsuccessful. Monsoonal rivers tend to change their beds yearly after annual heavy flooding. In Punjab, those changes meant that, each year, small pieces of land were transferred from one side of a river to the other. (Riverbed changes also caused problems in Bengal, where *chars*, sandbars or small sandy islands, appeared or disappeared each year, raising with them questions about whether they were Indian or Pakistani territory.[2]) Finally, in the early 1950s, India and Pakistan agreed to a settlement assigning areas on the Indian side of such rivers to India and those on the Pakistani side to Pakistan.[3] For a time, the Sutlej and Ravi Rivers became *de facto* boundaries.[4]

As noted above, the new boundary largely followed colonial administrative divisions, indicating that Radcliffe read these maps as primarily indicating administrative space, which he sought to preserve. However, the administrative divisions that stood out so definitively on maps were not necessarily clear on the ground. As an official in Bengal complained, 'There is nothing to demarcate the boundary line except an imaginary one supported by settlement maps showing the border of villages.'[5] The very lines that, from the perspective of Radcliffe's office in New Delhi, contributed much-needed clarity, actually added to the confusion in some local areas.[6]

Although these complexities posed serious challenges, the fundamental problem with the boundary was that it left millions of people as minorities in areas where they were subject to ethnic cleansing. The combination of large minorities, ethnic cleansing and economic disruption contributed to immediate and lasting conflict between India and Pakistan. Would any other boundary have functioned more effectively? Could the risk to minorities, the threat to Sikh security or the danger of international clashes between India and Pakistan have been alleviated if the line had been located elsewhere? Addressing these questions requires a counterfactual analysis of alternative boundary proposals.

Although counterfactual history, which asks, 'what if events had unfolded differently?' can be a useful tool to examine the impact of any one event or decision, historians have traditionally been wary of this method.[7] Counterfactual thinking can clarify the repercussions of a chosen decision, through comparison with the repercussions that

[141]

might have resulted from a different decision. In this section, I examine a number of counterfactual cases in an effort to better understand the impact of Radcliffe's line. Under the circumstances that prevailed in the summer of 1947, would alternative lines have resulted in less violence, less economic disruption or less tension between India and Pakistan?

To begin with, criticism of the Radcliffe boundary commission and of Radcliffe's award raises the following question: how could the line have been improved? In other words, if Radcliffe had drawn a different line, would it have been better? 'Better' is a vague term, and this analysis requires specificity. Based on the most common complaints about the boundary – that it provoked violence, that it caused avoidable economic and social disruptions, and that it was unfair to one side or the other, leaving lasting resentment and/or disadvantage – we can define a 'better' line as one that, in the short term, would have resulted in:

(a) less violence;
(b) fewer disruptions to infrastructure and other economic networks;
(c) lower tension between India and Pakistan.

As possible alternatives, I consider the various proposals submitted to the boundary commission in the weeks before partition. I also examine the 'notional' boundary, which was based solely on demographic data from the 1941 census. Finally, I analyse the sketch map line, an alternative that, the evidence indicates, Radcliffe considered only days before submitting his award.

Beginning with the westernmost line, I discuss the likely repercussions of the Sikh claim, which called for a boundary following the Chenab River in the west. Next is the Congress proposal, which included Lahore and several large salients of central Punjabi territory. In central Punjab, I examine the sketch map line of 8 August, which ran through the middle of the province, with a detour west into Ferozepur. The notional boundary, which followed the district majorities as laid out in the 1941 census, is slightly east of the sketch map. Finally, I consider the Muslim League proposal, which left most of Amritsar district as an Indian enclave surrounded by Pakistani territory and extended several small salients into eastern Punjab. For comparison's sake, the Radcliffe line falls roughly in the middle of these proposals; it is further east (i.e. allots more territory to Pakistan) than the Sikh and Congress claims, but further west (i.e. allots more territory to India) than the League, notional or sketch map lines.

In appraising these alternatives, I have applied the following principles, based on the conditions prevailing in 1947. First, given the scale and efficiency of the ethnic cleansing that occurred, the presence of large minority populations on the 'wrong' side of the line would result in high numbers of deaths. It is difficult to enumerate counterfactual casualties, but the lack of reliable numbers even for the actual death toll in 1947 renders such estimates largely irrelevant. For this analysis, a rough discussion of the likelihood of mass violence must suffice. The second principle holds that a line cutting through infrastructure networks or across trade routes would contribute to economic disruption. Finally, a line that is perceived as unfair, or in violation of the commission's terms of reference, would aggravate tensions between India and Pakistan, as would perceptions of military insecurity. In particular, salients, strips of land that jut into foreign territory, provide a significant military advantage by enabling the forward deployment of troops and equipment. The presence of salients can contribute to military insecurity and even prompt pre-emptive strikes.

Contemporary observers offered a number of critiques of each of the alternative plans discussed here, which indicate how they might have been received had they been finalized. These critiques are significant not only as predictors of possible results, but also as indicators of local expectations. Even if critics' gloomy predictions had not come true, such negative perceptions could well have prompted one side or the other to attack in order to pre-empt an attack by the other side.

The Sikh claim

The Sikh claim (map 4a) would have left large areas of land with unquestioned Muslim majorities in India. Its primary merit is that it would have satisfied Sikh demands and therefore reduced Sikh militants' perception of the need to make pre-emptive attacks. However, its drawbacks are far more numerous. It would have violated the basic terms of reference given to the commission; only the most elastic interpretation of the importance of 'other factors' would have allowed the commissioners to override the primary mandate of determining 'contiguous majority areas' to this extent. As a result, the basic legitimacy of this line would have been open to question.

The economic consequences of this award would have been damaging not only for Pakistan but also, surprisingly, for the Sikh homelands. India would have controlled a much larger portion of the Punjabi irrigation system. But Pakistan would have retained the headworks that regulated the water supply to the Sikh canal colonies of central Punjab. As Aloys Michel's excellent analysis of the Indus waters system notes, 'the Sikh proposal would have left the key to the irrigation of their treasured lands in Lyallpur and Montgomery districts in the hands of a disgruntled (to say the least) Pakistan. Viewed in the light of its effect on the irrigation system, the Sikh proposal would have created a far worse situation than that which actually resulted from Partition.[8] But Pakistan would also have suffered other economic setbacks. With Lahore in India, Pakistani Punjab would have had no major cities and therefore no communications or transportation hub. The loss of the canal colonies would have drastically reduced the agricultural potential of Pakistani Punjab, damaging the entire country's food supply. Limited access to major transportation networks would have restricted the ability of farmers to get even their reduced yield to market.

It seems unlikely that Pakistan would have accepted this award. Muslim militants, who were already armed and organized for resistance, would have seen it as a serious threat to the nation and a call to action. It seems likely that extensive fighting between Muslims and Sikhs (and, to a lesser extent, Hindus) would have resulted. It is difficult to calculate how this line would have changed the balance of fighting. Would Muslims, a larger minority in the united Punjab than they were in the actual West Punjab of 1947, have been better able to resist in this counterfactual case? Would Sikhs, their claims to an ancestral homeland validated by this award, have fought even more fiercely? Would ethnic cleansing have verged on genocide, as each side fought without quarter to stake its claim to central Punjab? It seems likely that this line would have provoked large-scale conflict between parties intent on claiming areas of Punjab. Although the precise results of such a counterfactual conflict are beyond this analysis, it is clear that the region would have emerged badly damaged.

The Congress claim

The Congress claim (map 4b) was less extreme than the Sikh proposal, but many of the same objections apply. Congress conceded Pakistan's right to the Muslim majority areas of south-western and western Punjab and generally confined its claims in the west to Lahore and Sialkot Districts, as well as a long finger of land stretching south-west through Sheikhupura and Lyallpur Districts. The irregular boundary delineated by this plan would have left the city of Lahore in India, and created a number of salients reaching into Pakistan. Between these spurs, of course, corresponding areas of Pakistani territory would have reached into India, including one that would have ended only a few miles from Lahore. Such salients would have proved a tempting starting point for border raids or even invasions to regain Lahore. This territorial interlacing would have left both countries feeling insecure about the defensibility of their Punjabi borders.

As noted above, the loss of Lahore to India would have left Pakistani Punjab with no major cities and truncated communication, transportation and irrigation systems. With less cropland and fewer canals, Pakistani Punjab's agricultural capacity would have been significantly reduced, although not to the extent dictated by the Sikh claim. This line also would have left large portions of the Muslim-majority districts Sialkot, Sheikhupura, Lyallpur and Lahore in India. With tense Indo-Pakistani relations resulting from Pakistani perceptions of this award, too, as unfair, the Muslim inhabitants of these areas would likely have fled for Pakistan or been killed if they tried to remain in their homes. Those who fled would have added to the overcrowding in Pakistani Punjab, as well as increasing the drain on limited resources there.

The notional boundary

The British established the 'notional boundary' (map 5b) as a sort of stand-in boundary, intended to facilitate planning in the months before the final boundary award. It was based solely on British administrative divisions, allotting those districts that the 1941 census had labelled as Muslim-majority to the west (Pakistan) while Hindu/Sikh-majority districts went to the east (India).

This line differed from the Radcliffe line in two significant ways: it would have given Pakistan all of Gurdaspur District and all of Lahore District. This arrangement would have left the city of Amritsar near the end of a salient of Indian territory that protruded into Pakistani land. Surrounded on three sides by Pakistan, Amritsar would have been vulnerable to attack. It is certain that Sikh militants would have reacted strongly to such a decision. It seems likely that they would have taken action to protect the city of the Golden Temple, although we can only speculate as to whether they would have done so through increased militarization of the border, assaults intended to capture Pakistani territory or ethnic cleansing of areas of the Pakistani borderlands. During the boundary commission's hearings, Congress asserted that with such a line, 'the three sided areas, viz., Amritsar would be immediately over-run'.[9] Whether or not Amritsar would really have been in danger from Pakistan, Sikh leaders *believed* that it would have been in danger. Accordingly, they prepared themselves to protect it. The use of the notional boundary would also have limited India's access to Kashmir. The contemporary strategic significance of such a move is unclear, however, given the fact that in the summer of 1947 the magnitude and significance of the Kashmir controversy were not yet evident. The loss of Gurdaspur would not have eliminated India's ability to move forces into Kashmir, given that in October 1947 it deployed its troops by air.

[145]

The 'sketch map' line

The sketch map line could have been disastrous. The sketch map (map 5a) showed the Radcliffe line as it was announced on 17 August, with one key difference: it included a salient extending some forty miles into the Indian district of Ferozepur. This salient comprised three *tehsils*: Ferozepur, Zira and Fazilka. The area contained an important military depot, but in fact the mere existence of this salient, even without the materiel in question, would have been of great strategic significance. Like the notional boundary discussed above, this line would have given Pakistan a strategically valuable piece of territory close to Amritsar, leaving that city enclosed on two sides by Pakistan. Again, this line would have left the Sikh community feeling vulnerable and threatened. The worst violence of 1947 began with the 9 August train attack, likely sparked by rumours about the sketch map line, particularly the Ferozepur salient. If this line had been finalized, Sikh militants would have reacted even more violently.

For different reasons, Patrick French calls this line 'an extraordinary proposal'. He argues that, 'like Afghanistan's Wakhan Corridor, it would have been an extremely vulnerable geographical anomaly, which ran the risk of being bisected at its western end in the event of military hostilities. Moreover, it was an obvious and provocative challenge to Sikh security.'[10] On military grounds, then, this salient would have caused more trouble than it resolved, even if it did bring valuable materiel to Pakistan through the Ferozepur arms depot. In fact, the presence of this depot would have rendered the salient even more threatening. French speculates that the Ferozepur salient may have been Radcliffe's attempt to compensate Pakistan for Muslim-majority areas of Gurdaspur and Lahore that went to India to buffer Amritsar. As such, 'the Ferozepur salient may have been an attempt to redress the balance, but it was a dangerously misguided one, and Radcliffe was right to alter it. Pakistan would in the long term have gained little benefit from having to defend a strip of land that was in such a strategically vulnerable position.'[11] Alternatively, this salient might have provided Pakistan with a military advantage, giving it a forward position deep within Indian territory from which to launch attacks. In either case, it would have been a destabilizing element in the Indo-Pakistani relationship.

[146]

The Muslim League claim

The fifth plan, proposed by the Muslim League, claimed most of Ferozepur District, most of Gurdaspur, and sections of Hoshiarpur, Jullundur, and Ludhiana Districts (map 5c). This proposal included a salient centred on the Sutlej River that stretched almost to the eastern edge of Punjab. The League did not attempt to claim the city of Amritsar, but proposed to leave it as a Sikh enclave. Needless to say, the prospect of Amritsar as an enclave, surrounded on all sides by Pakistani territory, would not have eased Sikh fears.

This claim would have given Pakistan sizeable Sikh and Hindu minorities. If the Pakistani state had been able to exercise effective authority, it might have been compelled by the presence of a larger number of Sikhs to protect them more effectively. But given that Pakistani (like Indian) resources were strained beyond the maximum in 1947, it is more likely that these minorities would have been killed or forced to flee.

In addition, Pakistan would have had two significant salients jutting into Indian lands. The Sutlej River salient would have given Pakistan increased control over a vital water source, allowing it further leverage over India. Both of these salients would also have been militarily useful. However, given India's relative military superiority and its proven willingness to invade recalcitrant localities like Hyderabad (in 1948) and later Goa (1961), it is possible that India would simply have taken over these valuable spits of land. Either way, the Muslim League line likely would have raised the probability of conflict between India and Pakistan.

Results of counterfactual analysis

In conclusion, there are serious objections to all of the major alternative proposals to the Radcliffe line. Any line, when taken in conjunction with the intense communal resentment that characterized the period, would have resulted in massive migration. The relative proportion of communal groups might have changed according to different lines, but the overall number of migrants would have remained in the millions. Although it may seem unlikely in light of the tremendous violence that occurred during partition, Radcliffe's line was in fact less problematic than any of the alternatives. Certainly the Radcliffe line was imperfect; unfortunately, it is difficult (if not impossible) to determine a significantly better line. In seeking ways to avoid, in similar situations, the troubles that plagued India and Pakistan in 1947, we must turn from boundary location to other factors.

[147]

A key factor in all these cases was Sikh anxiety about, and determination to pre-empt, threats to their community. Decisions that Sikh militants considered unacceptable would almost certainly have provoked further violence as they protested with rifle and spear. In addition, claims that left very large Muslim minorities in Indian territory would also have prompted violence, for Muslim private armies had also proved themselves to be effective killers. Another problem was the fact that any line would cut through the Punjab's road, rail and canal networks. Finally, any line other than the notional boundary would have indicated a greater departure from the primary factor indicated in the commission's terms of reference – contiguous majority areas – than did Radcliffe's final award. This fact would have left the legitimacy of the new boundary open to question.

It is certainly true that improvements were possible at the local level. In some cases, the Radcliffe line cut farmers' homes off from their fields, and even (although primarily in Bengal, not in Punjab) divided homes in two. But such problems, according to the best contemporary boundary-making practices, should have been accounted for in the demarcation phase, when the line could be adjusted to meet local needs. Requiring Radcliffe to create any line in six weeks was asking a great deal; asking him to delineate a perfect line, one that demarcators could simply mark on the ground without any adjustment, amounted to a request for the impossible.

The violence that accompanied partition relates more directly to British efforts to project a false image of order in the midst of chaos than it does to the location of the boundary. Certainly there is an important relationship between violence and the boundary commission, but it runs in a different direction than one might assume. In reaction to the simmering violence of 1946 and early 1947, the British constructed a façade of control, of which the Radcliffe commission was a central part. This pretence was useful in the short term, allowing the British to carry out their hasty withdrawal, but it also had serious repercussions, both short- and long-term. The fact that British leaders were content to focus on maintaining an appearance of order, rather than making real preparations to reduce conflict, contributed to the mass killing that erupted during partition. The location of the line itself played a less significant role in this violence than did the larger set of attitudes and priorities that drove Britain's approach to its withdrawal.

Notes

1   IOR Mss Eur R 150, 'Interview #16, Judge H.C. Beaumont.'
2   Chatterji, 'Fashioning', pp. 222–5.
3   S. Wajahat Husain, personal interview, 30 July 2000.
4   Satya Rai, *Partition of the Punjab: A Study of its Effects on the Politics and Administration of the Punjab (I) 1947–56* (Bombay: Asia Publishing House, 1965), p. 175.
5   Inspector's 'Report on border intelligence of Nadia District', 23 April 1948, Government of [West] Bengal, Intelligence Branch, File No. 1238–47 (Nabadwip), cited in Chatterji, 'Fashioning', p. 221.
6   See Chapter 8 for an examination of the local repercussions of the boundary.
7   For a discussion of historians' attitudes towards counterfactual analysis, see Niall Ferguson, 'Introduction', in *Virtual History: Alternatives and Counterfactuals* (London: Picador, 1997), esp. pp. 4–20.
8   Michel, p. 176.
9   Sadullah, vol. 2, p. 35.
10 French, p. 328.
11 French, pp. 329–30.

CHAPTER EIGHT

'In between, on a bit of earth which had no name': the development of the Indo-Pakistani borderlands

In Saadat Hasan Manto's short story 'Toba Tek Singh', a man from a village in the Indo-Pakistani borderlands refuses to choose between the two states and dies in the no-man's-land along the boundary. The West Punjabi town of Toba Tek Singh, from which Manto's tale takes its name and its protagonist his nickname, was one of many affected by the Indo-Pakistani boundary. The term 'borderland' refers to the area surrounding the boundary, a loosely defined zone including territory in both India and Pakistan that is directly influenced by the boundary. Manto's story, written in 1948, reflects the difficult border development that followed partition. Villages in this area suddenly found themselves on a new frontier, on land that was contested – or sometimes jointly neglected – by India and Pakistan. In addition to dramatizing the confusion about which people and which villages belonged to which country, Manto's powerful story also highlights the physical manifestations of the boundary's demarcation. Although there was confusion over the boundary's exact location immediately after independence, barbed wire, boundary posts and remembered resentments soon marked the new line and separated the region's inhabitants.

The burgeoning field of borderlands studies has only recently begun to deal in detail with Punjab. This chapter builds on recent work in other borderlands, particularly scholarship on Bengal, to describe and analyse the development of the Punjabi boundary and the territory surrounding it. Beginning with the violence and mass migration of partition, I examine the division's impact on areas near the border, both immediately after partition and in the years that followed. After tracing the evolution of the boundary disputes that arose from the Radcliffe award, I conclude with a brief discussion of the state of the borderlands at the beginning of the twenty-first century.

A boundary is a line, while a border is the area adjacent to that line.[1] The term 'borderlands' refers to border areas on both sides of a boundary. Although most existing border studies focus on the US–Mexico border or, to a lesser extent, European borders, analyses of African and Asian borders also provide useful comparative insights.[2] South Asian borderlands research has tended to focus on the Pakistan–Afghanistan region and the Indo-Bangladesh border.[3] We know much more about the Radcliffe boundary commission's impact on the development of the Bengali borderlands than we do about Punjab. Joya Chatterji has rightly emphasized the disruption caused by the Radcliffe line for local communities in Bengal, particularly in agricultural areas.[4] However, the Bengal border also provided new opportunities for local residents. Although it was a barrier to some areas of work, it was also a workplace in itself, employing new categories of labourers like smugglers and border guards.[5] For the Punjabi borderlands, Ian Talbot and other scholars have produced pioneering recent work examining issues such as the comparative development of Lahore and Amritsar and the nature of the Wagah-Attari checkpoint that is the sole border crossing between the two countries.[6]

The Indo-Pakistani borderland displays many characteristics of an 'alienated borderland':[7] it is militarized, border-crossing traffic is rigidly controlled, and legal cross-boundary exchange is extremely limited. In other ways, however, it does not fit this model. During times of peace, there is a great deal of illegal cross-border exchange. In addition, many areas of the borderlands, on both sides, are densely populated and heavily cultivated – one legacy of the Radcliffe line, which drove through the middle of a thickly settled and agriculturally valuable region. Certainly the Punjabi borderlands bear the marks of the hostile yet intimate relationship between India and Pakistan.

Borderlands research requires gathering information on both sides of the boundary, a tall order for contested borderlands controlled by hostile governments. For the Indo-Pakistani borderlands, this dual research is particularly challenging, in part because a great deal of information on border areas, even historical records over fifty years old, remains classified. A further problem inherent in comparative borderlands research is the fact that it is nearly impossible to obtain comparable sources for the areas to be examined.[8] Extensive research in archives in both India and Pakistan, as well as Britain, is necessary to address the development of the Punjabi borderlands.

Early borderlands formation

This section examines life on the India–West Pakistan border in the months following partition, attempting to reconstruct perspectives of people on both sides of Radcliffe's line. Life on the border held numerous dangers, particularly for farmers, who had to protect not only their fields but also their livestock. Uncertainties over the exact location of the boundary, combined with raids by rivals who in some cases were former neighbours, complicated the picture. As local residents and national security forces sought to protect themselves and the infrastructure systems on which Punjabi agriculture depended, the border became increasingly militarized.

A great many border incidents involved livestock. Livestock wandered or were driven across the boundary, accidentally or on purpose; they were stolen in cross-border raids; and individuals attempting to gather fodder for their livestock mistakenly wandered across the boundary, intentionally crossed the line or were abducted while working near the boundary. Farmers could not abandon activities like feeding and herding animals, despite the new dangers they involved, and so they – and the resulting problems – continued.[9] The importance of livestock is further highlighted by the fact that government situation reports on boundary incidents dutifully recorded the deaths of animals as well as human beings.[10]

Many incidents were little more than cattle rustling but had international consequences because they involved crossing the new boundary. On 23 September 1947, for example, Muslim refugees grazing their cattle on the borderlands of Lahore District were set upon by Sikh villagers, who drove away their herd. An encounter between the Indian villagers and Pakistani troops ensued; the troops fired on the Sikhs and recovered the stolen cattle.[11] Such raids could result in human deaths, as happened the next day, when Indian villagers attacked Pakistani herdsmen grazing their cattle in the Kasur area. In the mêlée, the Sikh raiders killed one Muslim and drove away six cattle.[12] Raiders themselves sometimes died in these attacks, as occurred on 8 October 1947, when nine Sikhs were killed by Pakistani police while their compatriots made off with fifty-two cattle from Pakistan's Kasur *tehsil*.[13] Even the river proved no barrier to such raids, as the villagers of Khiwa discovered in mid-November when 'three Mahtam Sikhs from Ferozepore swamped across the Sutlej and took away 7 heads of cattle found grazing on the river bank'.[14] Although the spark for each of these incidents was provided by livestock, the end result often cost both human lives and concerted government effort to enforce the new boundary.

In this intensely cultivated area, it was necessary to seek animal fodder even in the dangerous zones nearest the boundary. On 22 September 1947, a group of refugees who had ventured towards the line in Lahore District in order to fetch grass for their cattle came under fire from Sikhs in India.[15] Around 6 October, a similar incident occurred, when residents of Sehjra village in Pakistan's Kasur *tehsil* went to the fields to cut fodder. Armed Indian Sikhs again assaulted them, killing two Pakistanis and abducting twenty-one other men. According to Pakistani police reports, the abductees were held for ransom in a police station in Indian Khem Karan and released only after paying a 'fee' of 1800 rupees.[16]

Continuing and parallel attempts to procure fodder could lead to confusions that might have been comic if they were not so often deadly. For example, one mid-November evening, forty-five cattle strayed into India, 'owing to the ignorance of graziers'. Sikh villagers quickly rounded up the animals, repulsing the attempts of the Pakistani police to recover them. Police officials from both sides arrived to negotiate the release of the Pakistani cattle, at which point nine Indian cattle conveniently strayed into Pakistani territory, where local peasants captured them. Seeing that they had lost the advantage, the Indian Sikhs exchanged twenty Pakistani cattle for the nine stray Indian cattle. They claimed, however, that the remaining twenty-five head originally had been theirs, having wandered from India into Pakistan at an earlier date.[17] Farmers living in such close quarters – whose livelihoods depended on animals that could not grasp the significance of the international boundary – were compelled to take part in ongoing negotiations of their needs.

Indian villagers also ventured near – and sometimes across – the boundary in their search for grazing lands. In late October, five Sikhs were arrested while grazing their cattle near the Pakistani border village of Rampura. In this case, police and military officials from India and Pakistan resolved the misunderstanding and the fortunate peasants in question were quickly released.[18] But such incidents could easily end in violence. A few days later, Pakistani police arrested four Indians in Kasur *tehsil*, having found them 'stealing' fodder from Pakistani territory. Indian military troops, apparently attempting a rescue, fired across the boundary. A bystander harvesting cotton in his fields was killed. The fate of the captured Indians was not recorded.[19]

Pakistani police patrols were inadequate to cover the entire border area, and on occasion agriculturalists were simply found dead. On 9 October 1947, the police reported: 'Being attracted by gun shots, Police and Troops from Wagha reconnoitered the border and found dead bodies of 3 Muslims near village Kacha Dhanoi across the border. Two of the dead bodies had gunshot wounds and one a spear wound. These Muslims are believed to have been grazing their cattle near the Wagha border.'[20] Unexplained and violent death, assumed to be the result of border raids, had become part of daily life for border residents.

Cattle were not only the goal of border raids but could be used as weapons themselves. In mid-October, a large group of Indian Sikhs drove their cattle to graze in a sugarcane field in the Pakistani village of Mohammadiwala. Local police who responded found the raiders well equipped, with two light machineguns set up in Pakistani territory, and apparently supported by Indian soldiers.[21] This incident highlights another aspect of agricultural disruption, the destruction of crops planted near the border, and demonstrates that crop damage was sufficient to spark a deadly incident.

Farmers cultivating their fields were also vulnerable to attack. In mid-October, two Sikhs attacked Pakistani peasants ploughing their fields and apparently tried to steal their plough-animals. The incident escalated into a clash between Indian and Pakistani troops, but no casualties resulted.[22] Living and working on the border were dangerous, but many farmers had no option. In addition, the value of this farmland to each state's agricultural success made both governments eager to keep farmers working the borderlands.

Border raids and livestock theft went both ways. Indian situation reports for September noted that 'border incidents continued to occur in Ferozepore and Amritsar districts. There were several instances of Muslim League National Guards and their West Punjab Police trespassing into East Punjab territory and taking away cattle and other property.'[23] Attacks worsened in the first half of October, as the monsoon rains eased and raiders found it easier to cross previously flooded rivers.[24] By early November, many border residents had concluded that the area was too unsettled; those who could afford transportation, which was still limited and therefore expensive, moved further east into India.[25] In short, agriculturists on both sides of the new border found themselves in a precarious position.

The borderland, therefore, took on contradictory new meanings, as a zone of danger for those who might fall victim to cross-border raids, and as a safe space for those who retreated back over it after venturing across the line to work their mischief. At least some, if not most, of these attacks were motivated by opportunism, rather than religious hatred. Muslims were not always the victims; Christian agriculturalists in Pakistan also lost their animals to cross-border raids.[26] Another factor was the close proximity of Indian and Pakistani villages; many of these incidents occurred in the Kasur area, where Radcliffe drew the boundary between villages rather than following district or *tehsil* boundaries as he did in other areas. Border raids continued into the new year but abated over the course of 1948.

Occasionally, uncertainties over the actual location of the boundary aggravated an already tense situation. As early as September, there were cases on both sides of the border of people crossing the line to seize possession of abandoned villages.[27] In mid-October, a group of Pakistani villagers were grazing their cattle on islands between two streams of the Sutlej River. A group of armed Sikhs, taking advantage of their vulnerable position, seized 120 head of cattle.[28] Even when a settlement had been negotiated, problems could suddenly arise, as happened in Kasur in mid-November. A situation report noted: 'Subsequent to a settlement between evacuees from village Jalloke and Baito Jagir of Kasur Sub-Division (Pak) which lies beyond river Sutlej and Sikh Mahtams of East Punjab who are now in occupation of these villages, some Muslims accompanied by a Police party of D.A.P. [District Armed Police?] went towards village Jalloke on the 9th but returned on the Mahtams' declining to carry out the agreement for restoring possession.'[29] On its way home, the Pakistani party was attacked. Its members fled back across the border, firing as they went, and killed three of their attackers in the process. Their retreat was rather undignified, however, as two police constables were forced to jump into the river, losing their weapons in the water.[30] For the moment, at least, the river continued to fall into both countries' spheres of control. As noted above, the boundary ran along the river for many miles, although Radcliffe had made clear that the *de jure* boundary line actually followed existing administrative divisions. In local practice, however, the Rivers Ravi and Sutlej became *de facto* boundaries, in the absence of any clear demarcation of the new line.

Visitors to the borderlands were particularly prone to trouble. In mid-November, a Muslim refugee family trying to locate the Pakistani village of Targa found themselves on the wrong side of the line. While riding in a *tonga* (a light horse-drawn cart), they 'ignorantly strayed into village Kals (East P[unja]b. [India]) where Sikhs took away the tonga and two women forcibly'. The driver escaped back into Pakistan and summoned help, and the two women ('as well as the tonga', the report notes) were recovered.[31]

Very few border incidents seem to have involved open attempts to claim territory. In early September, however, one such episode occurred, when a group of Sikhs 'assisted by Sikh military men from the same area looted and turned out Muslims' from villages that lay in Pakistani territory on the eastern side of the Sutlej River. Eight Muslims were killed in this operation, which seems to have been an attempt by Indians to claim for their own purposes this vulnerable land across the river from Pakistan.[32] In late September, a river figured in another attempt to move the Pakistani border further west. An Indian military platoon reportedly forced the inhabitants of two Pakistani hamlets in Sialkot District (bordering Kashmir) 'to evacuate beyond the old Ujh river bed'.[33] Nearly a month later, further south in the Pakistani district of Kasur, a group of heavily armed Sikhs moved into Pakistani territory. When they were reportedly joined by Indian military men, 'they also pitched two flags in the Western Punjab area and when Police attempted to remove them the encounter became brisk in which 5 Sikhs were killed and 3 injured by our Police'. By that night, the raiders had recognized the precarious nature of their position and decamped, taking the flags with them.[34] These three incidents are the only such cases reported in the Pakistani records, however, showing that territorial seizures seem to have been the exception and conflicts relating to agriculture the rule.

In a number of cases, raiders and victims knew each other. In one incident in early October, Indian raiders attacked farmers in the fields of Sehjra village in Pakistani Kasur, taking away a mare. Victims identified one of the raiders by name as 'Kahan Singh, uncle of Iqbal Singh of Khem Karan'.[35] A few days later, several Sikhs carried out a cattle-rustling operation in the village of Dhinkia, in Lahore District. Again, the victims were able to report the name and home village of one of the men, Makhan Singh of Danka village, to police.[36]

Some incidents involved refugees returning to their home villages in order to retrieve their property or exact revenge. In October, a well-organized and well-armed group of Sikhs attacked the Kasur *tehsil* village of Mohammdiwala. Throwing a grenade, they killed a man and wounded three others, as well as abducting a Muslim woman. In the attack's aftermath, some of the raiders were identified, and the reports on this raid implied that it was the handiwork of a local criminal boss who had emigrated to India: 'Six of the raiders were identified as original residents of this village under not[o]rious gangster Lakha Singh, originally of Kahna Kachha, who shifted to East Punjab after the Partition.'[37] At this remove, it is difficult to disentangle criminal motives from the desire for revenge.

In other cases, one can only guess at the motivations of cross-border 'raiders'. In late October, Pakistani border forces responded to reports of 'some armed Sikhs moving about in the deserted village Sarja Marja'.[38] Left unsaid was the fact that a deserted village was most likely a formerly Sikh or Hindu village, and that these interlopers might well be returning refugees hoping to recover lost belongings. Another incident demonstrates that desperate or vengeful migrants did indeed return to their home villages. One night at the end of October, a large group of Sikhs, 'including some previous residents of village Lehl', in the Kasur area of Pakistan, raided Lehl. They looted the village and killed two Muslims before making off with twenty-six cattle.[39] In this incident (as in a number of others), local villagers were apparently able to identify the Indian villages from which the attackers came, again suggesting a certain degree of familiarity between the various parties involved.

Another confrontation involving a returning refugee occurred in mid-November, again in the Kasur area. Two Sikhs and a Hindu from the village of Theh Sheikhan 'who had evacuated returned to the village and assaulting the Muslim occupant of the house of [the] Hindu dug out and took away some buried ornaments besides some Khadar cloth belonging to the Muslim'.[40] Many refugees had buried valuables in their fields or family compounds before fleeing, hoping to return home and dig them up. The vast majority of such migrants lived out their lives in exile and never returned home to claim their goods. But homes near the border, as seen here, were within striking range of those refugees angry or desperate enough to attempt to recover their property.

In other cases, Indian raiders were motivated by the desire for revenge rather than a need to recover lost belongings. In mid-December 1947, a dozen Sikhs raided the village of Nath, near Lahore. There, they entered the house of a local goldsmith and 'compelled the Muslim goldsmith to point out the house of Noori, a bad character, whom they suspected of killing many Sikhs during the disturbances'. The goldsmith refused to provide any information, and the raiders shot at him in frustration, injuring his son. The shot attracted other villagers, including the notorious Noori; Noori fired his own weapon at the interlopers, who disappeared.[41] We have no further details on Noori's role in the partition violence, but it is evident that enmities created during partition had lasting effects.

In another case, refugees' local knowledge helped them conduct an effective raid on a Pakistani border village in Kasur. In mid-February 1948, a party of armed Indians drove away thirty-one cattle. They were identified as Sikhs who had been evacuated from the local area, and the police report noted that 'they were fully acquainted with all routes leading to the interior and thus managing to avoid Police pickets and nakabandi points [checkpoints]'.[42] This incident makes clear that local residents on both sides of the boundary had intimate knowledge not only of the territory but also of their neighbours on the other side of this invisible and often porous barrier.

Although the importance of infrastructure and the vulnerability of the divided canal system led to official fears about the possibility of sabotage, reports on border incidents record remarkably little damage to irrigation. In fact, Pakistani reports on 'Aerial and Land Incursions' include only one such case, in mid-September 1947, when 'Sikh inhabitants of villages Doode, Khalera and Khalsian [East Punjab] made a cut in the bank of a canal within our border'.[43] Apparently, the damage was not remarkable enough to record in further detail.

Indian reports show that flooding brought on by the belated monsoon of 1947 caused infrastructure problems and added to the miseries suffered by border residents and refugees alike.[44] Transportation was extremely limited for months, as refugees swamped rail and road networks. All non-emergency journeys were curtailed, and the authorities introduced a permit system to regulate train travel.[45] In some cases, however, assailants deliberately impeded fleeing refugees, even using canals as weapons. A PBF contingent sent to escort Muslim refugees from Kapurthala state (a princely state within Indian Punjab) found that Sikh attackers had cut an irrigation canal in order to render the refugees' escape route impassable.[46] The infrastructure system Radcliffe had been so anxious to preserve was now turned against the very people it had previously nourished.

Both states felt a pressing concern with boundary defence. In Pakistan, contemporary reports paint a consistent picture of a highly militarized society on the border. Given the continuing violence and their dangerous position so close to India, most male inhabitants of the Punjabi borderlands carried arms as they went about their daily activities. These arms ranged from *lathis*, spears and, for Indian Sikhs, *kirpans* (edged weapons carried in accordance with religious tradition), up through rifles and other firearms, all the way to sophisticated military weaponry. On more than one occasion, Indian attackers used bren guns and grenades. In one case, the Indian military reportedly used a two-inch mortar – albeit without causing any casualties – to silence cross-border firing.[47]

The Indian Government cited fears of Pakistani militarization as justification for its own defensive arrangements. In early September, a Punjabi situation report claimed that Pakistani authorities were distributing arms in Indian border districts.[48] Later that month, it was alleged that Pakistan had settled members of the Pathan ethnic group, regarded as fierce and warlike, in a belt of border villages and that the Pakistani Army was transferring troops to Lahore. Intelligence reports asserted that the Indian public took these moves as evidence of Pakistani preparations for invasion.[49] These fears rose through early October, fed by reports that Pakistan was arming its civilian population; 'in consequence of this, a demand for raising a national militia has grown and the introduction of compulsory military training for all youngmen is being advocated freely. Since the border remained disturbed, there has also been a great demand for drafting of more troops into that area.'[50] The Indian Government was concerned not only with threats from across the border, but also with potential unrest among its own borderlanders, who were living in constant anxiety.

[158]

The Indian Government rapidly put into place civil defence measures of its own. By early November, 'village defence licensees', who had been granted arms licences, were offering effective resistance to Pakistani raiders.[51] However, unlicensed weapons were still easily available, and local police efforts to confiscate them were largely unsuccessful. Volunteer defence organizations also sprang up, especially in the vicinity of Amritsar. These groups, some of them openly political, included 'the Punjab Frontier Corps, the Punjab Defence Force, the Congress Sewa Dal, the Student Home Guards and the Sher-i-Punjab Dal', and their leaders engaged in vigorous recruitment efforts. Members of the RSS, a militant group active even before partition, continued 'their usual exercises', arming volunteers with rifles and hand grenades.[52] When the Congress Party called for such volunteer organizations to disband, there was widespread discontent in Sikh militant circles. In early December, a government situation report noted that 'in spite of what has been said and done by the Government, the public, especially the well-to-do classes, remained obsessed with the inadequacy of defensive arrangements on the border and were very critical about them'.[53] The border situation was no longer merely a security risk, but had become a political liability for the new Indian Government.

Reports about border incursions reveal governmental attitudes towards these borderlands and towards the government across the line. They also highlight problems inherent in using government documents to understand the realities of border life. Indian intelligence reports make no attempt to disguise their anti-Pakistani bias. One report, part of a series that emphasizes Indian fears of an imminent Pakistani invasion, asserts, 'Muslim politicians seldom speak without mental reservations', a delicately phrased accusation of mendacity.[54] Emphasizing Pakistan's militarization of the border area, these documents portray Indian planning as purely defensive, a response to public pleas for help. It is not always clear whether the reports are simply summarizing public opinion or are themselves advocating for increased border defence. For example, the late October situation report argues, 'the demand for the issue of more arms under the Village Defence Scheme and the posting of more troops in that area became persistent and a feeling continued to grow that slow action of the Government in strengthening the border was putting the security of East Punjab in great jeopardy'.[55] The subsequent report takes a different tack, however, stating, 'there were complaints by ill-informed people about the disturbed state of the boundary with Pakistan and inadequacy of defensive arrangements'.[56] These sources must be read with a careful eye to their authors' perspectives, including possible national biases.

What is clear is that Government of India anxiety about these border areas was very real. This anxiety concerned not only threats from Pakistan but also problems with Indian residents of the border-lands, whose increasing insecurity made them restive. The perceived lack of governmental support was a constant theme in Indian situation reports from late 1947 onward. These reports were initially classified as 'confidential' but were upgraded to 'secret' in early October as their significance became clear. Demands for increased military presence and fears of a Pakistani invasion rose through October and November 1947. In December, with Indo-Pakistani conflict over neighbouring Kashmir heating up, there was 'considerable panic all along the border area. This gave a further fillip to the movement of well-to-do classes into the interior of the country and placed a further strain on the already slender transport arrangements.' Businesses suffered as well, and 'there were reports of businessmen winding up their assets in the border towns of Amritsar, Gurdaspur, Ferozepore, Fazilka, and Abohar. The Rai Sikhs, settled along the west bank of the Sutlej, were also thinking in terms of moving away after the next crop had been harvested.'[57] The one bright spot was the fact that the number of border raids decreased as 'unruly elements' in Pakistan appeared preoccupied with Kashmir.[58] Given East Punjab's struggle to resettle migrants from Pakistan, however, the prospect of border residents fleeing into the interior posed a serious danger to stability. The Government of India therefore kept close tabs on its unsettled Punjabi borderlands.

For their part, Government of Pakistan documents consistently emphasize Indian aggression, stating in almost every case that Indians fired first and that Pakistanis merely responded. In addition, Pakistani situation reports highlight the role of Indian officials, both military and police. The implication is that the Indian state approved, supported and even took part in these illegal and unprovoked incursions into Pakistan's sovereign territory. The real picture was undoubtedly more complicated, and although it seems likely that officials played a part in some cases, villagers in the Indian borderlands possessed the equip-ment, training and motivation to carry out such raids on their own. However, these reports offer valuable insight into the Government of Pakistan's early perceptions of itself as a victim of repeated, state-sponsored aggression from its larger neighbour.

This attitude is apparent from the beginning. The third entry in the 'Aerial and Land Incursions' report, for early September 1947, notes that 'Khem Karan Police (East Punjab) injured a Muslim' in a Pakistani village, abducted three villagers and took away some cattle.[59] In late September, a 'non-Muslim military platoon from East Punjab' reportedly helped force inhabitants out of two Pakistani villages.[60] On numerous other occasions over the next several months, local officials reported that Indian officials were behind raids on Pakistani territory. For example, after a late September raid that left one Muslim dead and three Muslim women abducted, it was reported that 'the raiders were accompanied by S.I. [Sub-Inspector] Hazara Singh – the last S.H.O. [Station House Officer] of Kot Nainan and F.C. [Foot Constable] Gurdial Singh'.[61] The phrases 'supported by military men' and 'supported by the Indian military' recur frequently in these reports.[62] Because many Punjabi men possessed uniforms left over from their wartime service with the Indian Army, however, it would have been difficult to tell civilians wearing old uniforms apart from active-duty troops.

If Pakistani reports are to be believed, there was a remarkable pattern of Indians firing first and Pakistanis firing almost exclusively in response to Indian provocation. Given the volatile situation on the border, however, it seems unlikely that the aggression would have been so one-sided. It is more likely that this reported pattern indicates that Pakistani officials either felt that Pakistan was – or wanted to portray Pakistan as – the victim of Indian-initiated attacks. An early example appears in the report for 23 September 1947, when invading 'miscreants fired about 7 rounds at the [Pakistani] Military Picket who also fired in response'.[63] Again in mid-October it is reported that when Sikh trespassers let loose their cattle on Pakistani land, 'the military men with the Sikhs opened fire on Police which was replied'.[64] Reports that do not clearly identify Indians as having fired first almost invariably note that the two sides 'exchanged firing': this phrase avoids identifying the side that initiated the firefight.[65] A rare exception occurred in mid-October, when, in response to an Indian attempt to drive away cattle grazing in Pakistan, mounted policemen 'engaged the raiders and fired seven rounds'.[66] Overall, these reports consistently portray Indians in the role of aggressors and Pakistanis as defenders.

Despite the tense atmosphere in which they worked, local officials occasionally cooperated to resolve problems without violence. As noted above, at least one incident involving villagers who had inadvertently crossed the border into Pakistan was resolved quickly and peacefully, when Indian and Pakistani police and military officials met to discuss the situation.[67] A few weeks later, two Pakistani women who were abducted after accidentally crossing the border in Kasur were recovered after a joint investigation by Indian and Pakistani police.[68] The Government of India even suggested that other states adopt the Punjabi model of periodic joint meetings.[69] However, resolutions like these appear only rarely in the surviving records.

The archives provide little information about the experiences of women in the borderlands. Indexes in the Lahore provincial archives show that documents relating to women, including women abducted during partition, were almost invariably categorized as so unimportant that they should be discarded after three years. Consequently, no such material survives. Women's experiences of borderlands development therefore remain a major lacuna.

Pakistani situation reports from 1947 and 1948 are slightly more revealing. In summaries of abductions and slayings, women are singled out from men. In some (though not all) cases, male victims are listed by religious affiliation, while women are simply 'women'. On 8 September 1947, for example, an incident that left six Pakistanis dead was recorded as 'killing four Muslims and two women'.[70] Casualty reports in many countries single out women and children, as a means of highlighting enemy brutality. But these particular reports indicate a deeper disconnect between the way the government thought about its male citizens and the way it perceived its female citizens. Female religious identity was not, apparently, a government concern to the extent that male religious identity was (and is; sixty years later, Pakistani national identity cards list the holder's religion). This may have been because in Pakistani society a woman's identity was tied so firmly to her father or husband's identity. (Even today, Pakistani – and Indian – governmental forms, such as passport and visa applications, require that any woman fill in information about her father or her husband.)

This is not to say that women were simply regarded as less important than men, however. The situation was more complex, for in certain situations, a woman might have been perceived as more important than a man, in terms of what her treatment implied about the honour of the larger community. Thus these reports assiduously note the abduction of women, in part because such assaults were considered an attack on a community's – as well as an individual woman's – honour. This concern continues to govern aspects of borderlands policy in the early twenty-first century. When tension between India and Pakistan rises, for example, women are among the first to be evacuated from border areas to the interior.[71] This is not an official policy but a tacitly agreed procedure, which holds true for both the Indian and the Pakistani borderlands.

Continuing borderlands development

In the years after partition, the number of cross-border raids decreased as the borderlands militarization increased. Occasional incidents of cattle lifting continued.[72] Even today, accidental border crossings by both animals and people remain a problem.[73] However, both countries continued to farm up to the borderline, making full use of the region's rich soil. As the conflict over Kashmir continued, flaring into open warfare in 1948, Punjabi districts such as Sialkot, which bordered Jammu and Kashmir, were particularly tense.

Pakistani border police in Sialkot complained that because they were not allowed to patrol within 500 yards of the border, that land was going fallow, while the Indians were gradually reclaiming agricultural land on their side of the Jammu and Kashmir line. Farming right up to their territorial limits was a point of pride for Pakistani officials, who noted, 'as a matter of fact it was remarked by U.N.O. Observers [United Nations personnel monitoring the situation in Jammu and Kashmir] that our boundary line was marked by the furrows of our ploughs'. Cattle theft remained a point of contention between security forces on the two sides. Pakistani police officials were anxious about the demoralizing effect of these incidents. As settlement and cultivation in Indian Kashmir moved closer to the border, they argued, 'the effect on [the] Pakistan side was that villagers suffered from lack of morale and several inhabited areas began to be deserted. Several incidents also occurred and the Indians considered the withdrawal of our Border Police as a signe [sic] of we[a]kness.'[74] Farming as near the border as possible was to be encouraged as a signal of Pakistani strength; conversely, Indian border cultivation was interpreted as demoralizing. It is not clear what farmers working in these areas thought of such dangerous but patriotic duties.

In 1948, the Government of Pakistan formed the Punjab Border Police to patrol the five-mile belt along the new boundary. Unfortunately, the Border Police were badly organized and poorly armed. Documents from the late 1940s and early 1950s reveal that they had to plead for more arms and ammunition, requests that were sometimes denied.[75] Patrols slept in the open or in buildings abandoned by refugees who had fled to India. One particularly plaintive memo from this period requests that the government at least supply rudimentary tents to this, its first line of defence.[76] (The request was granted.) Not surprisingly, the Border Police were inefficient and prone to corruption.[77]

By late 1948, it was more difficult to cross the border. Indian social workers employed in the recovery of abducted women had to request special permits to ease their movement across the boundary.[78] In 1949, India introduced a permit system intended to discourage Muslim emigrants from returning to India. Citing difficulties in settling Hindu and Sikh immigrants from Pakistan, the Government of India declared that, as of 19 July 1949, Muslims wishing to resettle in India would have to apply for permission. Even then, the government apparently anticipated lifting such restrictions on movement in the near future, for it announced, 'The Government of India regret that they have to impose this restriction. It will be removed as soon as conditions settle down.'[79] A displeased Government of Pakistan threatened retaliatory measures.[80] In September, Pakistan announced the Pakistan (Control of Entry) Ordinance, which required permits for entry into its territory.[81]

Those who overstayed their permits were subject to arrest and could quickly find themselves in an uncomfortable position. For example, in India's Patiala and East Punjab States Union, an amalgamation of former princely states, administrators reported that eight Muslims had entered without permits and one permit-holder had overstayed. State officials regarded these unfortunates with suspicion, noting that 'the motive of three Muslims was to resettle in this Union and of others to search [for] the lost members of their families but it is possible that their motive might have been to work as spies'.[82] Borderlands residents seeking to reunite with family members on the other side of the line faced not only bureaucratic obstacles to travelling through territory where they had previously moved freely but also government suspicion once they had crossed the boundary.[83]

By August 1948, India's augmented border defence included limitations on the distribution of maps and aerial photography of border areas.[84] When the East Punjab Public Works Department requested aerial photography of certain towns in order to build new townships, the Survey of India denied its request, citing Ministry of Defence orders.[85] Paradoxically, this attempt to make the boundary invisible, at least on maps, helped render it more real. The Government of India's refusal to allow images of the boundaries to be freely made or distributed was part of the process of making the Punjabi boundary more than just a line on a map, transforming it into a politico-military barrier. With the boundary hidden from view, it became more of a barrier – not only to administrators who were denied knowledge of India's sensitive border areas, but also to civilians wishing to cross back into what had once been their homeland but was now a hostile alien power.

Border raids into Pakistan continued through the late 1940s and early 1950s (see Table 8.1), although the threat they posed diminished steadily. In response to these raids, Pakistan developed its border defences. Punjab police enforced a 'Punjab Village and Small Town Patrol Act' in selected border villages through 1954. Other villages were responsible for their own defence.[86] In 1949, the Government of Pakistan considered a proposal to fence the boundary with barbed wire, but concluded that it was too expensive.[87] Although the borderlands had unique security issues, border incidents were not the only problem facing the Pakistani Punjab; crime continued to be a major problem province-wide. Punjabi locales that bordered tribal areas had to contend not only with Indian raids but also with attacks by Pathan tribesmen.

Despite Pakistan's implementation of border defence measures, an association of ex-servicemen expressed concern about the lack of arms for border residents as late as 1951, writing, 'it is now over three years since we are trying to get free arms for the settlers on the border'. The organization's assistant secretary complained that

> even the pickets who do night patrolling have no arms on them. They carry lathis [wooden batons] and spears. Very few have got guns on them but that [sic] are also not sufficient at all to serve the purpose. The original scheme was that every one (adult member) must carry arms wherever he goes within the border limit similarly to those of tribal areas of N.W.F.P. [Pakistan's largely autonomous North West Frontier Province]. Personally I would like to see our fit women carry light arms on them so that they may be able to protect themselves against any surprise attack.[88]

Border residents, who saw themselves as the country's first line of defence, sometimes felt neglected by the central government. The provincial government's correspondence about this complaint highlighted differences between the expectations of border residents and governmental plans. There were no plans to arm every adult on the border, officials noted, although immediately after partition weapons had been withdrawn from other provinces and reallocated to border areas. In addition, gun licence fees had been waived for licensees who lived within five miles of the border. The government admitted, however, that the number of arms distributed to border residents was 'no doubt not an adequate supply in comparison to the population on our border'.[89] The inhabitants of the borderlands continued to live in insecurity.

Boundary disputes

Although local residents bore the brunt of border problems, the two central governments had their own border concerns. In addition to lower-level boundary incidents, four major territorial disputes resulted from the Radcliffe award.[90] These disputes concerned (from north to south) three villages along the Amritsar–Lahore border: Theh Sarja Marja, Rakh Sardar Hardit Singh and Pathenke; Chak Ladheke in Kasur *tehsil*; the headworks area at Hussainiwala in Ferozepur; and the canal headworks at Sulemanke (see maps 6, 7 and 8). In addition, the lack of physical markers such as pillars to indicate the boundary line made life more difficult for local residents and security forces alike. In 1960, India and Pakistan finally settled their outstanding disputes over the

Table 8.1 *Impact of border raids on Pakistani Punjab 1948–55*

	Murder			Dacoity [Banditry]			Burglary			Robbery		
	Due to border raids	Due to Pathan raids	Punjab total[a]	Due to border raids	Due to Pathan raids	Punjab total[a]	Due to border raids	Due to Pathan raids	Punjab total[a]	Due to border raids	Due to Pathan raids	Punjab total[a]
1948	n/a	n/a	n/a	93	124	n/a	20	59	932	n/a	n/a	n/a
1949	12[b]	n/a	1120	27	5	98	5	8	704	48	4	10,770
1950	5	1	n/a	14	0	72	1	1	586	15	1	9,817
1951	3	2	1126	7	3	65	1	2	554	10	0	10,422
1952	1	0	1098	6	0	43	0	1	445	4	1	9,490
1953	0	3	1232	8	1	112	2	1	481	0	1	9,533
1954	0	3	1169	6	1	37[c]	2	2	376[d]	1	0	7,898[e]
1955	0	9	2373	1	5	211	2	2	734	0	0	11,063

n/a – not available

[a] Reported cases; includes cases unrelated to border or Pathan raids.

[b] 6 in Lahore, 2 each in Kasur and Sialkot, 1 each in Montgomery and Sheikupura.

[c] Conflicting information appears in the 1954 and 1955 reports; the 1955 report gives the total number of dacoities for 1954 as 260. Breakdown for 1954 dacoities committed in the course of border raids and by Pathans is the same in both reports.

[d] Conflicting information appears in the 1954 and 1955 reports; the 1955 report gives the total number of robberies for 1954 as 907. Breakdown for 1954 robberies committed in the course of border raids and by Pathans is the same in both reports.

[e] Conflicting information appears in the 1954 and 1955 reports; the 1955 report gives the total number of burglaries for 1954 as 12,662, but does not provide a breakdown of 1954 burglaries committed in the course of border raids and by Pathans.

Sources: Report on Police Administration, 1949; Report ... 1950; Report ... 1951; Report ... 1952; Report ... 1953; Report ... 1954; Report ... 1955.

Radcliffe line, completing the demarcation of the Punjabi boundary by April 1960. As it happened, the first major conflict arising from the Radcliffe award concerned not the distribution of territory but the sharing of water.

The distribution of water between India and Pakistan was initially governed by a standstill agreement, signed on 18 December 1947. That agreement expired on 31 March 1948, and the following day India cut off Pakistan's water supplies from the Hussainiwala headworks and the Upper Bari Doab canal. This interruption came during the planting season for the summer crop and shut down a large portion of Lahore's municipal water supply, causing severe disruptions in Pakistani Punjab. As the upper riparian, India was in a stronger position, and Pakistan agreed, on 4 May 1948, to pay India 'such *ad hoc* sum as may be specified by the Prime Minister of India'. In exchange, India reopened the closed canals.[91] This temporary agreement lasted until 1960, when these problems were largely resolved by the Indus Waters Treaty, a notable success story in Indo-Pakistani relations. The treaty divided the river system of the Punjab in two, giving India rights to all the waters of the three eastern rivers, while Pakistan relied on the three western rivers. Pakistan subsequently constructed link canals to carry water from these western rivers to eastern Punjab, making it less dependent on Indian cooperation.[92]

As for territorial disputes, a 1951 meeting of the Chief Secretaries of East and West Punjab produced encouraging results. The delegates agreed that a clearly demarcated boundary was necessary. Furthermore, they acknowledged the 'difficulties that arise on account of some villages belonging to one Dominion being on the wron[g] side of the river in the other Dominion'. They offered no immediate solution but laid out extensive cooperative procedures intended to improve the situation. These guidelines, which called for warnings to border security forces not to assist raiders, show that each side suspected the other of aiding rather than preventing cross-border attacks.[93]

In April 1956, police officials from East and West Punjab agreed on a policy to deal with riverbed changes. Their agreement provided that

> if in future a river changes its course and land in possession of one side is thrown on the other side of the river, as a result thereof no attempt shall be made by nationals of either side or their armed forces to exercise or establish control or possession of the area in question. The matter will at once be reported to the two Inspectors General who will meet and make suitable recommendations to their respective Governments. At the same time, they will take adequate steps to ensure that the local problem does not develop into a dispute involving firing or other use of force.

Enacting this accord required the approval of both central governments, however, and the Government of Pakistan took no action.[94]

As border incidents continued, cooperation gave way to other priorities. The Government of Pakistan became concerned about the effect on national morale of firing on the border and directed its provincial governments to respond more aggressively: 'A feeling of frustration is sometimes created by reports in Press that Pakistani forces did not reply to Indian fire or other [sic] they retaliated at very end. Firing across border is an aggressive action to which immediate reply should be made.' Furthermore, the central government directed that Indian prisoners should not be returned except in exchange for Pakistani captives.[95]

In August 1958, Indian and Pakistani officials revisited their boundary disputes at a conference in Karachi. The conferees reached no agreement on any of the Punjabi disagreements, each side citing its own interpretation of the Radcliffe award to support its claims. India contended that Pakistan had to clarify its claim to the Sulemanke headworks before Radcliffe's direction that 'this boundary line should ensure that the canal headworks at Sulemanke will fall within the territorial jurisdiction of the West [Pakistani] Punjab' could be applied.[96] For Hussainiwala, Pakistan asserted that joint control of the headworks should precede demarcation of the boundary, while India took the opposite position. In regard to Chak Ladheke, an area of Kasur *tehsil*, disagreements arose as to whether Radcliffe's text or the local map annexed to his award took precedence. Radcliffe had stated that he had attached the provincial map to his award for illustrative purposes only and that the text took precedence, but India pointed out that he had neglected to make a similar statement for the Kasur *tehsil* map (see map 3).[97] Finally, India maintained that Radcliffe's statement that he had made 'small adjustments of the Lahore–Amritsar boundary' indicated that three villages (Theh Sarja Marja, Rakh Sardar Hardit Singh and Pathenke) belonged to India, while Pakistan pointed out that the Radcliffe award specified the Lahore *tehsil* line as the boundary in this area. The plot thickened when Pakistan claimed that the Deputy Commissioners of Amritsar (India) and Lahore (Pakistan) Districts had agreed to a territorial exchange in 1948. Pakistan asserted that it had given India the area of Jhugian Noor Mohammad in 1949, but that India had failed to hand over the promised areas of Theh Sarja Marja. India professed itself bewildered and noted that it had uncovered no evidence of any such agreement. Both sides left the bargaining table unsatisfied.[98]

The importance of the Sulemanke headworks is readily apparent on a 1953 map produced by the Survey of Pakistan.[99] The legend for this map, a small scale (1 inch: 50 miles) depiction of the whole of Pakistan, does not include canal headworks. However, on the map itself, the 'Sulaimanke Headworks' are clearly marked on the Indo-Pakistani boundary. The italicized type used to indicate the Sulemanke equipment puts it on a par with small cities like Toba Tek Singh. No other canal headworks are marked, either in Pakistan or in India. Yet the Sulemanke headworks appear, presumably because of their national-level significance. Including them on a national map also strengthened Pakistan's claim.

In February 1959, Pakistani and Indian delegates met again in Karachi to revisit the Sulemanke and Hussainiwala headworks disputes. Disagreement over the definition of 'headworks' impeded progress, but a sub-committee of engineers was appointed to discuss the point. Not surprisingly, given Pakistan's desire to claim as much of this territory as possible and India's desire to restrict Pakistani claims, the two sides emerged with different definitions. However, both delegations agreed that the Radcliffe award mandated some adjustment of territory in the Sulemanke area. In regard to the Hussainiwala headworks, India maintained that Radcliffe's recommendation of 'joint control' did not require territorial adjustments, while Pakistan insisted that it meant that Radcliffe had not actually delineated a boundary in this area. The two sides were unable to reach any agreement on boundary adjustments or joint control.[100]

Not all parties were disappointed at this failure. Pakistani documents demonstrate that there was more than irrigation equipment at stake in these disputes; defence needs also played a role. During the preparations for the February 1959 conference, Pakistani defence officials 'pointed out that the Hussainiwala Headworks ha[d] substantial strategic value. They were situated on the soft belly of West Pakistan defences.' Because their loss would leave Pakistan vulnerable, and because it was felt that Pakistan could well lose these headworks if the dispute went to arbitration, the status quo was preferable. As for the Sulemanke headworks, Pakistani engineers believed that Pakistan had a strong claim but were prepared to continue the stalemate if military interests so required: 'the engineers felt that if due to defence requirements it was necessary to continue the dead-lock, in the Sulemanke Headworks our present position was not uncomfortable'. Plans were made to prolong the standoff by linking any Indian demands for arbitration with conditions unacceptable to India.[101]

The next year finally brought a breakthrough. Mian Muhammad Sadullah, who had served as superintendent on the Punjab boundary commission before going on to a lengthy career in government, participated in the Indo-Pakistan boundary negotiations. Sadullah recalls that

India insisted that the boundary follow the deep channel (or thalweg) of nearby rivers. Such an arrangement, he says, would have been to India's advantage, because India held more Pakistani territory in their 'adverse possession' than vice versa.[102] This situation resulted from the fact that monsoon floods in Punjab annually cut away at the western (Pakistani) bank, meaning that Pakistan lost territory every year. In a memo drafted for Pakistani negotiators, Sadullah argued that Radcliffe had intended to 'freeze' the boundary in alignment with the existing administrative lines mentioned in his award, so that the meanderings of the river would make no difference.[103]

In January 1960, India and Pakistan finally resolved their Punjabi boundary disputes. A preliminary meeting on 4 January 1960 brought settlements on all four disputes with relatively little difficulty; these agreements were codified on 11 January. The villages of Theh Sarja Marja, Rakh Sardar Hardit Singh and Pathenke went to Pakistan, based on administrative boundaries laid down by the British in 1939. Chak Ladheke went to India, in accordance with the division of Kasur *tehsil* as outlined on the map Radcliffe attached to his award. The members of the Pakistani delegation were pleased with this outcome, since their guidance had authorized them to give up their claims not only to Chak Ladheke but also to the other three villages.[104] In light of its own irrigation development and World Bank efforts to settle Indus Valley canal disputes, Pakistan relinquished its claims to the Hussainiwala headworks. The Pakistani delegates offered this concession, subject to a resolution of the Sulemanke dispute, in exchange for Indian guarantees that the status quo would be maintained until all canal disputes had been settled. The Sulemanke area required more negotiation, but after both sides modified their claims, Pakistan won control of most of the headworks area. India undertook to maintain the portion of the protective banks, vital to the proper operation of a headworks, that remained in its control.[105] However, as a Pakistani summary noted, 'had we not been in possession of some area at Hussainiwala it is doubtful whether the Indians would have agreed to our claim at Sulemanki Headworks'.[106] The final agreement also clarified that territory would not switch sides due to post-monsoon riverbed changes: 'where, due to the change in the course of a river, territory of one country is thrown on the other side, such change will NOT affect either the de jure or de facto position of the territory'.[107] Areas held in the 'adverse possession' of one country were to be returned to the rightful owner by 15 October 1960; in fact, this handover was delayed until January 1961.[108]

In addition, the two governments agreed on detailed ground rules for border security forces on both sides. No troops or border posts were to be stationed within 150 yards of the boundary, or 'zero line', although security forces could patrol within this restricted zone, as well as pursue offenders up to the boundary. These ground rules acknowledged the likelihood of civilians wandering over the boundary, noting that, 'In the case of local population, inadvertent crossings are likely to take place along[ ]with border. The border security forces, after satisfying themselves that the crossing was done inadvertently, shall immediately return the persons concerned to the opposite commanders at officer level.' They also recognized that cattle theft was a continuing problem and outlined procedures for the resolution and prevention of such episodes. The ground rules also attempted to provide for the safety of farmers, asserting their right to farm land up to the boundary itself: 'nationals of both the countries, while cultivating land up[ ] to the de facto boundary of the country concerned shall not be interfered with by the border security forces of the other side'.[109] Both India and Pakistan placed great importance on maintaining the borderlands' agricultural productivity.

At the time of the treaty's signing in January 1960, only 252 miles out of the 325-mile-long Punjabi boundary had been demarcated. Once the Radcliffe disputes had been settled, however, India and Pakistan made demarcation of the remaining line a priority. With the Survey of India and the Survey of Pakistan working together, the Punjabi boundary was completely demarcated by the end of April.[110] This accomplishment marked the end of serious dispute over the Radcliffe award for Punjab. Border tensions continued, especially during the 1965 and 1971 wars; in 1965, Indian tanks crossed the Lahore border in force and stopped only a few miles outside the city. After the war, however, India and Pakistan agreed to return all captured territory and restore the status quo ante.[111] The Radcliffe line was fixed, from a state perspective; for local residents, negotiating life in the borderlands was an ongoing process.

Conclusion

The post-partition experience of border residents was, to a certain extent, a continuation of previous patterns, in which attackers from the north-west frontier occasionally swept down onto the plains, stealing cattle and committing murder.[112] Raids by Pathan tribesmen continued even after partition, placing Pakistani border dwellers in the uncomfortable position of anticipating attacks both from across the boundary and from Pakistan's interior. In addition, international tension periodically worsened the situation in the borderlands.

In 1962, Pakistan replaced its marginally effective Border Police with the Pakistan Rangers. This federally run civilian force is commanded by officers who rotate in from the regular Army. They patrol the international boundary in Sindh and Punjab, while in Kashmir the working boundary (the line between Pakistani Punjab and Jammu and Kashmir state) and the Line of Control (the ceasefire line between Indian- and Pakistani-controlled Kashmir) are under the direct control of the Army. The Rangers' Indian equivalent is the Border Security Force (BSF), which replaced State Police guards after the 1965 war.[113]

In addition to local problems, inhabitants of the Punjabi borderlands have been caught up in larger national and international conflicts. In both the 1965 and 1971 wars, Indian and Pakistani troops fought along this border. From the early 1980s through the early 1990s, when Sikh radicals waged an intense struggle in Indian Punjab against the Indian Government, India accused Pakistan of waging a proxy war by assisting the militants. For their part, Pakistani officials cite Indian mistreatment of prisoners and recall the headless bodies of Sikh victims floating down the Sutlej River into Pakistan.[114] In other words, the central governments of both sides have used the borderlands to further their own ends, including attempts to score points against the other side.

In the 1980s, fearing that Pakistan would provide cross-border support to the Sikhs, India erected a border fence, as Pakistan had considered doing in the 1950s. After fencing its boundary with Pakistan from the Arabian Sea up until the point where the working boundary starts, India began fencing the working boundary in late 2001.[115] The Punjabi fence runs along the Indian side of the border, 150 yards from the zero line. Despite the cost and scarcity of electricity, large portions of this fence are lit at night by powerful floodlights. There are 560 gates in the fence, which BSF officers open at 8.00 in the morning, to allow farmers to reach their fields, and close at 4.00 in the afternoon.[116]

In border areas near Lahore, civilian fields run almost all the way up to the zero line. In peacetime, the land seems eerily normal, as farmers work in their fields, animals graze near the border and dogs wander across the zero line, although armed border guards perch in observation posts every few hundred yards along the line. The last ten feet before the border, on each side, are reserved for a dirt track, which each side monitors for footprints left by border-crossers. Border guards watch this final ten-foot dirt track carefully in order to prevent farmers from eking out an extra foot or two of farmland.

Although the Punjabi border is now clearly demarcated and even fenced, and all Punjabi boundary disputes have been settled, it remains tense. There is constant smuggling along the entire international boundary, in both the Rajasthan/Sindh and Punjab borderlands. Most of this smuggling involves gold, drugs or alcohol, a banned substance in Muslim Pakistan. There are also weekly shootings, as border guards intercept border-crossers. It is likely that many of the victims are smugglers, although the Rangers assert that most are Indian intelligence agents. Although the level of suspicion on the border is extremely high, there are cooperative arrangements in place. The two countries' border forces have regular meetings, which range from low-level conferences between patrols to biannual general staff-level gatherings. Officially, any person who crosses the border, even inadvertently, must be detained and interrogated. However, local commanders do have the discretion to resolve – and a tradition of resolving – such problems on the ground, before they escalate into international incidents. Calling a flag meeting, by raising a white flag and walking up to the zero line, they hold an informal conference with officers on the other side. When the person who has crossed the line is a local resident known to the guards, they are usually able to resolve the situation and return the individual within twenty-four hours. If it takes longer than twenty-four hours, the unfortunate farmer in question must be handed over to the intelligence agencies. Relations between counterparts in the border forces are formal, not friendly, but the two organizations seem to have a fairly effective working relationship during peacetime.[117]

Increased international hostility still imposes additional difficulties on borderlands residents. In the winter of 2001–2, for example, rising Indo-Pakistani tensions led both governments to mine their entire international boundary. Coming immediately after planting for the *rabi* (wintertime) crop, the mining deprived affected farmers not only of their harvest but also of their lands. Poorly marked minefields and mine-related accidents killed a number of civilians as well as some 150 soldiers, and stray livestock were also killed.[118] In October 2004, India reported that it had removed 99 per cent of the mines laid in 2001–2.[119] This episode provides a vivid reminder that, sixty years past partition, life in the borderlands remains volatile.

Notes

1 J. R. V. Prescott, *Political Frontiers and Boundaries* (London: Allen & Unwin, 1987), pp. 13–14. See also S. Whittemore Boggs, *International Boundaries* (New York: Columbia University Press, 1940), pp. 6, 22.
2 Notable among these is Peter Sahlins's *Boundaries: The Making of France and Spain in the Pyrenees* (Berkeley: University of California Press, 1989), which demonstrates the possibility and the value of combining local history with analysis of state-level processes. For Africa, see Anthony Asiwaju, *Borderlands Research: A Comparative Perspective* (El Paso, TX: University of Texas at El Paso, 1983).
3 See for example Ainslie T. Embree, ed., *Pakistan's Western Borderlands: The Transformation of a Political Order* (Durham, NC: Carolina Academic Press, 1977).
4 Chatterji, 'Fashioning.'

5   Willem van Schendel, 'Working through partition: Making a living in the Bengal borderlands', *International Review of Social History* 46 (2001), pp. 393–421.
6   See Ian Talbot, *Divided Cities: Partition and Its Aftermath in Lahore and Amritsar 1947–1957* (Oxford: Oxford University Press, 2006), as well as Virinder S. Kalra and Navtej K. Purewal, 'The strut of the peacocks: Partition, travel and the Indo-Pak border', in *Travel Worlds: Journeys in Contemporary Cultural Politics*, eds Raminder Kaur and John Hutnyk (London: Zed Books, 1999), pp. 54–67. See also Gurdit Singh and Carol C. Fair, 'The partition of Punjab: Its impact upon Sikh sacred and cultural space', pp. 253–68; Shinder S. Thandi, 'The unidentical Punjab twins: Some explanations of comparative agricultural performance since partition', pp. 298–324; and Mohammad Waseem, 'Partition, migration and assimilation: A comparative study of Pakistani Punjab', especially pp. 218–25; all in *Region and Partition: Bengal, Punjab and the Partition of the Subcontinen*, eds Ian Talbot and Gurharpal Singh (Oxford: Oxford University Press, 1999). Vazira Fazila-Yacoobali Zaminder, *The Long Partition and the Making of Modern South Asia: Refugees, Boundaries, Histories* (New York: Columbia University Press, 2007) deals primarily with figurative boundaries but includes a useful discussion of border surveillance and control.
7   Oscar J. Martinez, *Border People: Life and Society in the U.S.–Mexico Borderlands* (Tucson: University of Arizona Press, 1994), pp. 5–10.
8   Asiwaju, p. 6.
9   The incidents discussed here were recorded in Pakistani Government documents and reflect a Pakistani viewpoint. Undoubtedly Indian Government records, were they open to researchers, would provide details of similar incidents on the Indian side of the line.
10 See for example IOR Mss Eur F 164/17, Mudie Papers, 'Aerial and land incursions from East Punjab into West Punjab' [hereafter ALI], Part I (Lahore: Government Printing, West Punjab, 1948), 22 October 1947, p. 6.
11 25 September 1947, ALI Part I, 2.
12 26 September 1947, ALI Part I, 2.
13 8 October 1947, ALI Part I, 3.
14 16 November 1947, ALI Part I, 9.
15 22 September 1947, ALI Part I, 1.
16 6 October 1947, ALI Part I, 3.
17 20 November 1947, ALI Part I, 9.
18 31 October 1947, ALI Part I, 7.
19 2 November 1947, ALI Part I, 8.
20 13 October 1947, ALI Part I, 4.
21 16 October 1947, ALI Part I, 5.
22 18 October 1947, ALI Part I, 5.
23 'Report on situation in East Punjab for the first half of September, 1947', NAI 10(16)-PR/47, corr. 1.
24 'Report on situation in East Punjab for the first half of October, 1947', NAI 10(16)-PR/47, corr. 6.
25 'Report on situation in East Punjab for the first half of November, 1947', NAI 10(16)-PR/47, corr. 13.
26 8 October 1947, ALI Part I, 3.
27 Described in the misleadingly headlined 'Border villages of East Punjab not occupied by Muslims', which reported that Muslims had occupied only a few east Punjab villages (*Pakistan Times* (7 September 1947), p. 7, col. 5).
28 20 October 1947, ALI Part I, 6.
29 12 November 1947, ALI Part I, 9.
30 12 November 1947, ALI Part I, 9.
31 17 November 1947, ALI Part I, 9.
32 3 September 1947, ALI Part I, 1.
33 26 September 1947, ALI Part I, 1.
34 22 October 1947, ALI Part I, 6.

35 N.d., ALI Part I, 4.
36 9 October 1947, ALI Part I, 4. For other incidents in which individual raiders were identified, see 11 November 1947, ALI Part I, 8; 14 November 1947, ALI Part I, 9; 14 December 1947, ALI Part I, 10; 24 December 1947, ALI Part I, 11; 25/26/27 December 1947, ALI Part I, 12.
37 22 October1947, ALI Part I, 6.
38 24 October 1947, ALI Part I, 7.
39 30 October 1947, ALI Part I, 7.
40 23 November 1947, ALI Part I, 10.
41 16 December 1947, ALI Part I, 11.
42 19 February 1948, ALI Part I, 17.
43 16 September1947, ALI Part I, 1.
44 'Report on situation in East Punjab for the 2nd half of September 1947', NAI 10(16)-PR/47, corr. 4.
45 'Report on situation in East Punjab for the first half of November, 1947', NAI 10(16)-PR/47, corr. 12.
46 Husain, 'Evacuation of Kapurthala state Muslims'.
47 21 January 1948, ALI Part I, 14.
48 'Report on situation in East Punjab for the first half of September, 1947', NAI 10(16)-PR/47, corr. 1.
49 'Report on situation in East Punjab for the 2nd half of September, 1947', NAI 10(16)-PR/47, corr. 4.
50 'Report on situation in East Punjab for the first half of October, 1947', NAI 10(16)-PR/47, corr. 6.
51 'Report on situation in East Punjab for the first half of November, 1947', NAI 10(16)-PR/47, corr. 12.
52 'Report on situation in East Punjab for the first half of November, 1947', NAI 10(16)-PR/47, corr. 13.
53 'Report on situation in East Punjab for the first half of December, 1947', NAI 10(16)-PR/47, corr. 18.
54 'Report on situation in East Punjab for the first half of October, 1947', NAI 10(16)-PR/47, corr. 6.
55 'Report on situation in East Punjab for the second half of October, 1947', NAI 10(16)-PR/47, corr. 10.
56 'Report on situation in East Punjab for the first half of November, 1947', NAI 10(16)-PR/47, corr. 12.
57 'Report on situation in East Punjab for the second half of December, 1947', NAI 10(16)-PR/47, corr. 21.
58 'Report on situation in East Punjab for the second half of December, 1947', NAI 10(16)-PR/47, corr. 22.
59 6 September 1947, ALI Part I, 1.
60 26 September 1947, ALI Part I, 1.
61 N.d., ALI Part I, 2.
62 For cases of reported military or police support to raiders, see 14 October 1947, ALI Part I, 4; 16 October 1947, ALI Part I, 5; 18 October 1947, ALI Part I, 5; 19 October 1947, ALI Part I, 6; 20 October 1947, ALI Part I, 6; 24 October 1947, ALI Part I, 7; 10 December 1947, ALI Part I, 10; 6 January 1948, ALI Part I, 12; 7 January 1948, ALI Part I, 13; 4 February 1947, ALI Part I, 15; 11 March 1947, ALI Part I, 20.
63 23 September 1947, ALI Part I, 2.
64 16 October 1947, ALI Part I, 5; see also two reports from 1 November 1947, ALI Part I, 7.
65 For an early example, see 6 September 1947, ALI Part I, 1.
66 17 October 1947, ALI Part I, 5.
67 31 October 1947, ALI Part I, 7.
68 17 November 1947, ALI Part I, 9.
69 NAI 4(110)-P/49, corr. 4–5.
70 8 September 1947, ALI Part I, 1.

71 Lieutenant-General Zarrar Azim, Pakistan Rangers (Punjab), personal interview, 13 July 2000.
72 See for example the December 1952 incident described in PPA, Punjab Government Civil Secretariat 1953, Home 8, p. 41.
73 During a 13 July 2000 visit to the Wagah border crossing, members of the Pakistan Rangers reported that fifty-one Pakistani farmers were then in Indian custody.
74 PPA 1954, Home/General 4, pp. 6–8.
75 PPA 1951, Home/Police 431; PPA 1951, Home/Police 389.
76 PPA 1951, Home/Police 334.
77 In his work on the Bengali borderlands, Schendel notes that corrupt border security guards are an intrinsic element of smuggling networks. 'Easy come, easy go: Smugglers on the Ganges', *Journal of Contemporary Asia* 23:2 (1993), p. 195.
78 NAI 1–G(R)/49, vol. I, p. 27.
79 'Permits for entry of people from Western Pakistan', *Times of India* (15 July 1949), Sardar Patel Papers, NAI Microfilm Reel 15, No. 233. The restriction did not apply to residents of east Pakistan.
80 'Pakistan's threat of retaliation: Free entry of Muslims into India demanded', *Amrit Bazar Patrika* (18 July 1948), Sardar Patel Papers, NAI Microfilm Reel 15, No. 230; 'Permit system for entry into India: Pakistan minister's reactions', *Indian Express* (19 July 1948), Sardar Patel Papers, NAI Microfilm Reel 15, No. 225.
81 'Control of entry into Pakistan ordinance promulgation: Provision for government to enforce in any area', *Amrit Bazar Patrika* (26 September 1948), Sardar Patel Papers, NAI Microfilm Reel 15, No. 136.
82 NAI 5(11)-R/49, p. 13.
83 For further discussion of permit and passport controls, see Zaminder, especially pp. 79–112 and 161–226.
84 NAI 32(25)-H/48, corr. 2.
85 NAI 14(1)-RHB/49.
86 *Report on Police Administration in the Punjab for the Year 1949* (Lahore: Superintendent Government Printing Punjab, 1952); *Report on Police Administration in the Punjab for the Year 1950* (Lahore: Superintendent Government Printing Punjab, 1953); *Report on Police Administration in the Punjab for the Year 1951* (Lahore: Superintendent Government Printing Punjab, 1953); *Report on Police Administration in the Punjab for the Year 1952* (Lahore: Superintendent Government Printing Punjab, 1955); *Report on Police Administration in the Punjab for the Year 1953* (Lahore: Superintendent Government Printing West Pakistan, 1957); *Report on Police Administration in the Punjab for the Year 1954* (Lahore: Superintendent Government Printing West Pakistan, 1958); *Report on Police Administration in the Punjab for the Year 1955* (Lahore: Superintendent Government Printing West Pakistan, 1958).
87 PPA 1951, Home/Police 470.
88 PPA 1951, Home/Police 302, p. 3.
89 PPA 1951, Home/Police 302, pp. 4–6.
90 South of the Radcliffe line, another dispute arose over the Rann of Kutch, on the Sindh/Gujarat border. This conflict later contributed to the 1965 war.
91 *India: Bilateral Treaties and Agreements*, vol. 1 (New Delhi: Ministry of External Affairs, Government of India, 1994), pp. 42–3.
92 This paragraph draws on the excellent analysis in Michel, pp. 195–204.
93 PPA 1951, Home/Police 361, pp. 2–6.
94 Private collection, South Asia.
95 Private collection, South Asia.
96 *TP* XII p. 749.
97 Radcliffe had written, 'for the purpose of identifying the villages referred to in this paragraph, I attach a map of the Kasur tahsil', but did not specify, as he did with his smaller-scale map, that the text should prevail in case of any divergence between the textual and cartographic boundary representations. *TP* XII p. 749.
98 Private collection, South Asia.

THE DEVELOPMENT OF THE INDO-PAKISTANI BORDERLANDS

 99 Survey of Pakistan, 'Map of Pakistan showing political divisions' [map], 2nd edn. 1:3,168,000 (Murree: Survey of Pakistan, 1953).
100 Private collection, South Asia.
101 Private collection, South Asia.
102 Mian Muhammad Sadullah, personal interview, September 2000.
103 Private information.
104 Private collection, South Asia.
105 Private collection, South Asia.
106 Private collection, South Asia.
107 *India: Bilateral Treaties*, vol. 3, p. 308. Emphasis in original.
108 Private collection, South Asia.
109 *India: Bilateral Treaties*, vol. 3, pp. 306–8.
110 M. N. A. Hasmi, *Survey of Pakistan Progress Report 1947 to 1961* ([Karachi?]: [Survey of Pakistan?], [1961?]), p. 31.
111 *India: Bilateral Treaties*, vol. 5, p. 309.
112 Philip Woodruff, *The Men Who Ruled India: The Guardians* (New York: St Martin's Press, 1954), p. 138.
113 [Government of India,] 'Border Security Force', http://bsf.nic.in/introduction.htm, accessed 29 February 2008.
114 Private communication.
115 Somini Sengupta, 'With wrath and wire, India builds a great wall', *New York Times* (2 January 2002), Sec. A, p. 1, col. 1.
116 Zarrar Azim, personal interview.
117 This paragraph is based on personal observations and interviews during fieldwork in summer 2000.
118 Human Rights Watch Backgrounder, 'Recent landmine use by India and Pakistan' (May 2002), www.hrw.org//backgrounder/arms/ind-pak-landmines.htm, accessed 3 March 2008.
119 CCW Amended Protocol II Article 13 Report, Form B, 14 October 2004, cited in International Campaign to Ban Landmines, 'Landmine Monitor Report 2005: India' (October 2005), www.icbl.org/lm/2005/india, accessed 12 June 2008.

CHAPTER NINE

Imperial epitaphs:
Cyril Radcliffe and the end of empire

Of all the individuals who play a role in this story, Cyril Radcliffe remains the central figure. As I have argued, Radcliffe's reputation as a great legal mind may have been a compelling factor for the nationalist leaders, many of them lawyers themselves, who endorsed his selection for the crucial boundary commission post. Congress's hesitation to approve Radcliffe, on the grounds that as a Conservative he would automatically side with the Muslim League, was ironic. In fact, Radcliffe had voted for the Labour Party in Britain's 1945 elections.[1] In these matters as well as in larger questions, it seems clear that the Indian leaders did not know Radcliffe as well as they thought they did. He was neither as ignorant of nor as disinterested about contemporary India as they had assumed.

Both Congress and Muslim League leaders perceived Radcliffe as impartial, in large part because he had never been a member of the Indian Civil Service. Radcliffe in fact had no direct knowledge of India, never having visited the subcontinent. As I have shown, however, he knew the Indian political scene and, most importantly, British interests in India, from his wartime work as a minister in the British Government. Although unfamiliar with Indian society, Radcliffe was certainly familiar with British imperial values. Radcliffe's previous and subsequent work demonstrated that his primary loyalty lay with the British Government and its interests.[2] The Indian leaders who agreed to Radcliffe's appointment as boundary commission chairman regarded him as a man of unimpeachable character, a highly respected barrister with a reputation for impartiality. All this was true, but Radcliffe had too many links to the British Government to be truly disinterested. These connections included Radcliffe's Ministry of Information colleague Monckton, who advised the Nizam of Hyderabad on constitutional matters during 1947, as well as Radcliffe's government experience during World War II.[3] Fundamentally, Radcliffe's loyalty was to the British state.

In agreeing to Radcliffe's selection, Muslim League and Congress leaders seem to have taken the view that ignorance of India could be taken as a guarantee of objectivity. This assumption was problematic for several reasons. First, even if it were true that ignorance translated directly into objectivity, it seems likely that local knowledge, as well as experience in the delineation of international boundaries, would be equally, if not more, valuable in a commissioner than neutrality. Radcliffe had neither local knowledge nor boundary-making expertise. Second, given his wartime access to intelligence reports on South Asian politics, Radcliffe was less ignorant than the Indian leaders assumed. Third, Radcliffe was not an objective, neutral observer in the sense that the Indian leaders seem to have believed; he was very much part of the British Government 'team'. One historian writes, 'Radcliffe was the insider's insider – the ultimate Establishment figure who could be trusted to put the interests of the state before any other consideration.'[4] Finally, and perhaps most seriously, the Indian leaders apparently failed to appreciate that the distribution of Hindus, Muslims and Sikhs in Punjab was such that no amount of rationality, objectivity or expertise could have produced a line that satisfied all parties, or, more importantly, guaranteed the safety of those on the ground.

Why did Radcliffe accept the government's request that he undertake a task so unfamiliar to him? Having done so, why did he not insist on more time to do the job properly, or resign his post once his impossible timetable became clear? Radcliffe's background, as outlined in Chapter 2, provides some clues. I argue that Radcliffe's strong sense of loyalty to the British Government impelled him not only to take the job, but to finish it, even under problematic conditions.

First, however, let us examine alternative explanations. Money might seem the obvious place to start, but Radcliffe did not accept the boundary commission job for purposes of financial gain. As a very successful barrister, he would have made far more at the bar than the British Government could offer him for his time in India. Before World War II, Radcliffe was earning some £20,000 annually. When he returned to the bar in 1946, he took in £36,188; in 1948 he earned over £50,000. In 1947, however, his earnings totalled only £19,963, indicating a substantial loss of income during his time in India.[5] The case he undertook immediately upon his return paid him £3,225 for only seven days' arbitration.[6] The British Government was well aware of the financial sacrifice Radcliffe would make in taking on a position in India. Lord Chancellor Jowitt observed, 'I should think he is making at least £60,000 a year and could, without very much difficulty, make much more if it were worth his while.' However, Jowitt noted, money was not an overriding concern for Radcliffe. Jowitt urged the Secretary of State for India to agree without hesitation to Radcliffe's terms about travel, lodging and living expenses, but concluded, 'If you want a bargain, bargain about salary and it may be that he would go out for no salary at all. Anyhow, he says he does not regard that as important.'[7] In the end, Radcliffe waived his fee after returning to England. All in all, his work on the boundary commission most likely resulted in a significant financial loss.

Similarly, it seems unlikely that a desire for prestige drew Radcliffe to India, because there was little of that to be had in what he ultimately regarded as Britain's rather regrettable exit from empire.[8] It is true that Radcliffe was awarded the rank of Knight Grand Cross of the British Empire (GBE) in 1948 for his services in India. The following year he was elevated to the House of Lords, as a Lord of Appeal in Ordinary; no barrister had vaulted to such heights directly from the bar for over sixty years.[9] Despite these honours, however, Radcliffe regarded the Indian decolonization with sadness. If not honour or financial gain, then what motivated Radcliffe to accept this assignment?

One possible explanation lies in the importance of the amateur ideal in the British administration of India.[10] In this school of thought, a talented but unprofessional all-rounder, such as Radcliffe, was preferred to the professional expert, who might know more, for example, about established methods of drawing boundaries.[11] But in arguing that Mountbatten must have tampered with Radcliffe's boundary decision, another historian of South Asia has advanced an opposing view: 'It was always improbable that the highly professional government of British India, even in its dying days, would leave matters of prime importance to amateurs like Sir Cyril Radcliffe.'[12] In any case, the amateurism theory might have explained why the British Government *offered* Radcliffe the job, but not why he accepted it. Nor did it explain why Radcliffe kept the job after it became clear what a difficult and thankless task it must be.

Another explanation for why Radcliffe accepted the job is that he thought himself up to the task. A very intelligent man, Radcliffe doubtless had a high opinion of his own ability to handle difficult and unfamiliar problems. In his work as a lawyer, he routinely confronted unfamiliar issues and then addressed them in detail and within a tight timeframe. He may have thought that he could deal adequately with the boundary problem. Given that even some high-level Indian officials apparently were taken by surprise when the Punjab exploded into mass killing, it is not at all clear that Radcliffe really understood all that was at stake, including the level of violence that might result. There are reports that Radcliffe was briefed in London before setting out, but there is no indication of how thorough – or frank – this briefing was.

The argument advanced here, however, provides a more satisfying answer than do the other explanations discussed above. Radcliffe was a man devoted to duty and devoted to serving the interests of the British Government. In fact, government officials first approached him about the possibility of heading the Arbitral Tribunal, a different committee entirely, only later asking him to chair the boundary commission instead. It is likely that this fact accounts for Radcliffe's expectation that he would have up to two years to do his work – as well as his apparent surprise at being told he must finish the job by mid-August.[13] Radcliffe was willing to serve the Crown in whatever capacity it preferred. He saw his primary calling as service to British interests, wherever the government needed him, rather than any specific job, like conducting arbitration or drawing a boundary. As one historian notes, '[Radcliffe's] duty was clearly to His Majesty's Government, which had retained him and in whose best interests, as he saw it, he acted: the barrister's first duty is to his client.'[14] Even when Radcliffe arrived in India and was finally, very late in the game, informed that he would have not two years, nor even six months, but a mere seven weeks to draw the boundary, he remained at his post. As quoted above, Radcliffe wrote, 'I have carried with me into the long years of growing up a settled admiration for that special kind of courage that, without illusion, sustains an unequal burden to whatever the end may be.'[15] I argue that Radcliffe regarded his work on the boundary commission as a burden to be carried to whatever end resulted, no matter the personal cost. Unfortunately, the millions of people who lost their lives or their property in the 1947 partition did not have that choice – and they risked far more than Radcliffe did.

As far as his role on the boundary commission is concerned, Radcliffe might most accurately be described as a scapegoat for the British Government. As one historian has argued, 'The Radcliffe Commission, it is clear, was a device to load the onus of the details of Partition on to the shoulders of a non-"Indian" so as to leave Mountbatten blameless of responsibility for unpopular decisions.'[16] Certainly Radcliffe understood the depth of his unpopularity in both Pakistan and India; when asked in the early 1960s whether he would like to return to India, he reportedly replied, 'God forbid. Not even if they asked me. I suspect they'd shoot me out of hand – both sides.'[17] Radcliffe was unconcerned with his popularity, however, let alone in South Asia. He once wrote to a friend, 'I have never, as you know, measured things much in terms of happiness.'[18] To such a man, it seems unlikely that public opinion would have mattered greatly.

Radcliffe's loyalty to the interests of the British Government and the keen sense of duty he displayed in all his public service illuminate his work as boundary commissioner. These elements of Radcliffe's character explain why he accepted this arduous task in the first place, as well as why he did not withdraw his services when Mountbatten finally made clear its impossible parameters. For the vital problem of the boundary, and for Britain's less explicit but no less important goal of avoiding domestic and international opprobrium, Radcliffe was the British Government's man on the spot. He worked within the current of history, subject, like the other major figures in this story, to the buffeting of larger historical forces, but left his individual mark on partition and its aftermath.

Mountbatten made clear to Radcliffe in their early meetings that it was absolutely necessary to have a boundary line drawn before the transfer of power took place.[19] Given his intimate connection with the British Government, Radcliffe likely would have understood – or had it explained to him – how urgently postwar Britain needed to cast off its Indian commitments. It seems probable that he concluded or was instructed that a boundary line was needed to save Britain further losses. Understanding the importance of this task to the British Government, he provided that line.

In addition, Radcliffe was experienced with problems of public and media perception, having handled censorship and press matters during World War II. He would almost certainly have been aware that his task was not only to address the boundary problem, but also to do so in a way that benefited the British in India and the government back home. Radcliffe's work at the Ministry of Information left him keenly conscious not only of American attitudes towards the raj, but also of American influence on British public opinion and American pressure on the British Government.

This perspective may offer one explanation for why Radcliffe did not insist on more time, or more expert advice, or a different process, for delineating the boundary. His job was to draw a line that allowed the British to leave, and to make the process of line-drawing look legitimate. In a rare statement on the subject, he told an interviewer that Mountbatten and the nationalist leaders 'told me that they wanted a line before or on 15th August. So I drew them a line.'[20] The fact that, from the British Government's point of view, Radcliffe had performed in a satisfactory manner in 1947 is demonstrated by the British Government's continued use of his services in a variety of temporary positions. The British Government trusted and relied upon Radcliffe, even in the most difficult and dangerous circumstances.

Radcliffe's responsibility for the violence that followed the 1947 division has been overstated. The record shows that other British decision-makers, in both Britain and South Asia, saw (or should have seen) the potential for mass violence. But it cannot be denied that Radcliffe played a central role in a violent historical episode, and he was haunted by regrets for the rest of his days. An interviewer who met him near the end of his life observed, 'he had never really recovered from his impossible task as the drawer of boundaries between India and Pakistan in 1947 and the bloodshed which ensued'.[21] For Radcliffe, duty had a price. But many residents of Punjab paid a much higher price for partition.

Radcliffe's views on Britain's imperial legacy

Although he did not visit India until the age of forty-eight, in his later life Radcliffe devoted a significant amount of thought to Britain's history in the subcontinent. *Not in Feather Beds*, a wide-ranging collection of Radcliffe's speeches and essays, includes four pieces directly related to India, compared to six which deal with aspects of the law, to which Radcliffe devoted his professional career.[22] He collected prints with Indian themes.[23] His work in India also gave him a deeper interest in the role Britain had played there and in the men who shaped British imperialism in South Asia. In short, Radcliffe's brief but intense visit to India made a lasting impression on him.

Radcliffe's Indian experience reinforced, rather than shook, his sympathy for imperialist values and actions. Radcliffe's comments after his return prompted his friend Robert Bruce Lockhart to record, 'I felt that he really regretted our leaving India now that he had seen things for himself.' Radcliffe told Bruce Lockhart that the British withdrawal had been unnecessary: 'We could have held India, he said, quite easily, but having let things go so far we had no alternative but to get out. He blames Parliament and the people at home for the lack of interest which they always took in India.' Furthermore, Radcliffe singled out the senior officials of the Indian Civil Service, a key mechanism of the British colonial state, for high praise. South Asians, in contrast, came in for criticism, as Radcliffe opined that 'the Sikhs and Moslems have behaved like savages'. In short, in Radcliffe's view, 'the division was a great mistake'.[24] Despite his central role in making partition possible, Radcliffe apparently disapproved of the decolonization.

Radcliffe's writings also demonstrate that his time in India strengthened his imperialist leanings. In a BBC address in late October 1947, he chided his listeners for their lack of interest in India, especially in British accomplishments there. His remarks convey a distinct nostalgia for an imperial past that was in danger of being forgotten in the hurry towards decolonization. In particular, he regretted domestic ignorance of Britons' achievements in India: 'It is easy to turn the page, now that the change has come, and rightly come, and forget the story of what they did in remembering what they failed to do. It must have called for great qualities exercised not only in crises, but day by day: courage, endurance, initiative, fortitude, responsibility.'[25] To Radcliffe, there were heroic aspects to the work of Britons in India, who sometimes gave their health and even their lives to uphold colonial undertakings. Although in public he stated that the decolonization was a change that had 'rightly come', his private conversations and other public statements demonstrate a more complex set of attitudes.

In keeping with his personal priorities, Radcliffe placed particular emphasis on duty, including the special imperial duty represented by the theory of stewardship. This paternalistic view held that Britons governed India in order to train Indians until they were capable of self-governance. In the introduction to his published lectures and writings, Radcliffe wrote of his 'deep admiration for the courage, endurance and selflessness with which in so many settings so many men have sustained the weary burdens of the world'.[26] Two of his lectures detailed the qualities that he admired, as personified by imperialists *par excellence* Mountstuart Elphinstone and Henry Lawrence, whom he singled out as part of the foundation of the British raj.[27] Elphinstone was British Resident in the crucial Maratha Confederacy and Governor of the Bombay Presidency. Lawrence was perhaps best known as an advocate of direct British rule in India, rather than indirect rule through indigenous princes. He was also a famous example of British imperial 'sacrifice', having died during the siege of the British Residency in Lucknow during the uprising of 1857.

Radcliffe cited the epitaph Lawrence chose for his tombstone: 'Here lies Henry Lawrence who tried to do his duty. May God have mercy on him.'[28] Radcliffe imagined the thoughts that passed through Lawrence's mind as, on his deathbed, he selected these words for his monument. Radcliffe surmised, 'His mind had turned, I think, to search for some statement of the meaning of his whole life in India, and India had indeed been his life, and he wanted the epitaph on his tomb to sum up in those few words the significance of his life and service.'[29] Earlier, Radcliffe noted, Lawrence had written to a friend, 'I know I have failed, as all of us must more or less, aliens as we are; but keeping a good standard before our eyes, we may at least try to do our duty.'[30] Radcliffe held this devotion to imperial duty in high regard.

Radcliffe felt that the empire suffered after the British Crown took over the government of British India in 1858. He wrote, 'there is a great deal to be said for the view that, while it was the Company and the Company's servants who made the British empire possible in India, it was the Parliament at Westminster and its successive emanations, the Viceroys, who made it certain that that empire must ultimately wither in sterility'.[31] Radcliffe's rather strong language about the empire's withering emphasizes his distaste for London-based armchair policy-makers, in contrast with what he saw as the vigorous, knowledgeable and dutiful soldier-statesmen of the EIC. (Contemporary officials did not escape Radcliffe's criticism. He confided to a friend that he 'never liked' Mountbatten, who was 'terribly ambitious', with a 'thirst for publicity'.[32]) Radcliffe's disdain for decision-makers unfamiliar with Indian realities is rather curious, coming as it did from a man who was perhaps the best-known outsider to take part in Indian decision-making. Perhaps this comment indicates an awareness on Radcliffe's part that he himself was ill suited to the task he undertook in 1947.

Radcliffe's observations on empire also offer some tantalizing glimpses of his views on decolonization. Intriguingly, Radcliffe quoted Lawrence's view that 'I have failed, as all of us must more or less, aliens as we are', which could be interpreted as foreshadowing the fall of empire.[33] His examination of Lawrence and Elphinstone touched repeatedly on their expectations about the form the end of the raj would take:

> If the long years of British rule in India had ended in something more fruitful than polite abdication it might matter very much today to record what he [Henry Lawrence], who knew Indians so well, had hoped that the outcome of it all might be. In one of his Essays he wrote that, with wisdom, England might retain India as a 'noble ally, enlightened and brought into the scale of nations under our guidance and fostering care'. We are too near the immediate events of 1947 and what followed to say how far his hope was realized by the generations that followed him. In so far as it was, the credit lies with that conception of the duty owed by the alien race to its subject peoples of which Lawrence was an exponent at once ardent and compelling.[34]

This passage highlights, once again, the importance of duty. It also, like Radcliffe's observation that misguided British policies ultimately caused the empire to 'wither in sterility',[35] suggests his disappointment with Britain's 'polite abdication' of its power in India in 1947. It seems that he would have preferred a 'more fruitful' result, although the exact nature of that result is left to the imagination. Finally, this passage assigns the credit for any Anglo-Indian alliance to the British, rather than their nationalist counterparts.

Radcliffe felt strongly about what he saw as the benefits of empire. Overall, Radcliffe depicted the British empire as a necessity and even a good, although not perhaps an unmitigated good. He discussed its merits in classical terms, as befitted his Edwardian upbringing and education. In his 1947 radio address on India, he described the benefits of British imperial rule in classical terms, asserting that 'the gifts we brought were Roman: peace, order, justice and the fruits that these things bring. Men are apt to prize them the less the longer they enjoy them.' Despite this lack of gratitude, Radcliffe seemed to argue, the empire's achievements were worthy of praise: 'Like the Romans, we brought and maintained a system of justice that we tried to make even-handed and a system of administration that we hoped was impartial.'[36] It is important to note, however, that Radcliffe followed his remarks on the many benefits of empire with a qualification: 'Of course such gifts are not everything ... It may be that somewhere on our course we mistook the means for the end, and absorbed in our practical tasks, we failed to penetrate to the heart or soul of India. It may be that the government of one people by another can never be the best government in the long run, since benevolence and fairness are no substitute for national inspiration.'[37] With lawyerly attention to a full range of implications, Radcliffe could not avoid the ambiguities of empire, and he made no attempt to deny them.

The historian Sunil Khilnani has offered Radcliffe's letter to his stepson Mark as a requiem for empire. In this letter, Radcliffe referred to the ceremonies that would mark the end of the raj, mentioned – rather disparagingly – the Indian flag that would replace the Union Jack, emphasized his desire to leave India and lamented, 'oh I have sweated the whole time'.[38] Khilnani writes, 'It is the weary, fearful, honest pathos of these private words, not the fine public speeches and pomp that accompanied the British departure, that is the true imperial epitaph.'[39] Certainly there is a great deal of truth to the idea that the real story of British decolonization lay not in its façade of order and control, pomp and circumstance, but in more honest behind-the-scenes appraisals of its failings.

These words may indeed provide an appropriate summation, but it is unlikely that Radcliffe himself would have wanted them to stand as an imperial epitaph. In his public speeches, he focused on the empire's heroic history, rather than on Britain's losses, consciously offering a far more confident judgement. In fact, as he concluded his 1947 remarks on 'India as the page is turned', Radcliffe explicitly took on the role of imperial elegist, with rather different results than in his earlier letter. Referring yet again to the death of Britons far from the British Isles, Radcliffe said: 'In all recorded history up to the present no people has ever so mixed its dust with the dust of the wide world. Eccentric, tiresome, interfering, if you like, but, surely too, adventurous, ingenious, courageous and enduring. And yes, for better or worse, very remarkable.'[40] This elegy mixes acknowledgement of criticisms of British imperialists – 'eccentric, tiresome, interfering' – with admiring praise for the imperial endeavour as a whole.

This is the epitaph that Radcliffe offered in public. If he had felt the freedom or the desire to display his private thoughts, how might this statement have been different? Radcliffe never spoke publicly about the Indo-Pakistani boundaries – a major element of Britain's imperial legacy in South Asia.[41] In private, however, he felt great regret for the events that accompanied Britain's withdrawal. A few months before his death, during a newspaper interview for a piece that focused on his long history of committee service, he impressed his interviewer with the genuine anguish he felt over the violence in Punjab in 1947.[42] It is unfortunate that we do not have a clear record of Radcliffe's thoughts on the legacy of his own work in India.

Although he was never a member of the administrative or military cadres that ruled India and never had extensive direct involvement in making British policy towards India, Radcliffe's imperial perspective was typical of many members of his class. He had close connections to a number of individuals playing active roles in the empire. His brother Geoffrey was directly involved in the military aspects of maintaining British imperial rule in India, and, even before he travelled to India, Radcliffe moved in British social circles that included many high-ranking imperialists. He had a professional acquaintance with Churchill, one of Britain's staunchest advocates of empire. His friend Bruce Lockhart's brother, Lieutenant-General Sir Rob McGregor Macdonald Lockhart, served in India as Army Commander and briefly as Acting Governor of the North West Frontier Province. In short, Radcliffe's pro-empire views fit his social milieu.

Radcliffe was not a reactionary imperialist. As noted above, he stated publicly that he thought the time for a transfer of power in India had come.[43] Yet he shied away from addressing the question of whether India was 'a state of native people being held in bondage by the British invaders', disclaiming the knowledge necessary to make 'so magisterial a generalization'.[44] In the end, he clearly admired Britain's activities in India. Radcliffe's imperialist values emerged intact, even strengthened, from his brush with the intricacies of colonial governance. Given his views, it is ironic that he should have played such a crucial role in the dismantling of the British raj. However, Radcliffe accepted the fact that the British Government had decided to leave India, and there is no evidence that Radcliffe sought to delay Britain's departure or to sabotage the two new states of India and Pakistan. As argued above, Radcliffe's primary loyalty was to the British Government, which had made it clear that its interests lay in leaving India as quickly as possible.

For the rest of Radcliffe's working life he practised law, with interludes to chair government committees or otherwise lend his skills to resolving problems facing the British Government. A historian of the British civil service writes that Radcliffe rose to 'unofficial number one' on the list of 'the Great and the Good' in 1952 and remained there until his death, twenty-five years later.[45] One official described the members of this list as 'the useful people'.[46] In 1955, a Home Office official advised Prime Minister Anthony Eden, 'Lord Radcliffe, who is in great demand, should be reserved for subjects which are more complex or difficult intellectually.'[47] To the government, it seems, Radcliffe was the most useful of the useful people.

For all his loyalty to the British Government, however, Radcliffe never tolerated fools kindly, even (or perhaps especially) governmental fools. In 1967, he felt compelled to criticize a government white paper on 'D' Notices (confidential government letters to media outlets that effectively censor a particular story), with a statement in the House of Lords. A contemporary account picturesquely described Radcliffe's scathing review: 'In a 25–minute speech he took apart the government's case with the artistry of a surgeon, and at the end left it scattered about the operating theatre headless and limbless. Lord Radcliffe said that he was not going to speak in a contentious spirit. The rest of his speech, amounting to a verdict that the White Paper was not worth the material it was written on, indicated that if ever Lord Radcliffe felt really peeved it would certainly be a sight worth seeing.'[48] Radcliffe was not blindly loyal to the government of the day or to its positions but sought to protect the broader interests of the British state.

The British Government's later use of Radcliffe showed it to be satisfied with his work in India. As a leader of the Great and the Good, he found himself summoned to chair government committees many times over the next three decades. His work included the Royal Commission on Taxation of Profits and Income, in 1952, and the Committee of Inquiry into the Monetary and Credit System, 1957–59. He led the 1956 effort to prepare a new constitution for Cyprus, which later experienced a *de facto* partition.[49] Radcliffe also chaired the Committee of Inquiry into Security Procedures and Practices in 1961 and the Tribunal of Inquiry into the Vassall espionage case of 1962.[50] The report of his 1975 Committee of Privy Councillors on Ministerial Memoirs proposed a voluntary code of conduct that would limit officials' right to publish memoirs in order to protect official secrets.[51] In all these undertakings, Radcliffe's sense of the importance of preserving British state interests stands out.

[188]

The working life outlined here is that of a man remarkable for his sense of duty. His biographer traces this quality to Radcliffe's childhood, noting that 'coming from a military family with a father and two brothers professional soldiers, he had many soldierly qualities, obedience to the call of duty, direct thinking and a dislike of waffle'.[52] Radcliffe's own recollections point to the formative influence of World War I, as noted in Chapter 2, while his life-long association with members of the British Establishment contributed to his sense of identification with British state interests and values. This loyalty to British aims was central to Radcliffe's decision to undertake the boundary commission work in 1947.

Notes

1   Young, p. 466.
2   French, p. 321.
3   Birkenhead, pp. 217–54.
4   French, p. 321.
5   Heward, p. 20. Heward (p. 21) records that Radcliffe had such a successful practice that his long-time clerk drove a Rolls-Royce and owned a flat in the south of France.
6   Heward, p. 22.
7   TP XI pp. 342–3.
8   The exception was the possibility for inclusion in the honours list, but a number of officials felt these honours were in bad taste. 'Pug' Ismay, Mountbatten's chief of staff, insisted that Mountbatten remove his name from the list of proposed honourees (Roberts, p. 130).
9   Heward, p. 63.
10 Chatterji, 'Fashioning', pp. 186–7.
11 David Potter, India's Political Administrators 1919–1983 (Oxford: Clarendon Press, 1986), pp. 74–5.
12 Alastair Lamb, letter, Daily Telegraph (25 February 1992), p. 16.
13 Mosley, p. 195.
14 Lamb, Incomplete Partition, p. 83.
15 Radcliffe, 'Introduction', in Not in Feather Beds, p. xvii. Emphasis added.
16 Lamb, letter, Daily Telegraph.
17 Mosley, p. 200.
18 Radcliffe, letter to John Sparrow, 22 August 1957, cited in Heward, p. 21.
19 TP XII p. 12.
20 Kirpal Singh, ed., Select Documents on Partition of Punjab – 1947: India and Pakistan: Punjab, Haryona and Himachal – India and Punjab – Pakistan (Delhi: National Book Shop, 1991), p. 744.
21 Peter Hennessy, Whitehall (London: Fontana Press, 1990), p. 567.
22 Radcliffe took his title from Sir Thomas More, who, according to More's son-in-law, habitually urged his family to bear their troubles steadfastly, saying: 'We may not look at our pleasure to go to heaven in feather beds, it is not the way.' William Roper, The Life of Sir Thomas More (London: Folio Society, 1980), p. 48.
23 Heward, p. 180.
24 Young, p. 624.
25 Radcliffe, 'Thoughts on India', in Not in Feather Beds, p. 5.
26 Radcliffe, 'Introduction', p. ix.
27 Radcliffe's admiration for Lawrence may be related to the fact that, at Haileybury,

Radcliffe was affiliated with Lawrence House, named for Henry Lawrence's brother John (Viceroy of India, 1864–69). A number of the Haileybury houses were named for East India College notables, including other examples of imperial sacrifice; Colvin House was named for Sir Auckland Colvin, Lieutenant Governor of the North West Provinces and another casualty of the 1857 uprising (Ashcroft, pp. 141–3). As a schoolboy, Radcliffe would have heard these names on a daily basis.

28 Radcliffe, 'Henry Lawrence', in *Not in Feather Beds*, p. 88.
29 Radcliffe, 'Henry Lawrence', p. 89.
30 Radcliffe, 'Henry Lawrence', p. 89.
31 Radcliffe, 'Henry Lawrence', p. 100.
32 Young, p. 624.
33 Radcliffe, 'Henry Lawrence', p. 89.
34 Radcliffe, 'Henry Lawrence', p. 93.
35 Radcliffe, 'Henry Lawrence', p. 100.
36 Radcliffe, 'Thoughts on India', p. 5.
37 Radcliffe, 'Thoughts on India', p. 5.
38 Radcliffe, letter to Mark Tennant, 13 August 1947, quoted in Heward, p. 42.
39 Sunil Khilnani, *The Idea of India* (London: Hamish Hamilton, 1997), p. 201.
40 Radcliffe, 'Thoughts on India', p. 6.
41 His one additional statement on the subject came in 1948, when he drafted the answer to a Parliamentary question (IOR/L/P&J/10/119, p. 92) (see above, pp. 112–13; also Heward, pp. 48–9). This statement was remarkable chiefly for how little it revealed.
42 French, p. 330.
43 Radcliffe, 'Thoughts on India', p. 5.
44 Radcliffe, 'Rudyard Kipling', in *Not in Feather Beds*, p. 251.
45 Hennessy, *Whitehall*, p. 566. The list's exact composition was secret. When one Whitehall denizen (Lord Rothschild) sought to examine the question of patronage, he concluded that 'the list of the Great and Good is jealously guarded, no doubt for good if not great reasons'. Nathaniel Rothschild, *Random Variables* (London: Collins, 1984), p. 74.
46 Hennessy, *Whitehall*, p. 552.
47 TNA, PREM (Prime Minister's Office) 11/824, Brook memo to Anthony Eden, 14 June 1955, cited in Hennessy, *Whitehall*, p. 548.
48 Hugh Noyes, '"D" Notice white paper savaged: Scathing attack by Lord Radcliffe', *The Times* (London) (7 July 1967), p. 1.
49 A contemporary news report described the proposed constitution as offering Cyprus 'a façade of self-government carefully designed to preserve what the British in India used to call their paramountcy' ('Proposed constitution', *Time* (31 December 1956) www.time.com/time/magazine/article/0,9171,867492,00.html, accessed 29 February 2008).
50 Heward, pp. 152–70.
51 Heward, pp. 211–20. William Vassall was a KGB spy at the British Admiralty in the 1950s and 1960s.
52 Heward, p. 2.

CONCLUSION

'No such deeds':
responsibility and remembrance

In a 1955 speech in Pakistan's Constituent Assembly, the Governor of West Punjab, Mushtaq Ahmed Gurmani, cited the well-known scholar of nationalism, Ernest Renan:

> 'The essence of the nation', as Renan puts it, 'is that all its individual members should have things in common; and also that all of them should hold many things in oblivion'. He asserts that forgetfulness, and even historical error, form an essential factor in the creation of a nation. 'Historical research, in fact', he suggests, 'bring back to the light the deeds of violence that have taken place at the commencement of all political formation, even those the consequences of which have been most beneficial'. Luckily, we have among ourselves no such deeds to re-count.[1]

This extraordinary statement, apparently delivered in all seriousness, demonstrates that some politicians in Pakistan, even eight years after the bloodbath of partition, were capable of denying their compatriots' role in that violence.[2] They were not alone in this forgetfulness; some of their Indian counterparts fell into the same trap. Because the violence that wracked Punjab in 1947 was the work of militants of all religions, laying blame on any one party is an inadequate approach. Unfortunately, this perspective is still widespread in India and Pakistan. Nationalist works that focus on British bad faith and allege that complex conspiracies took place are also inadequate. As we have seen, Congress and Muslim League leaders acceded to a number of disastrous policies in the months leading up to independence, in some cases under British pressure and in others out of a desire to secure their own political gains.

Differences in Indian and Pakistani historiographies of partition are to be expected. In India, there is a greater sense of loss associated with the division, while in Pakistan one sees the reverse side of the same coin: a sense of gain, of pride in a newly created state. But in

[191]

Pakistani historiography as well there is a sense of loss; as the historian Hugh Tinker writes, 'Pakistan is unique as a country with a sense of bitterness and grievance for territories that have never formed part of its polity.'[3] Immediately after partition, the Radcliffe commission proved a convenient scapegoat for the three major parties involved. In the years that followed, nationalist historiography in both India and Pakistan, but particularly in Pakistan, has continued to offer skewed versions of the commission's work, implying that the unfair nature of the Radcliffe award was a key to the country's subsequent misfortunes.[4] The truth is rather more painful to contemplate. As one Pakistani observer (who believes that the notional boundary would have been better than Radcliffe's final line) bitterly concludes, 'Even the right boundary would not have been helpful. With the bad administrators we had, nothing would have changed.'[5] The role of the individual is at least as important as the larger structural forces at play.

This work calls for a move away not only from histories that seek to lay all blame at the feet of one party or another, but also from imperialist works that blame Indian political discord for the disastrous aftermath of partition. One of the primary arguments I have made in this book is that the British played a greater role than is readily apparent in determining the path towards partition. The Radcliffe boundary commission offers one example; from the outside, it appeared that the British, the Muslim League and Congress all cooperated in drawing up the boundary commission's terms of reference, personnel and procedure. In reality, the British guided key elements of this process, steering the party leaders towards approving Radcliffe as chairman. It is true that the nationalist leaders agreed to his appointment. Jinnah, for example, protested that he would have preferred personnel selected by the UN but assented to the boundary commission plan because he, like the other leaders, valued speed. But the British made good use of the atmosphere of pressure and fatigue in which all the leaders operated to move events in the direction most favourable to British interests. They were able to do so in part because the nationalist leaders were all eager for a speedy resolution; these leaders, therefore, must share responsibility with the British for sacrificing a more rigorous process in favour of a fast result.

By 1947, none of the decision-makers in Delhi, whether British or South Asian, had the political will or the resources to disarm the heavily militarized groups or subdue the inflammatory rhetoric of the political leaders who contributed to the violence in Punjab. All of them preferred to rely on a 'hostage' approach to the problem of minority security, assuming that the existence of large minorities in each country would guarantee the safety of minorities across the line. They repeatedly refused to implement plans for an orderly exchange of populations, even as a temporary measure. The result was an unplanned, chaotic and bloody migration, in which hundreds of thousands died and millions more lost their homes. One might wish that the nationalist leaders had displayed greater political will, but the fact remains that they were operating within the constraints of the British imperial system.

This is not to say that partition was a British conspiracy or that the British dictated the entire division. On the contrary, I have argued that the British were rapidly losing control of South Asia (which made them all the more eager to project the appearance of order). Both communal tension and nationalist triumph were eating away at the power of the raj. Certainly Congress and the Muslim League played a central role in the shaping of the Indian and Pakistani polities. Congress in particular seems to have had the upper hand; Ayesha Jalal has argued that Congress drove the division of India, frustrating Jinnah's desire for an equal share of power within independent India.[6] Furthermore, boundary-making was only one element – albeit a crucial one – of an immensely complicated division. That said, we must recognize what the boundary episode reveals about British efforts to stage-manage their difficult and in many ways humiliating retreat. The British, recognizing the significance of the new border, worked hard to keep key decisions about it under their control to the greatest extent possible, while disguising that control beneath a cloak of cooperation.

For some, the violence of partition led to horror at the damage each community had inflicted on the others. One historian asserts that by 1948, and particularly after Gandhi's murder in January 1948, 'most [Hindus] were prepared to share the guilt and atone for it ... the national mood was one of reconciliation. For a time, Hindus tried to bury the past and to co-exist with their Muslim neighbours as fellow human beings.'[7] These contradictory desires to atone and to 'bury the past' persist in modern South Asia. Other contradictions have arisen as partition passes into history. Krishna Sobti, an Indian writer and partition refugee, says, 'Partition was difficult to forget but dangerous to remember.'[8] Building on this theme, Urvashi Butalia argues that 'while it may be dangerous to remember, it is also essential to do so – not only so that we can come to terms with it, but also because unlocking memory and remembering is an essential part of beginning the process of resolving, perhaps even forgetting'.[9] As this vital work progresses, care must be taken to put these memories to constructive use. There is a vital difference between history written with integrity and propaganda that merely digs up old wrongs in order to support new aggression.

Reflections on 1947 naturally raise the question of how the partition process might have been improved. The first possibility is perhaps the most obvious: decision-makers could have devoted more attention to territorial issues. In 1947, all parties were content to discuss partition without getting down to territorial specifics until very late in the process. Congress had no desire to discuss potential lines because it did not wish to legitimize the possibility of partition. The British paid little heed to Wavell's efforts to force discussion of the borders of a potential Pakistan. For Jinnah, defining Pakistan would inevitably disappoint some supporters; it was more politically useful to allow people to imagine the Pakistan they most desired. Another possible explanation for the leaders' lack of interest in the boundary issue is that, from their perspective, the 1947 partition was less about territory than it was about political power. Political battles took on specific territorial dimensions only later. In many cases, these territorial effects, including the creation and hardening of a boundary, had a greater impact on local people than previous high-level political struggles had. For many borderlanders, partition aggravated problems rather than resolving them; it intruded, sometimes fatally, on the lives of individuals who otherwise had little reason to care about the political tussles that resulted in partition.

Second, British and South Asian leaders could have recognized and attempted to compensate for the role of politics. Shielding the processes of partition from all political influences would have been difficult at best. But rather than ignoring political pressures or simply wishing fervently that they would go away, the leaders could have acknowledged and incorporated conflicting demands – particularly Sikh requirements.

Third, these leaders could have made more serious arrangements for a worst-case outcome. In 1947, doing so would have required all parties to make fuller preparations to deal with mass violence and to grapple with the inevitability of infrastructure disruptions. If it proved impossible to separate infrastructure systems fully, they could have laid down clear guidelines for resolving future infrastructure-related disputes – and made a commitment to follow those guidelines. If preparing for a worst-case outcome seemed too overwhelming, perhaps the leaders should have explored alternatives to partition once again.

Finally, the British could have allowed adequate time. Many have argued that speed avoided worse calamities in 1947; from this perspective, a death toll of half a million to a million was a relative success.[10] This argument does not hold much water as a policy recommendation. It amounts to saying, 'Because we left things until the last minute, when we had no choice but to move quickly, we had no choice but to move quickly.' This approach cannot excuse the failures that resulted from the high-speed division; acting sooner, difficult though it might have been, would have been preferable. Moving too quickly in order to compensate for moving too late proved dangerous, because preparations for potential consequences were neglected. In addition, the British created a situation in which leaders on all sides had to work under conditions of high stress, while deeply fatigued, and with little time for reflection. These circumstances did not lend themselves to good decision-making. The paradox was that, at least according to the traditional imperialist view, violence seemed so imminent that British leaders judged it impossible to allow more time. Unfortunately, implementing the suggestions outlined here would have required a great deal of time, cooperation and political will – precisely the ingredients that were lacking in 1947.[11]

The lack of cooperation, and the inherent contradictions of partition, come through clearly, even in contemporary observations. As Ismay commented on the interim government of 1947, 'I do not suppose that in the history of the world there had ever been a Coalition so determined not to cooperate with each other.'[12] And as early as 1943, Penderel Moon, an experienced Indian administrator, had pointed out the problems with a Punjabi partition with uncanny prescience. He addressed in detail the question, 'Is partition of the Punjab practicable?' Lahore and Amritsar must be divided, he wrote, but there was 'no natural dividing line' between them. Any line in this area 'would be geographically, ethnographically and economically wholly artificial'. A boundary of this type might be acceptable on the provincial level, but it would not be adequate as an international frontier. Moon concluded that only the creation of a new independent state would necessitate the creation of such a line, emphasizing that 'the necessity for division, therefore, only arises in circumstances in which division would be impracticable'.[13] This irony proved fatal to many Punjabis in 1947.

Four intertwining themes have run through the course of this narrative: haste, the thin façade of order, Britain's concern for its international reputation and the British desire to present nationalist leaders as bearing primary responsibility for decisions over which, in reality, British leaders had done their best to maintain real control. Each of these issues impacts on the others. In the first case, the British were successful; they were able to extricate themselves by 15 August. The second issue, the pretence of order, quickly turned to chaos, particularly after the British officially relinquished power. On the third point, the British were surprisingly successful at presenting partition positively in the eyes of the world, even during the course of the Punjab massacres. This success was related to the final theme, Britain's skilful portrayal of the nationalist leaders as the driving forces behind partition and therefore responsible for its aftermath.

British leaders clearly regarded the South Asian withdrawal as a success, with honours going to key officials (except those who refused them, like Ismay). In September, with the Punjabi violence at brutal heights, Prime Minister Attlee presented Britain's departure from the subcontinent as a useful model to guide its actions in another major trouble-spot, the Palestine Mandate. He told his Cabinet that

> in his view there was a close parallel between the position in Palestine and the recent situation in India. He did not think it reasonable to ask the British administration in Palestine to continue in present conditions, and he hoped that salutary results would be produced by a clear announcement that His Majesty's Government intended to relinquish the Mandate and, failing a peaceful settlement, to withdraw the British administration and British forces.[14]

In other words, the approach adopted in India – establishing a firm deadline for withdrawal, come what may – had worked well enough for British interests that Attlee could advocate its use again.

While a full comparison of the Bengal and Punjab divisions would require a separate book, an examination of key differences between the boundary-making process in these two cases highlights several important points: the role of extreme boundary claims, Radcliffe's varying influence, the position of provincial political parties and the lack of direction from the central leadership of Congress or the Muslim League.

The first difference involves the moderate claims advanced in Bengal and the more extreme positions argued in Punjab. The Bengal Congress wanted a post-partition state in which its hold on power would be secure; to that end, it proposed a line that would minimize the number of Muslims left in West Bengal.[15] In Punjab, by contrast, the major parties advanced maximalist positions. The fear generated by claims such as the Muslim League's call for the territory surrounding Amritsar or the Sikh demand for much of central Punjab, arguably contributed to the high level of tension and of violence in Punjab. The 9 August train attack, which was apparently prompted by rumours that the Ferozepur salient would go to Pakistan, provides the clearest evidence that expansive boundaries could lead directly to violence.

This disparity led directly to a second significant point: the fact that Radcliffe played a greater role in Punjab than in Bengal. In Bengal, the final line followed the Congress Plan closely.[16] In Punjab, however, Radcliffe's line differed significantly from each of the major proposals.

In other words, Congress clearly played a major role in shaping the Bengal border, while in Punjab the stark differences between the party proposals, combined with the fact that each commission member loyally supported his party's line, left Radcliffe in the role of arbiter. The Punjab parties' extensive demands had the ironic effect of diminishing their influence over the final boundary and of increasing the importance of the chairman's role.

The Bengal Congress's skilful calculation contrasts with the weakness of Punjabi political parties, marking a third important disparity between the two cases. Although the power of the Bengali *bhadralok* (gentlefolk) had diminished in the decades preceding independence, undercutting Congress's power in the province, the political situation in Punjab was much worse. The imposition of governor's rule had swept Punjabi politicians out of power, leaving their parties in disarray. The organization and savvy political reckoning of the Bengal Congress's boundary presentation stand in stark contrast to the disorganization of the groups arguing before the Punjab commission.

The difference in tactics adopted by the Bengali and Punjabi parties also highlights the lack of direction from each party's central leadership. Only at the end of the process did top-ranked leaders take an active interest in the boundary question; as we have seen, Nehru forwarded protests about the Ferozepur salient to Mountbatten, while Patel objected to the planned allocation of the Chittagong Hill Tracts to Pakistan. The party leaders' decision not to involve themselves in the substance of the claims made before the Bengal and Punjab commissions left individuals at the provincial level to make decisions that would have nationwide impact.

Punjab paid the highest immediate price for Britain's speedy withdrawal, but the Bengali division too had terrible costs. Bengal experienced less violence in the short term but was seriously disrupted demographically and economically over a longer period. India's border with East Pakistan remained porous far longer than its border with West Pakistan and has experienced greater confusion and unrest, particularly over issues like the many tiny enclaves left by partition.[17] The disruption to the Bengali borderlands ran just as deep as the Punjabi catastrophe.

British officials' desire for order drew in part on Britain's long association with India, an association supported by complex paternalistic ideologies. Many officials sincerely believed in the benefits, particularly unity and law and order, bestowed by empire. Partition was a grave blow to those who took pride in the British unification of South Asia. Churchill stridently berated the Labour Government for its policy of 'scuttle'. In March 1947, he declaimed, 'In handing over the Government of India to these so-called political classes we are handing over to men of straw, of whom, in a few years, no trace will remain.' Leaving aside Churchill's woefully flawed assessment of South Asia's nationalist leaders, his views on the dishonour of the withdrawal were widely shared, and not just by those who thought Britain should have stayed on. Churchill concluded, 'Let us not add – by shameful flight, by a premature, hurried scuttle – at least, let us not add, to the pangs of sorrow so many of us feel, the taint and smear of shame.'[18] Many British officials felt that the 1947 partition amounted to little more than abandonment of peoples who had placed their trust in British rule.[19] But a façade of order was a crucial part of domestic political calculations as well as those in the international arena; if the British had not at least appeared to make an effort to hand over intact what they saw as the 'benefits' of the imperial legacy, the protests from both within and without could have endangered the Labour Party's legitimacy and hold on power.

The boundary commission's legalistic approach was a key element of this façade of order, and it was one that retained a special appeal to the nationalist leaders, even after August 1947. Nehru apparently remained convinced of the value of legal experience, although he came to regret the structure of the boundary commission. In the chaotic weeks that followed partition, he proposed that two-man teams of observers, one Hindu and one Muslim, should patrol East and West Punjab. Specifically, he suggested the selection of 'men of high standing, e.g. with High Court experience'. Nehru put this idea to Liaquat Ali Khan, who suggested the addition to each team of a British observer. Here Nehru drew the line: 'it was too reminiscent of what had happened in the Boundary Commission, when Hindu and Moslem judges had disagreed and Sir Cyril Radcliffe had had to give the casting vote'.[20] Nehru recognized that the boundary commission's format had, in the end, worked against real South Asian influence, at least in Punjab.

On the global level, the international audience was crucial because the British were struggling to maintain their position as a world leader in difficult postwar circumstances. Simply abandoning India, without a pretence at orderly withdrawal, would have undermined their efforts to maintain or even expand the imperial position elsewhere, particularly the Middle East and Africa.[21] It would have amounted to an admission that imperialism was exploitative and illegitimate. The British transfer of power was largely an exercise in public relations – particularly with Mountbatten, ever aware of his public image, at the helm. This fundamental interest in public perceptions led to decisions, for example about the boundary question, that had little to do with defining a workable basis for two independent nation-states.

In addition, abandoning India might have created a power vacuum. Communist powers could have found an opening in the region, particularly if warring parties Balkanized the subcontinent. Even before Anglo-American suspicions of Soviet aims reached Cold War levels, the British were deeply concerned about the communist threat in South Asia.[22] In short, a number of factors relating to imperial values and concern for international prestige drove the British attempt to 'transfer power' in an orderly fashion – or at least to depict as orderly their rush to leave.

In short, the British made the calculation that implementing partition would be the easiest way to get the nationalist parties to cooperate in the decolonization process. That cooperation was crucial to the British plan to project a strong image to international observers, even – or perhaps especially – at the end of empire. The British had a reputation to protect. In fact this reputation was already badly damaged, but the British still felt a need to project an image of power and control to key allies, particularly Arab powers in the Middle East. Their South Asian empire had disappeared, but decision-makers in London fervently hoped that Britain had a long future ahead of it in other regions.

Creating the appearance that nationalist leaders had control over key aspects of decolonization was a vital element of the British effort to legitimate the whole process. But they were unwilling to give up control of the most important elements, particularly elements that were crucial to keeping to the aggressive timetable laid down by Mountbatten. At the same time, they hoped to avoid shouldering the blame if things went badly. In the end, things went very badly indeed: hundreds of thousands died, millions more were exiled from their native lands and criticism of Britain mounted, especially in Pakistan. The question of responsibility was murky enough, however, that the British were able to escape immediate condemnation. As Punjab smouldered, Nehru wrote to Mountbatten to express his feelings of helplessness: 'I suppose I am not directly responsible for what is taking place in the Punjab. I do not quite know who is responsible.'[23] Even those closest to events found themselves puzzled as to where real responsibility lay.

But the façade of order and rationality was already crumbling. In an address to the Pakistani nation at the end of August 1947, Jinnah lamented the fact that the Radcliffe decision 'may not be a judicial but political award'.[24] This realization that the Radcliffe award was not entirely 'judicial' comes as something of a surprise from the keen Muslim League lawyer. Did Jinnah really believe that the commission was removed from the political sphere? Or did he simply find it expedient to demonstrate public outrage at the decision despite his private understanding of *realpolitik*? Radcliffe had to find a middle ground between politically motivated parties with conflicting claims. It is difficult to conceive of a situation in which the boundary award could have been completely free of politics.

Radcliffe's loyalty to British interests is key to understanding his work in 1947. The party leaders, both Congress and League, fundamentally misunderstood this aspect of Radcliffe's position. Radcliffe endeavoured to divide territory fairly, according to religious demographics, but other factors played a role as well. In attempting to buffer Amritsar and in allowing Mountbatten to persuade him that the Ferozepur salient would cause more trouble than it was worth, he demonstrated a concern for geopolitical matters. In the end, he was not a ruthlessly objective judge, but a lawyer who considered his client's view of the difficult matters confronting him. It is misguided to protest that Mountbatten should not have advised Radcliffe on these points; as others have argued, 'Radcliffe was a barrister following a brief,'[25] and Mountbatten was his client. Rather, criticism should be directed at the partition process as a whole, including the façade of rationality that enabled the transfer of power to take place so quickly. As the French geographer Jacques Ancel wrote, 'La volonté de l'homme est l'élément déterminant. Il n'y a pas de "bonne" ou de "mauvaise" frontière: cela depend des circonstances.' ('Human will is the determining element. There are no "good" or "bad" boundaries; it all depends on the circumstances.')[26] I have argued that Radcliffe's line was superior to the major alternatives proposed at the time, but this is not to say that it was a 'good' boundary in any absolute sense. It was the flawed product of a deeply flawed process, whose repercussions continue to plague South Asia today.

Notes

1 15 September 1955, [Government of Punjab,] *Integration of West Pakistan* (Karachi: Ferozesons, [1955?]), p. 2.
2 Nothing in the context of this passage or in the rest of the speech, an extended plea for national unity, suggests irony.
3 'Pressure, persuasion, decision: Factors in the partition of the Punjab, August 1947', *Journal of Asian Studies* 36:4 (August 1977), p. 695.
4 See the example cited in K. K. Aziz's powerful *The Murder of History*, p. 74.
5 Private information.
6 Jalal, *The Sole Spokesman.*
7 Ian Copland, 'The further shores of partition: Ethnic cleansing in Rajasthan 1947', *Past & Present* 160 (1998), pp. 203–39.
8 Cited in Urvashi Butalia, *The Other Side of Silence* (New Delhi: Viking, 1998), p. 269.
9 Butalia, *Other Side of Silence* (New Delhi: Viking, 1998), p. 269.
10 See for example Ziegler, *Revisited*, p. 22.
11 For further discussion of the complications inherent in partition, see Lucy Chester, 'Factors impeding the effectiveness of partition in South Asia and the Palestine

mandate', in *Order, Conflict, and Violence*, eds Stathis N. Kalyvas, Ian Shapiro and Tarek Masoud (Cambridge: Cambridge University Press, 2008), pp. 75–96.

12 Hastings Lionel Ismay, 'India, 1947: A personal story', *United Empire* (July–August 1948), p. 195.

13 Rhodes House Library, Reginald Coupland Papers, Mss Brit Emp s 403, Box 5, Folder 2, Memo from Moon to Coupland, 1 December 1943, fols. 64–6.

14 TNA CAB 128/10, Cabinet meeting minutes, 20 September 1947, p. 19.

15 Chatterji, *Spoils*, pp. 39–46.

16 Chatterji, *Spoils*, pp. 59–60.

17 See Chatterji, 'Fashioning' and *Spoils*, as well as Schendel's extensive work in this area, including 'Working through partition', 'Easy come, easy go' and *The Bengal Borderland: Beyond State and Nation in South Asia* (London: Anthem Press, 2005). For the Indo-Bangladeshi enclaves, see Brendan Whyte, *Waiting for the Esquimo: An Historical and Documentary Study of the Cooch Behar Enclaves of India and Bangladesh*, vol. 8, *Research Papers of the School of Anthropology, Geography and Environmental Studies* (Melbourne: University of Melbourne, 2002).

18 Great Britain, House of Commons Debates, vol. 434, 1946–47, 5th series, cols 674 and 678.

19 Arthur Williams, the District Magistrate in Lahore in 1947, regarded the British withdrawal as 'an act of betrayal and even cowardice; one does not leave in the lurch and to bloody slaughter people who trusted in one's will and ability to protect them' (IOR Mss Eur F 180/70, cited in Roberts, pp. 114–15).

20 LHA, Ismay Papers, 3/7/68/3a, Ismay notes on talk with Nehru, 2 October 1947.

21 John Kent, 'Bevin's imperialism and Euro-Africa, 1945–49', in *British Foreign Policy, 1945–56*, eds Michael Dockrill and John Young (New York: St Martin's Press, 1989), pp. 47–76.

22 Brecher, *Nehru*, p. 372.

23 S. Gopal, ed., *Selected Works of Jawaharlal Nehru*, 2nd series, vol. IV (New Delhi: Jawaharlal Nehru Memorial Fund, 1986), pp. 25–6.

24 Zaidi, vol. V, p. 175.

25 Lamb, quoted in French, p. 322.

26 Jacques Ancel, 'Les frontières: Étude de géographie politique', *Recueil des cours* 55 (1936), p. 210.

BIBLIOGRAPHY

Note on sources

During my research, I spoke with several interviewees who preferred to remain anonymous. I was also allowed to see material that is not open to public access. I have cited information gained from these interviews and this material as 'private information' or 'private collection'. The private collection cited has no connection with any person named in the text.

Archival sources

Britain

Cambridge University South Asian Archive

Arthur Papers
Bell Papers
Benthall Papers
Brendon Memoirs
Collier Papers
Cowley Memoirs
Darling (M. L.) Papers
Dash Memoirs
Derrick-Jehu and Somerset Papers
Goodman Papers
Heaney Papers
Holland Memoirs
Hubback Memoirs
Hudson (H. B.) Papers
Hume Papers
MacNabb Memoirs
Medd Papers
Perry-Keene Memoirs
Reynolds Papers
Somerset Memoirs
Spate Papers
Stephens Papers
Talbot Papers
Taylor (S. G.) Memoirs
Tennyson Papers

India Office Library, British Library (London)

India Office Records (IOR)
L/MIL/17/5
L/P&J/8/663
L/P&J/10/117
L/P&J/10/118
L/P&J/10/119
R/3/1/157
R/3/1/176
V/27/314/573
Y/101, Y/104

Private Papers
Mss Eur A 221 (Jenkins Papers)
Mss Eur C 645 (Jenkins–Abbott Correspondence)
Mss Eur D 718 (Christie Diary)
Mss Eur D 807 (Jenkins Papers)
Mss Eur F 164 (Mudie Papers)
Mss Eur Photo Eur 279 (Zafrullah Khan Memoirs)
Mss Eur R 150 (Beaumont Interview)

Liddell Hart Centre for Military Archives (King's College London) (LHA)

Ismay Papers

National Archives of the United Kingdom (Kew) (TNA)
CAB 127
CAB 128

Rhodes House Library (Oxford University)

Coupland Papers

University of Southampton Libraries Special Collections

Mountbatten Papers

India

Nehru Memorial Museum and Library (New Delhi) (NMML)

All India Congress Committee Papers
Hindu Mahasabha Papers
Mahajan (M. C.) Papers
Nehru (Rameshwari) Papers

National Archives of India (New Delhi) (NAI)

Government records
Legislative
  Reference 1948

Reform 1947
Ministry of External Affairs [MEA] and Commonwealth Relations
OS (I, III, V) 1947, 1948
Pakistan (I) 1948
Ministry of Home Affairs
H 1948
RH 1953
RHB 1949, 1950
Political Department/Ministry of States
G(R) 1949
IA (States) 1947
IB 1947
K 1948, 1951, 1952
P 1949
PA 1951
PR 1947
R 1949

Private papers
Patel Papers
Prasad (Rajendra) Papers

Pakistan

National Archives of Pakistan (Islamabad)
S-415: Police Abstract of Intelligence 1947

Punjab Provincial Archives (Lahore) (PPA)
Civil Defence 1951
Food Supplies 1948, 1949, 1951
Home 1953
Home/Gazette 1947, 1950, 1951
Home/General 1947, 1950, 1952, 1954, 1955
Home/Judicial and Jails 1947, 1948, 1949, 1950
Home/Military 1951
Home/Passport 1947, 1949
Home/Police 1947, 1951
Home/Police and Military 1948
Industries 1947, 1951
Judicial and Jails 1951
Medical 1949, 1950, 1951
Passport 1949, 1951
Public (Health) 1949

United States

Stanford University Libraries (Palo Alto)
Central Map Collection

Other unpublished primary sources

Documents remaining in their authors' possession
Beaumont, Christopher. 'The partition of India.' Unpublished manuscript, n.d.
Husain, S. Wajahat. 'Woman in the pond!: Reminiscences [of] Punjab Boundary Force Operations '47.' Unpublished manuscript, n.d.

Published primary sources

Bata Footwear. Advertisement. *Times of India* (15 August 1947), p. 4.
Batalvi, A. H., ed. *The Forgotten Years: Memoirs of Muhammad Zafrullah Khan*. Lahore: Vanguard, 1991.
Boggs, S. Whittemore. *International Boundaries*. New York: Columbia University Press, 1940.
Bowra, C. M. *Memories 1898–1939*. London: Weidenfeld and Nicolson, 1966.
Burrard, Sidney Gerald. *Completion of the Link Connecting the Triangulations of India and Russia 1913*. Dehra Dun: Trigonometrical Survey, 1914.
Campbell-Johnson, Alan. *Mission with Mountbatten*. New York: Atheneum, 1985.
Coldstream, W. M. *Records of the Survey of India, Vol. XII: Notes on Survey of India Maps and the Modern Development of Indian Cartography*. Calcutta: Survey of India, 1919.
Din Muhammad. 'Din Muhammad on Radcliffe's boundary award in the Punjab.' In *Pakistan Resolution to Pakistan 1940–1947: A Selection of Documents Presenting the Case for Pakistan*, ed. Latif Ahmed Sherwani, pp. 276–9. Karachi: National Publishing House, 1969.
[Gandhi, Mohandas K.] *The Collected Works of Mahatma Gandhi*. 90 vols. New Delhi: The Publications Division, Ministry of Information and Broadcasting, Government of India, 1979.
Godrej. Advertisement. *Times of India*, Supplement (15 August 1947), p. 9.
Gopal, S., ed. *Selected Works of Jawaharlal Nehru*. 2nd series, vol. IV. New Delhi: Jawaharlal Nehru Memorial Fund, 1986.
[Government of Punjab.] *Integration of West Pakistan*. Karachi: Ferozesons, [1995?].
Great Britain, House of Commons. Parliamentary Debates (Hansard). 5th series, vol. 434. London: HMSO, 1947.
——, Parliamentary Debates (Hansard). 5th series, vol. 440. London: HMSO, 1947.
Hamid, Shahid. *Disastrous Twilight: A Personal Record of the Partition of*

India by Major-General Shahid Hamid, Private Secretary to Field Marshal Sir Claude Auchinleck. Barnsley, South Yorkshire: Leo Cooper, 1986.

Hasmi, M. N. A. *Survey of Pakistan Progress Report 1947 to 1961.* [Karachi?]: [Survey of Pakistan?], [1961?].

Heaney, G. F. 'Preface.' In *Survey of India Technical Report 1947.* Dehra Dun: Survey of India, 1949.

Husain, S. Wajahat. 'The evacuation of Kapurthala state Muslims.' *Dawn* (14 August 1992), p. VII.

India: Bilateral Treaties and Agreements. 10 vols. New Delhi: Ministry of External Affairs, Government of India, 1994–97.

Intelligence Reports Concerning the Tribal Repercussions to the Events in the Punjab, Kashmir and India. Lahore: Superintendent Government Printing West Punjab, 1948.

Ismay, Hastings Lionel. 'India, 1947: A personal story.' *United Empire* (July–August 1948), pp. 195–8.

——. *The Memoirs of General Lord Ismay.* London: Heinemann, 1960.

Jones, Stephen B. *Boundary-Making: A Handbook for Statesmen, Treaty Editors and Boundary Commissioners.* Washington, DC: Carnegie Endowment for International Peace, 1945.

Khan, Rashid Ahmad. *Map of Kasur Tahsil* [map]. 1:126,720. Lahore: Kapur Art Printing Work, [n.d.]. British Library, India Office Records, L/P&J/10/117, Map 1.

Khan, Saleem Ullah, comp. *The Journey to Pakistan: A Documentation of Refugees of 1947.* Islamabad: National Documentation Centre, 1993.

Khosla, G. D. *Stern Reckoning: A Survey of Events Leading up to and Following the Partition of India.* Oxford: Oxford University Press, 1989.

[Labour Party.] 'Let us face the future.' New York: League for Industrial Democracy, 1945.

Mahajan, Mehr Chand. *Looking Back: The Autobiography of Mehr Chand Mahajan Former Chief Justice of India.* London: Asia Publishing House, 1963.

Mansergh, Nicholas et al., eds. *Constitutional Relations between Britain and India: The Transfer of Power 1942–7.* 12 vols. London: HMSO, 1970–83.

Moon, Penderel, ed. *Wavell: The Viceroy's Journal.* London: Oxford University Press, 1973.

——. *Divide and Quit: An Eyewitness Account of the Partition of India.* New ed. Delhi: Oxford University Press, 1998.

Morgan, J. Cumming. 'A labour company at Ypres.' In *Everyman at War: Sixty Personal Narratives of the War,* ed. C. B. Purdom, pp. 130–5. New York: E. P. Dutton, 1930.

Munir, Muhammad. *Highways and Bye-Ways of Life.* Lahore: Law Publishing Company, n.d. [1978].

——. *From Jinnah to Zia.* Lahore: Vanguard Books, 1980.

——. 'Partition of the Punjab', *Times of India* (19 August 1947), p. 7.

——. 'Radcliffe award announced', *Pakistan Times* (19 August 1947), p. 1.

Radcliffe, Cyril. *The Problem of Power: The Reith Memorial Lectures 1951.* London: Secker and Warburg, 1952.

——. *The Law and Its Compass.* London: Faber & Faber, 1960.

——. [No title], *The Haileyburian Centenary Magazine* (1962), pp. 58–9.

——. *Not in Feather Beds: Some Collected Papers*. London: Hamish Hamilton, 1968.

——. *Government by Contempt*. London: Chatto and Windus, 1967.

Report on Police Administration in the Punjab for the Year 1949. Lahore: Superintendent Government Printing Punjab, 1952.

Report on Police Administration in the Punjab for the Year 1950. Lahore: Superintendent Government Printing Punjab, 1953.

Report on Police Administration in the Punjab for the Year 1951. Lahore: Superintendent Government Printing Punjab, 1953.

Report on Police Administration in the Punjab for the Year 1952. Lahore: Superintendent Government Printing Punjab, 1955.

Report on Police Administration in the Punjab for the Year 1953. Lahore: Superintendent Government Printing West Pakistan, 1957.

Report on Police Administration in the Punjab for the Year 1954. Lahore: Superintendent Government Printing West Pakistan, 1958.

Report on Police Administration in the Punjab for the Year 1955. Lahore: Superintendent Government Printing West Pakistan, 1958.

Sadullah, Mian Muhammad et al., eds *The Partition of the Punjab – 1947*. 4 vols. Lahore: Sang-e-Meel Publications, 1993.

Sain, Kanwar. *Reminiscences of an Engineer*. New Delhi: Young Asia Publications, 1978.

Setalvad, Motilal C. *My Life: Law and Other Things*. London: Sweet & Maxwell, 1971.

Singh, Kirpal, ed. *Select Documents on Partition of Punjab – 1947: India and Pakistan: Punjab, Haryana and Himachal – India and Punjab – Pakistan*. Delhi: National Book Shop, 1991.

Spate, O. H. K. 'The partition of Punjab and of Bengal.' *Geographical Journal* 110 (1947), pp. 201–22.

——. 'The partition of India and the prospects of Pakistan.' *Geographical Review* 38 (1948), pp. 5–29.

——. *On the Margins of History: From the Punjab to Fiji*. Canberra: National Centre for Development Studies, Australian National University, 1991.

Survey of Pakistan. 'Map of Pakistan showing political divisions' [map]. 2nd edn. 1:3,168,000. Murree: Survey of Pakistan, 1953.

Thyer, Donald C. 'The partition of India – A personal account.' *Royal Engineers Journal* 111 (December 1997), p. 263.

Tuker, Francis. *While Memory Serves*. London: Cassell, 1950.

Union Life Assurance. Advertisement. *Times of India* (Bombay) (15 August 1947), p. 3.

Wheeler, Oliver. *The Survey of India during War and Early Reconstruction, 1939–1946*. Dehra Dun: Survey of India, 1955.

Williams, Francis. *A Prime Minister Remembers: The War and Post-War Memoirs of the Rt. Hon. Earl Attlee, Based on his Private Papers and on a Series of Recorded Conversations*. London: Heinemann, 1961.

Zaidi, Z. H. et al., eds *Jinnah Papers*. Islamabad: Quaid-i-Azam Papers Project, 2000.

Personal interviews

Azim, Zarrar. Lieutenant-General, Pakistan Army; Director-General, Pakistan Rangers. Personal interview: 13 July 2000.

Beaumont, Christopher. Private secretary to Cyril Radcliffe, 1947. Personal interviews: 8 and 29 February 2000.

Husain, S. Wajahat. Major-General (Ret.), Pakistan Army; Lieutenant, Punjab Boundary Force, 1947. Personal interview: 30 July 2000.

Janjua, Adnan. Colonel, Pakistan Army; Wing Commander, Pakistan Rangers. Personal interview: 1 September 2000.

Kirmani, Ahmed Sayed. Member, Muslim League legal team, Punjab Boundary Commission, 1947. Personal interview: 3 September 2000.

Sadullah, Mian Muhammad. Superintendent, Punjab Boundary Commission, 1947. Personal interview: September 2000.

Tennant, Mark. Stepson of Cyril Radcliffe. Personal interview: 9 February 2000.

Newspapers

Pakistan Times
Times of India

Secondary sources

Ahmed, Ishtiaq. 'The 1947 partition of Punjab: Arguments put forth before the Punjab Boundary Commission by the parties involved.' In *Region and Partition: Bengal, Punjab and the Partition of the Subcontinent*, eds Ian Talbot and Gurharpal Singh, pp. 116–67. Oxford: Oxford University Press, 1999.

Aiyar, Swarna. '"August anarchy": The partition massacres in Punjab, 1947.' In *Freedom, Trauma, Continuities: Northern India and Independence*, eds D. A. Low and Howard Brasted, pp. 15–38. Walnut Creek, CA: AltaMira Press, 1998.

Ali, Imran. *The Punjab under Imperialism, 1885–1947*. Princeton: Princeton University Press, 1988.

Ancel, Jacques, 'Les frontières; Étude de géographie politique.' *Recueil des cours* 55 (1936), pp. 203–97.

Anderson, Benedict. *Imagined Communities: Reflections on the Origin and Spread of Nationalism*. Rev. ed. London: Verso, 1991.

Ashcroft, R. L. *Haileybury, 1908–1961*. N.p.: The Haileybury Society; Frome: Butler & Tanner, 1961.

Asiwaju, Anthony. *Borderlands Research: A Comparative Perspective*. El Paso, TX: University of Texas at El Paso, 1983.

Auden, W. H. 'Partition.' In *City without Walls and Other Poems*, pp. 86–7. New York: Random House, 1969.

Aziz, Khursheed Kamal. *A History of the Idea of Pakistan*. 4 vols. Lahore:

Vanguard Books, 1987.
——. *The Murder of History: A Critique of History Textbooks Used in Pakistan*. Lahore: Vanguard, 1993.
Banga, Indu, ed. *Five Punjabi Centuries: Polity, Economy, Society and Culture, c. 1500–1990*. New Delhi: Manohar, 2000.
Basu, Aparna. 'Uprooted women: Partition of Punjab 1947.' In *Nation, Empire, Colony: Historicizing Gender and Race*, eds Ruth Roach Pierson and Nupur Chaudhuri, with the assistance of Beth McAuley. Bloomington, IN: Indiana University Press, 1998.
Baud, Michiel and Willem van Schendel. 'Toward a comparative history of borderlands.' *Journal of World History* 8:2 (1997), pp. 211–42.
Bhalla, Alok, ed. *Stories about the Partition of India*. 3 vols. New Delhi: HarperCollins, 1994.
Birkenhead, Frederick. *Walter Monckton: The Life of Viscount Monckton of Brenchley*. London: Weidenfeld & Nicolson, 1969.
Black, Jeremy. *Maps and Politics*. London: Reaktion Books, 1997.
Blackwell, Michael. *Clinging to Grandeur: British Attitudes and Foreign Policy in the Aftermath of the Second World War*. Westport, CT: Greenwood Press, 1993.
Bolitho, Hector. *Jinnah: Creator of Pakistan*. London: John Murray, 1954.
Bose, Pradip Kumar. 'Memory begins where history ends.' In *Reflections on Partition in the East*, ed. Ranabir Samaddar, pp. 73–86. New Delhi: Vikas Publishing House, 1997.
Bose, Sugata and Ayesha Jalal. *Modern South Asia*. London: Routledge, 1998.
Boyle, Andrew. *Poor, Dear Brendan: The Quest for Brendan Bracken*. London: Hutchinson, 1974.
Brecher, Michael. *Nehru: A Political Biography*. London: Oxford University Press, 1959.
——. Rev. of *Last Days of the British Raj*, by Leonard Mosley. *Pacific Affairs* 35:3 (Autumn 1962), pp. 295–6.
Briggs, Asa. *History of Broadcasting in the United Kingdom*. Vol. 2, *The War of Words*. London: Oxford University Press, 1970.
Brines, Russell. *The Indo-Pakistani Conflict*. London: Pall Mall Press, 1968.
Brown, Judith. *Gandhi: Prisoner of Hope*. New Haven: Yale University Press, 1989.
Butalia, Urvashi. 'Muslims and Hindus, men and women: Communal stereotypes and the partition of India.' In *Women and Right-Wing Movements: Indian Experiences*, eds Tanika Sarkar and Urvashi Butalia, pp. 58–81. London: Zed Books, 1995.
——. *The Other Side of Silence*. New Delhi: Viking, 1998.
——. 'Community, state, and gender: Some reflections on the partition of India.' In *Inventing Boundaries: Gender, Politics and the Partition of India*, ed. Mushirul Hasan, pp. 178–207. New Delhi: Oxford University Press, 2000.
Cain, P. J. and Anthony Hopkins. *British Imperialism: Innovation and Expansion, 1688–1914*. London: Longman, 1993.
——. *British Imperialism: Crisis and Deconstruction, 1914–1990*. London: Longman, 1993.

Chakrabarty, Dipesh. 'Remembered villages: Representations of Hindu–Bengali memories in the aftermath of the partition.' In *Freedom, Trauma, Continuities: Northern India and Independence*, eds D. A. Low and Howard Brasted, pp. 133–52. Walnut Creek, CA: AltaMira Press, 1998.

Chatterji, Joya. 'The fashioning of a frontier: The Radcliffe Line and Bengal's border landscape, 1947–1952.' *Modern Asian Studies* 33:1 (1999), pp. 185–242.

——. *The Spoils of Partition: Bengal and India, 1947–1967.* Cambridge: Cambridge University Press, 2007.

Chaudhri, Nazir Hussain, ed. *Chief Justice Muhammad Munir: His Life, Writings and Judgments.* Lahore: Research Society of Pakistan, University of the Punjab, 1973.

Chester, Lucy. 'Mapping imperial expansion: Colonial cartography in North America and South Asia.' *The Portolan* 45 (Fall 1999), pp. 9–24.

——. 'The mapping of empire: French and British cartographies of India in the late eighteenth century.' *Portuguese Studies* 16 (October 2000), pp. 256–75

——. 'Factors impeding the effectiveness of partition in South Asia and the Palestine mandate.' In *Order, Conflict, and Violence*, eds Stathis N. Kalyvas, Ian Shapiro and Tarek Masoud, pp. 75–96. Cambridge: Cambridge University Press, 2008.

Cohn, Bernard. 'The census, social structure and objectification in South Asia.' In *An Anthropologist among the Historians and Other Essays*. Delhi: Oxford University Press, 1987.

Collins, Larry and Dominique Lapierre. *Freedom at Midnight*. New York: Simon and Schuster, 1975.

——. *Mountbatten and Independent India*. 3rd edn. New Delhi: Vikas Publishing House, 1989.

——. *Mountbatten and the Partition of India*. New Delhi: Vikas Publishing House, 1999.

Copland, Ian. 'The further shores of partition: Ethnic cleansing in Rajasthan 1947.' *Past & Present* 160 (1998), pp. 203–39.

Coupland, Reginald. *The Indian Problem: Report on the Constitutional Problem in India*. New York: Oxford University Press, 1944.

Das, Veena. 'National honour and practical kinship: Of unwanted women and children.' In *Critical Events: An Anthropological Perspective on Contemporary India*. Delhi: Oxford University Press, 1995.

——. 'Official narratives, rumour, and the social production of hate.' *Social Identities* 4:1 (1998), pp. 109–30.

Donnan, Hastings and Thomas M. Wilson. *Borders: Frontiers of Identity, Nation and State*. Oxford: Berg, 1999.

Edney, Matthew. *Mapping an Empire: The Geographical Construction of British India, 1765–1843*. Chicago: University of Chicago Press, 1997.

Edwardes, Michael. *The Last Years of British India*. Cleveland: World Publishing Company, 1963.

——. *Nehru: A Political Biography*. New York: Praeger Publishers, 1971.

Ellis, Roger. 'Abell, Sir George Edmond Brackenbury (1904–1989).' Rev. *Oxford*

Dictionary of National Biography. Oxford: Oxford University Press, 2004. www.oxforddnb.com/view/article/39894. Accessed 29 February 2008.

Embree, Ainslie T., ed. *Pakistan's Western Borderlands: The Transformation of a Political Order.* Durham, NC: Carolina Academic Press, 1977.

——. 'Frontiers into boundaries: The evolution of the modern state.' In *Imagining India: Essays on Indian History,* ed. Mark Juergensmeyer, pp. 67–84. Delhi: Oxford University Press, 1989.

Fay, Peter Ward. *The Forgotten Army: India's Armed Struggle for Independence 1942–1945.* Ann Arbor: University of Michigan Press, 1993.

Ferguson, Niall, ed. *Virtual History: Alternatives and Counterfactuals.* London: Picador, 1997.

French, Patrick. *Liberty or Death.* London: HarperCollins, 1997.

Gilmartin, David. *Empire and Islam: Punjab and the Making of Pakistan.* Berkeley: University of California Press, 1988.

——. 'Scientific empire and imperial science: Colonialism and irrigation technology in the Indus basin.' *Journal of Asian Studies* 53:4 (November 1994), pp. 1127–49.

——. 'Partition, Pakistan, and South Asian history: In search of a narrative', *Journal of Asian Studies* 57:4 (November 1998), pp. 1068–95.

Goethals, Helen. 'Poetry and history in the context of W. H. Auden's poem "Partition"'. Paper delivered at the fourth meeting of the Société Anglo-Indienne et Histoire de l'Inde Britannique et Contemporaine, 'La route des Indes', 3–4 September 1999.

Goldenberg, Suzanne. 'Memories of Mountbatten.' *Guardian* (7 August 1997), p. 3.

Gole, Susan. *Early Maps of India.* New York: Humanities Press, 1976.

——. *India within the Ganges.* New Delhi: Jayaprints, 1983.

——. *Indian Maps and Plans.* New Delhi: Manohar Publications, 1989.

[Government of India.] 'Border Security Force.' http://bsf.nic.in/introduction. htm. Accessed 29 February 2008.

[Government of Pakistan.] 'Pakistan Rangers (Punjab).' www.pak.gov.pk/ public/govt/reports/punjab_rangers.htm.

Grewal, J. S. and Indu Banga, eds *Punjab in Prosperity and Violence: Administration, Politics and Social Change 1947–1997.* Chandigarh: Institute of Punjab Studies, 1998.

Hansen, Anders Bjørn. *Partition and Genocide: Manifestation of Violence in Punjab 1937–1947.* New Delhi: India Research Press, 2002.

Harley, John Brian. *The New Nature of Maps.* Baltimore: Johns Hopkins University Press, 2001.

Hasan, Mushirul, ed. *India's Partition: Process, Strategy and Mobilization.* Delhi: Oxford University Press, 1993.

——, ed. *India Partitioned: The Other Face of Freedom.* 2 vols. New Delhi: Roli Books, 1995.

——. *Inventing Boundaries: Gender, Politics, and the Partition of India.* New Delhi: Oxford University Press, 2000.

Hayden, Robert. 'Schindler's fate: Genocide, ethnic cleansing, and population transfers.' *Slavic Review* 55:4 (Winter 1996), p. 739.

[211]

Hennessy, Peter. 'The eternal fireman.' *The Times* (London) (30 January 1976), p. 16.

——. *Whitehall*. London: Fontana Press, 1990.

Herschy, Reg. *Disputed Frontiers*. Lewes, Sussex: Book Guild, 1993.

Heward, Edmund. *The Great and the Good: A Life of Lord Radcliffe*. Chichester: Barry Rose Publishers, 1994.

Hodson, H. V. *The Great Divide: Britain – India – Pakistan*. 1969. Jubilee Series ed. Karachi: Oxford University Press, 1997.

Howarth, T. E. B. *Prospect and Reality: Great Britain 1945–1955*. London: Collins, 1985.

Human Rights Watch. 'Recent landmine use by India and Pakistan.' May 2002. www.hrw.org//backgrounder/arms/ind-pak-landmines.htm. Accessed 3 March 2008.

'India before partition.' [map]. 1:15,840,000. In *The Transfer of Power 1942–7*. Vol. XII, eds Nicholas Mansergh and Penderel Moon. London: HMSO, 1983.

International Campaign to Ban Landmines. 'Landmine Monitor Report 2005: India.' October 2005. www.icbl.org/lm/2005/india. Accessed 12 June 2008.

Islam, M. Mufakharul. *Irrigation, Agriculture and the Raj: Punjab, 1887–1947*. New Delhi: Manohar, 1997.

Jalal, Ayesha. *The Sole Spokesman*. Cambridge: Cambridge University Press, 1985.

- ——. *Self and Sovereignty: Individual and Community in South Asian Islam Since 1850*. New Delhi: Oxford University Press, 2001.

Jeffrey, Robin. 'The Punjab Boundary Force and the problem of order, August 1947.' *Modern Asian Studies* 8:4 (1974), pp. 491–520.

Kalra, Virinder S. and Navtej K. Purewal. 'The strut of the peacocks: Partition, travel and the Indo-Pak border.' In *Travel Worlds: Journeys in Contemporary Cultural Politics*, eds Raminder Kaur and John Hutnyk, pp. 54–67. London: Zed Books, 1999.

Kamtekar, Indivar. 'The military ingredient of communal violence in Punjab, 1947.' *Abstracts of Sikh Studies* 4:1 (2002), pp. 48–52.

Kant, Surya. *Administrative Geography of India*. Jaipur: Rawat Publications, 1988.

Kaufmann, Chaim. 'Possible and impossible solutions to ethnic civil wars.' *International Security* 20:4 (Spring 1996), p. 137.

Kent, John. 'Bevin's imperialism and Euro-Africa, 1945–49.' In *British Foreign Policy, 1945–56*, eds Michael Dockrill and John Young, pp. 47–76. New York: St Martin's Press, 1989.

Khan, Nighat Said. 'Identity, violence and women: A reflection on the partition of India 1947.' In *Locating the Self: Perspectives on Women and Multiple Identities*, eds Nighat Said Khan, Rubina Saigol and Afiya Shehrbano Zia, pp. 157–71. Lahore: ASR Publications, 1994.

Khan, Yasmin. *The Great Partition: The Making of India and Pakistan*. New Haven: Yale University Press, 2007.

Khilnani, Sunil. *The Idea of India*. London: Hamish Hamilton, 1997.

——. 'India's mapmaker.' *Observer* (London) (22 June 1997), p. 7.

Krishna, B. *Sardar Vallabhbhai Patel: India's Iron Man*. New Delhi: Harper-Collins, 1996.

Kudaisya, Gyanesh. 'From displacement to "development": East Punjab countryside after partition, 1947–67.' In *Freedom, Trauma, Continuities: Northern India and Independence*, eds D. A. Low and Howard Brasted, pp. 73–90. Walnut Creek, CA: AltaMira Press, 1998.

Kumar, Radha. *Divide and Fall?* London: Verso, 1997.

Lamb, Alastair. Letter. *Daily Telegraph* (25 February 1992), p. 16.

——. *Birth of a Tragedy: Kashmir 1947*. Hertingfordbury: Roxford Books, 1994.

——. *Incomplete Partition: The Genesis of the Kashmir Dispute 1947–1948*. Hertingfordbury: Roxford Books, 1997.

Lapierre, Dominique. *A Thousand Suns: Witness to History*. New York: Warner Books, 1999.

Louis, Wm. Roger. *The British Empire in the Middle East, 1945–1951*. Oxford: Clarendon Press, 1984.

Lysaght, Charles. *Brendan Bracken*. London: Allen Lane, 1979.

Madan, P. L. *Indian Cartography: A Historical Perspective*. New Delhi: Manohar, 1997.

Mahajan, Vidya Dhar. *Chief Justice Mehr Chand Mahajan (The Biography of the Great Jurist)*. Lucknow: Eastern Book Company, 1969.

Major, Andrew J. '"The chief sufferers": Abduction of women during the partition of the Punjab.' In *Freedom, Trauma, Continuities: Northern India and Independence*, eds D. A. Low and Howard Brasted, pp. 57–72. Walnut Creek, CA: AltaMira Press, 1998.

Manto, Saadat Hasan. *Mottled Dawn: Fifty Sketches and Stories of Partition*. New Delhi: Penguin, 1997.

Martinez, Oscar J. *Border People: Life and Society in the U.S.–Mexico Borderlands*. Tucson: University of Arizona Press, 1994.

Mayaram, Shail. 'Speech, silence and the making of partition violence in Mewat.' In *Subaltern Studies IX: Writings on South Asian History and Society*, eds Shahid Amin and Dipesh Chakrabarty, pp. 126–64. Delhi: Oxford University Press, 1996.

Menon, Ritu. 'Reproducing the legitimate community: Secularity, sexuality, and the state in postpartition India.' In *Appropriating Gender: Women's Activism and Politicized Religion in South Asia*, eds Patricia Jeffery and Amrita Basu, pp. 15–32. New York: Routledge, 1998.

Menon, Ritu and Kamla Bhasin. *Borders and Boundaries: Women in India's Partition*. New Brunswick, NJ: Rutgers University Press, 1998.

——. 'Recovery, rupture, resistance: The Indian state and the abduction of women during partition.' In *Inventing Boundaries: Gender, Politics and the Partition of India*, ed. Mushirul Hasan, pp. 208–35. New Delhi: Oxford University Press, 2000.

Metcalf, Barbara D. and Thomas R. Metcalf. *A Concise History of India*. Cambridge: Cambridge University Press, 2002.

Metcalf, Thomas. *Ideologies of the Raj*. Cambridge: Cambridge University Press, 1995.

Michel, Aloys. *The Indus Rivers: A Study of the Effects of Partition*. New Haven: Yale University Press, 1967.

Mishra, Prabhakar. 'Cadastral surveys in India – A critique.' *GISDevelopment*, n.d. www.gisdevelopment.net/application/lis/policy/lisp0001.htm. Accessed 3 March 2008.

Moore, Robin J. *Escape from Empire: The Attlee Government and the Indian Problem*. Oxford: Clarendon Press, 1983.

——. 'India in the 1940s.' In *Oxford History of the British Empire*, ed. Robin W. Winks. Vol. V. Oxford: Oxford University Press, 1999.

Morris-Jones, W. H. Rev. of *Last Days of the British Raj*, by Leonard Mosley. *Journal of Modern History* 35:2 (June 1963), pp. 223–4.

——. 'Thirty-six years later: The mixed legacies of Mountbatten's transfer of power.' *International Affairs* 59:4 (Autumn 1983), pp. 621–8.

Mosley, Leonard. *The Last Days of the British Raj*. New York: Harcourt, Brace & World, 1962.

Murphy, Richard McGill. 'Performing partition in Lahore.' In *The Partitions of Memory: The Afterlife of the Division of India*, ed. Suvir Kaul, pp. 183–207. Delhi: Permanent Black, 2001.

Noorani, A. G. 'Ayodhya in reverse.' *Frontline* 18:3 (3–16 February 2001). www.flonnet.com/fl1803/18030890.htm. Accessed 3 March 2008.

Noyes, Hugh. '"D" Notice white paper savaged: Scathing attack by Lord Radcliffe.' *The Times* (London) (7 July 1967), pp. 1, 5.

'Old journeys revisited', *The Economist* (12 February 2000), pp. 86–8.

Pandey, Gyan. 'The prose of otherness.' In *Subaltern Studies VIII*, eds David Arnold and David Hardiman, pp. 188–221. Delhi: Oxford University Press, 1994.

——. *Remembering Partition: Violence, Nationalism and History in India*. Cambridge: Cambridge University Press, 2001.

'Partition boundaries in the Punjab' [map]. Approximately 1:2,661,120. September 1948. In *The Transfer of Power 1942–7*, Vol. XII, eds Nicholas Mansergh, Nicholas and Penderel Moon. London: HMSO, 1983.

Pelling, Henry. *The Labour Governments, 1945–51*. London: Macmillan Press, 1984.

Philips, C. H. and Mary Doreen Wainwright. *The Partition of India: Policies and Perspectives, 1935–1947*. London: Allen & Unwin, 1970.

Plummer, Simon Scott. 'How Mountbatten bent the rules and the Indian border.' *Daily Telegraph* (24 February 1992), p. 10.

Potter, David. *India's Political Administrators 1919–1983*. Oxford: Clarendon Press, 1986.

Prescott, J. R. V. *Boundaries and Frontiers*. London: Croom Helm, 1978.

——. *Political Frontiers and Boundaries*. London: Allen & Unwin, 1987.

Rai, Satya. *Partition of the Punjab: A Study of its Effects on the Politics and Administration of the Punjab (I) 1947–56*. Bombay: Asia Publishing House, 1965.

Roberts, Andrew. 'Lord Mountbatten and the perils of adrenalin.' In *Eminent Churchillians*. London: Phoenix, 1994.

Roper, William. *The Life of Sir Thomas More*. London: Folio Society, 1980.

Roth, Andrew. 'On the Sikh–Moslem Frontier.' *Nation* 165:12 (20 September 1947), p. 282.

Rothschild, Nathaniel Mayer Victor. *Random Variables*. London: Collins, 1984.

Rushdie, Salman. *Midnight's Children*. New York: Knopf, 1981.

Sahlins, Peter. *Boundaries: The Making of France and Spain in the Pyrenees*. Berkeley: University of California Press, 1989.

Schendel, Willem van. 'Easy come, easy go: Smugglers on the Ganges.' *Journal of Contemporary Asia* 23:2 (1993), pp. 189–213.

——. 'Working through partition: Making a living in the Bengal borderlands.' *International Review of Social History* 46 (2001), pp. 393–421.

——. *The Bengal Borderland: Beyond State and Nation in South Asia*. London: Anthem Press, 2005.

Schofield, Victoria. *Wavell: Soldier and Statesman*. London: John Murray, 2006.

Sengupta, Somini. 'With wrath and wire, India builds a great wall.' *New York Times* (2 January 2002), Sec. A, p. 1, col. 1.

Sidhwa, Bapsi. *Ice-Candy-Man*. New Delhi: Penguin, 1988.

Singh, Darbara. 'Justice Teja Singh.' In *Ten Eminent Sikhs*. Amritsar: Literature House, 1982.

Singh, Gurdit and Carol C. Fair. 'The partition of Punjab: Its impact upon Sikh sacred and cultural space.' In *Region and Partition: Bengal, Punjab and the Partition of the Subcontinent*, eds Ian Talbot and Gurharpal Singh, pp. 253–68. Oxford: Oxford University Press, 1999.

Singh, Khushwant. *A History of the Sikhs*. Vol. 2. Princeton: Princeton University Press, 1966.

——. *Train to Pakistan*. New York: Grove Press, 1990.

Spear, Percival. 'Britain's transfer of power in India.' *Pacific Affairs* 31:2 (June 1958), pp. 173–80.

Sukhwal, B. L. *India: A Political Geography*. Bombay: Allied Publishers, 1971.

Talbot, Ian. *Freedom's Cry: The Popular Dimension in the Pakistan Movement and Partition Experience in North-West India*. Karachi: Oxford University Press, 1996.

——. *Khizr Tiwana, the Punjab Unionist Party and the Partition of India*. Richmond: Curzon Press, 1996.

——. 'Literature and the human drama of the 1947 partition.' In *Region and Partition: Bengal, Punjab and the Partition of the Subcontinent*, eds Ian Talbot and Gurharpal Singh, pp. 228–52. Oxford: Oxford University Press, 1999.

——. *Divided Cities: Partition and Its Aftermath in Lahore and Amritsar 1947–1957*. Oxford: Oxford University Press, 2006.

Tan Tai Yong. '"Sir Cyril goes to India": Partition, boundary-making and disruptions in the Punjab.' *International Journal of Punjab Studies* 4:1 (1997), pp. 1–20.

——. *The Garrison State: Military, Government and Society in Colonial Punjab, 1849–1947*. New Delhi: Sage Publications, 2005.

BIBLIOGRAPHY

Tan Tai Yong and Gyanesh Kudaisya. *The Aftermath of Partition in South Asia*. London: Routledge, 2000.

Tanwar, Raghuvendra. *Reporting the Partition: Press, Public, and Other Opinions*. New Delhi: Manohar, 2006.

Thandi, Shinder S. 'The unidentical Punjab twins: Some explanations of comparative agricultural performance since partition.' In *Region and Partition: Bengal, Punjab and the Partition of the Subcontinent*, eds Ian Talbot and Gurharpal Singh, pp. 298–324. Oxford: Oxford University Press, 1999.

Tinker, Hugh. *Experiment with Freedom: India and Pakistan, 1947*. London: Oxford University Press, 1967.

——. 'Pressure, persuasion, decision: Factors in the partition of the Punjab, August 1947.' *Journal of Asian Studies* 36:4 (August 1977), p. 695.

Tufte, Edward. *Envisioning Information*. Cheshire, CT: Graphics Press, 1990.

——. *Visual Explanations: Images and Quantities, Evidence and Narrative*. Cheshire, CT: Graphics Press, 1997.

——. *The Visual Display of Quantitative Information*. 2nd ed. Cheshire, CT: Graphics Press, 2001.

United States Army Map Service. NH 43–6, 'Ferozepore' [map]. Edition 1–AMS. 1:250,000. Series U502. Washington: Army Map Service, 1959.

——. NH 43–2, 'Lahore' [map]. Edition 2–AMS. 1:250,000. Series U502. Washington: Army Map Service, 1963.

Venkataramani, M. S. and B. K. Shrivastava. *Roosevelt–Gandhi–Churchill: America and the Last Phase of India's Freedom Struggle*. New Delhi: Radiant Publishers, 1983.

von Tunzelmann, Alex. *Indian Summer: The Secret History of the End of an Empire*. New York: Henry Holt and Company, 2007.

Waseem, Mohammad. 'Partition, migration and assimilation: A comparative study of Pakistani Punjab.' In *Region and Partition: Bengal, Punjab and the Partition of the Subcontinent*, eds Ian Talbot and Gurharpal Singh, pp. 203–27. Oxford: Oxford University Press, 1999.

Whyte, Brendan. *Waiting for the Esquimo: An Historical and Documentary Study of the Cooch Behar Enclaves of India and Bangladesh*. Vol. 8, *Research Papers of the School of Anthropology, Geography and Environmental Studies*. Melbourne: University of Melbourne, 2002.

Wilson, Thomas M. and Hastings Donnan, eds. *Border Identities: Nation and State at International Frontiers*. Cambridge: Cambridge University Press, 1998.

Winichakul, Thongchai. *Siam Mapped: A History of the Geo-Body of a Nation*. Honolulu: University of Hawaii Press, 1994.

Wolpert, Stanley. *A New History of India*, 3rd ed. New York: Oxford University Press, 1989.

——. *Shameful Flight: The Last Years of the British Empire in India*. Oxford: Oxford University Press, 2006.

Woodruff, Philip [Philip Mason]. *The Men Who Ruled India: The Guardians*. Vol. 2. New York: St Martin's Press, 1954.

Xydis, Stephen George. *Cyprus: Conflict and Conciliation, 1954–1958*. Columbus: Ohio State University Press, 1967.

[216]

Young, Kenneth, ed. *The Diaries of Sir Robert Bruce Lockhart*. Vol. 2. London: Macmillan London Limited, 1980.

Zafar, Rukhsana, comp. *Disturbances in the Punjab 1947*. Islamabad: National Documentation Centre, 1995.

Zaminder, Vazira Fazila-Yacoobali. *The Long Partition and the Making of Modern South Asia: Refugees, Boundaries, Histories*. New York: Columbia University Press, 2007.

Ziegler, Philip. *Mountbatten: The Official Biography*. New York: Harper & Row, 1985.

———. *Mountbatten Revisited*. Austin, TX: Harry Ransom Humanities Research Center, The University of Texas at Austin, 1995.

Unpublished theses

Aiyar, Swarna. 'Violence and the State in the Partition of Punjab: 1947–48.' Unpublished Ph.D dissertation, University of Cambridge, 1994.

Hasan, Masuma. 'The Transfer of Power to Pakistan and Its Consequences.' Unpublished Ph.D dissertation, University of Cambridge, 1967.

INDEX

Note: References in *italic* refer to illustrations, while 'n.' after a page reference indicates the number of a note on that page.

natural boundaries 55, 61–2, 77–8,
114, 195
Nehru, Jawaharlal 5, 9–10, 12, 93,
133, 136, 198–9
boundary commission formation
and 26–33, 61–2, 79
fatigue 16, 51
irrigation concerns 69, 81, 92,
120, 197
'notional boundary' 12–13, 56, 65,
74–6, 108, 142, 145–6, 148,
192, *map 2*

Palestine 2, 13, 59, 196
partition
announcement of plan for 27–8
attitudes to 6, 12, 16, 35, 51, 79,
82, 195, 197–200
historiographies of 6, 99, 191–3
misleading portrayal of 6, 15, 22,
25, 27–8, 37, 65, 92–3, 108, 111,
125, 148, 181, 195–200
possible improvements in
handling of 97–8, 194–5
process of 1–4, 15, 28, 73, 79, 83,
90, 97–100
Partition Council 17, 37, 50, 55–6,
62, 112
Patel, Vallabhbhai 5, 9, 16, 26, 28, 60,
119, 133
protests over boundary 93, 101,
197
Pethick-Lawrence, Frederick 10, 12
private armies 11, 129–33, 145, 148
see also Muslim League
National Guard; Rashtriya
Swayamsevak Sangh
Punjab Boundary Force 131–3, 135–6,
158

'Quit India' movement 10, 17, 60

Radcliffe, Antonia 45, 48–9
Radcliffe, Cyril 1, 5–8, 26, 33–70
passim, 100, 105n.111, 112,
178, 198
interest in and opinions on Indian

affairs and imperialism 44–5,
48–9, 183–7
in later life 188–9
motivation of 179–82, 189
responsibility for mass violence
182–3
as a scapegoat 110–11, 181, 192
service to the British state 40–9,
76–7, 178–82, 187–9, 200
see also maps, use of by Radcliffe
Radcliffe award
advance notice of 89–92, 107
alternative lines 140–8, 200, *maps
4–5*
announcement of 106–8, 120, 125,
130, 134–6, 139n.39, 140
balancing of elements within 74,
80, 122, 124–5, 140, 146
disputes and disruption arising
from 97, 137, 140–1, 150,
165–71, *maps 6–8*
formulation of 73–88
Mountbatten's influence on
112–25
reception of 101, 109–12
sketch map of 73, 77, 83, 90–5,
103n.49, 112, 120–1, 124, 142,
146, *map 5a*
Radcliffe Commission 1–6, 15, 25–
40, 50–1, 110–11, 181
negotiations over formation of
27–40
procedure of 58–9, 62–3, 117–19,
192
terms of reference of 26–8, 32–3,
35, 38–9, 50, 55–6, 62, 65, 69,
74–82 *passim*, 92, 112, 114,
116, 143, 148, 192
Radcliffe, Geoffrey 44, 187
railway communications 11, 43, 64,
80, 82, 140–1, 146, 148, 158
attacks on 129–31, 196
on maps 66–7, 95–8
Rashtriya Swayamsevak Sangh (RSS)
132–3, 159
Rees, Thomas ('Pete') 57, 110, 131,
133, 136

CPSIA information can be obtained at www.ICGtesting.com
Printed in the USA
LVOW01s1702200415

435336LV00006B/177/P